AF594154
Did you know that Benjamin Franklin started our nation's first public library? He also invented lightning rods, swim fins, and bifocal eyeglasses.

HARCOURT

Social Studies

Our Communities

www.harcourtschool.com

Our Communities

Series Authors

Dr. Michael J. Berson
Professor
Social Science Education
University of South Florida
Tampa, Florida

Dr. Tyrone C. Howard
Associate Professor
UCLA Graduate School of Education & Information Studies
University of California at Los Angeles
Los Angeles, California

Dr. Cinthia Salinas
Assistant Professor
Department of Curriculum and Instruction
College of Education
The University of Texas at Austin
Austin, Texas

Series Consultants

Dr. Marsha Alibrandi
Assistant Professor of Social Studies
Curriculum and Instruction Department
North Carolina State University
Raleigh, North Carolina

Dr. Patricia G. Avery
Professor
College of Education and Human Development
University of Minnesota
Minneapolis/St. Paul, Minnesota

Dr. Linda Bennett
Associate Professor
College of Education
University of Missouri–Columbia
Columbia, Missouri

Dr. Walter C. Fleming
Department Head and Professor
Native American Studies
Montana State University
Bozeman, Montana

Dr. S. G. Grant
Associate Professor
University at Buffalo
Buffalo, New York

C. C. Herbison
Lecturer
African and African-American Studies
University of Kansas
Lawrence, Kansas

Dr. Eric Johnson
Assistant Professor
Director, Urban Education Program
School of Education
Drake University
Des Moines, Iowa

Dr. Bruce E. Larson
Professor
Social Studies Education
Secondary Education
Woodring College of Education
Western Washington University
Bellingham, Washington

Dr. Merry M. Merryfield
Professor
Social Studies and Global Education
College of Education
The Ohio State University
Columbus, Ohio

Dr. Peter Rees
Associate Professor
Department of Geography
University of Delaware
Wilmington, Delaware

Dr. Phillip J. VanFossen
James F. Ackerman Professor of Social Studies Education
Associate Director, Purdue Center for Economic Education
Purdue University
West Lafayette, Indiana

Dr. Myra Zarnowski
Professor
Elementary and Early Childhood Education
Queens College
The City University of New York
Flushing, New York

Classroom Reviewers and Contributors

Connie Bingham
Teacher
Elm Tree Elementary
Bentonville, Arkansas

Lisa Johnson
Teacher
Whitely County School District
Corbin, Kentucky

Sheila McCoy
Teacher
Karns Elementary School
Knoxville, Tennessee

Charla Uhles
Teacher
Eastlake Elementary School
Oklahoma City, Oklahoma

Maps
researched and prepared by

2008 Edition

Printed in the United States of America

ISBN 13: 978-0-15-348583-1
ISBN 10: 0-15-348583-3

3 4 5 6 7 8 9 10 048 15 14 13 12 11 10 09 08 07

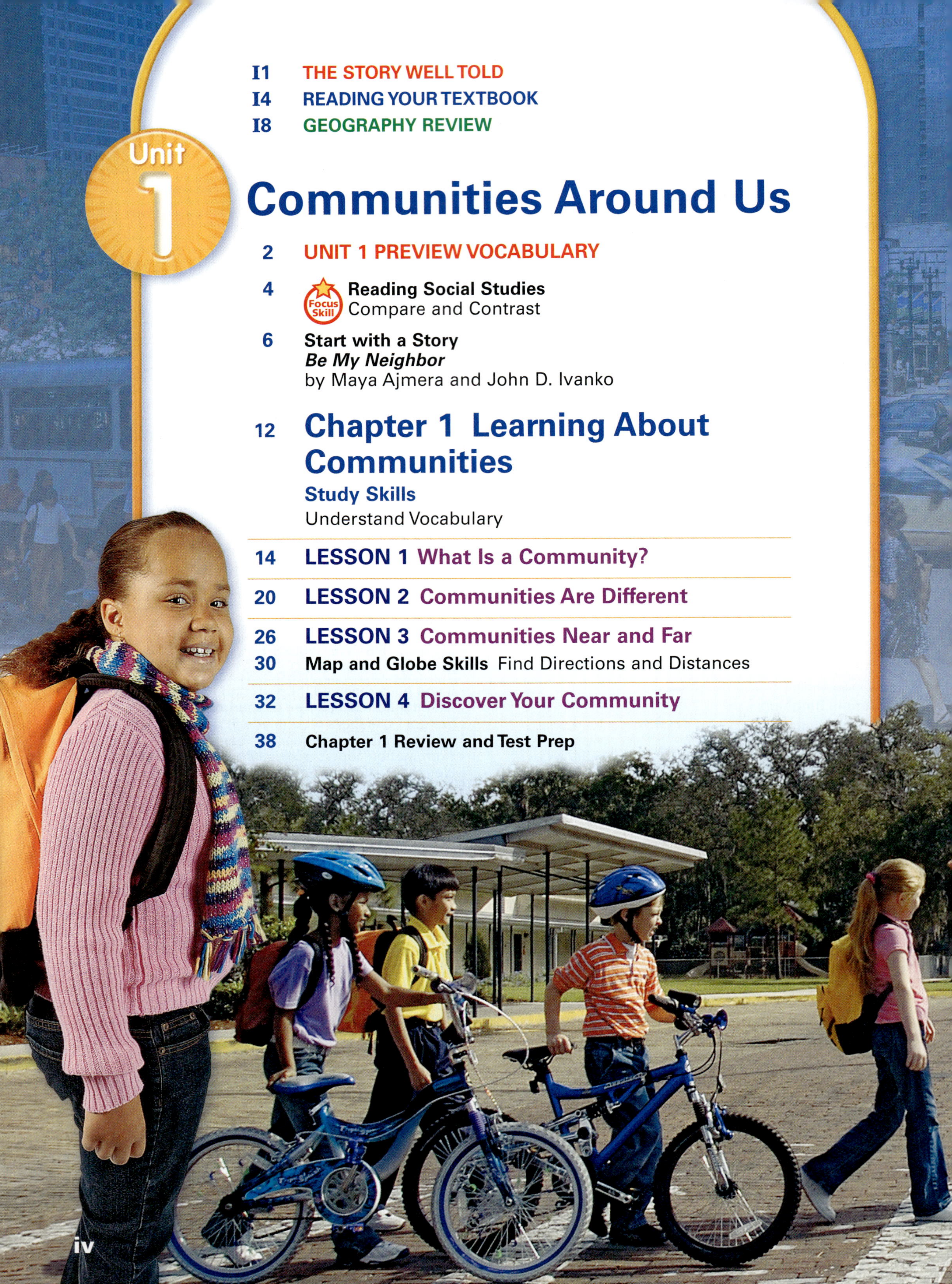

Unit 1

Communities Around Us

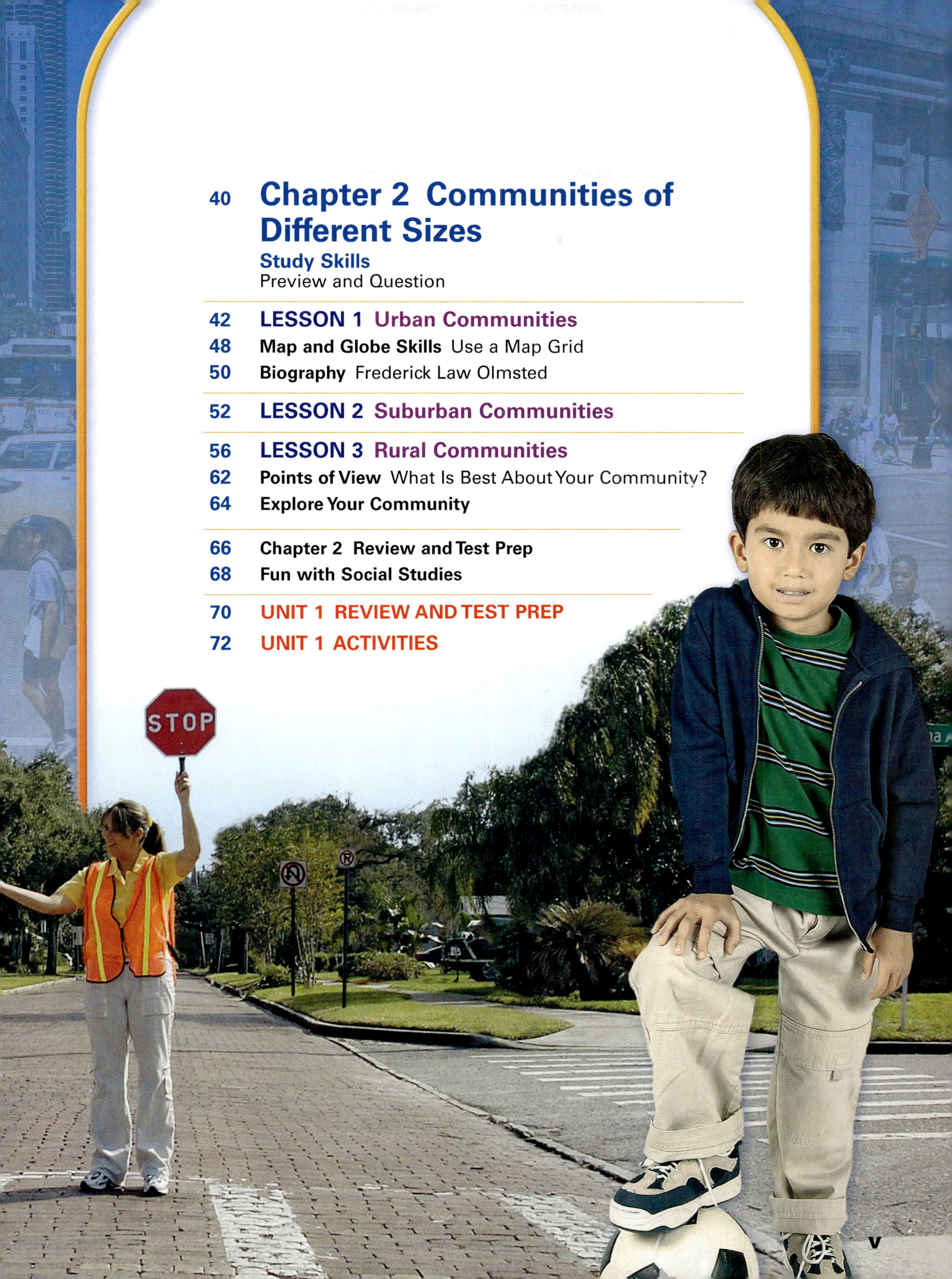
STOP

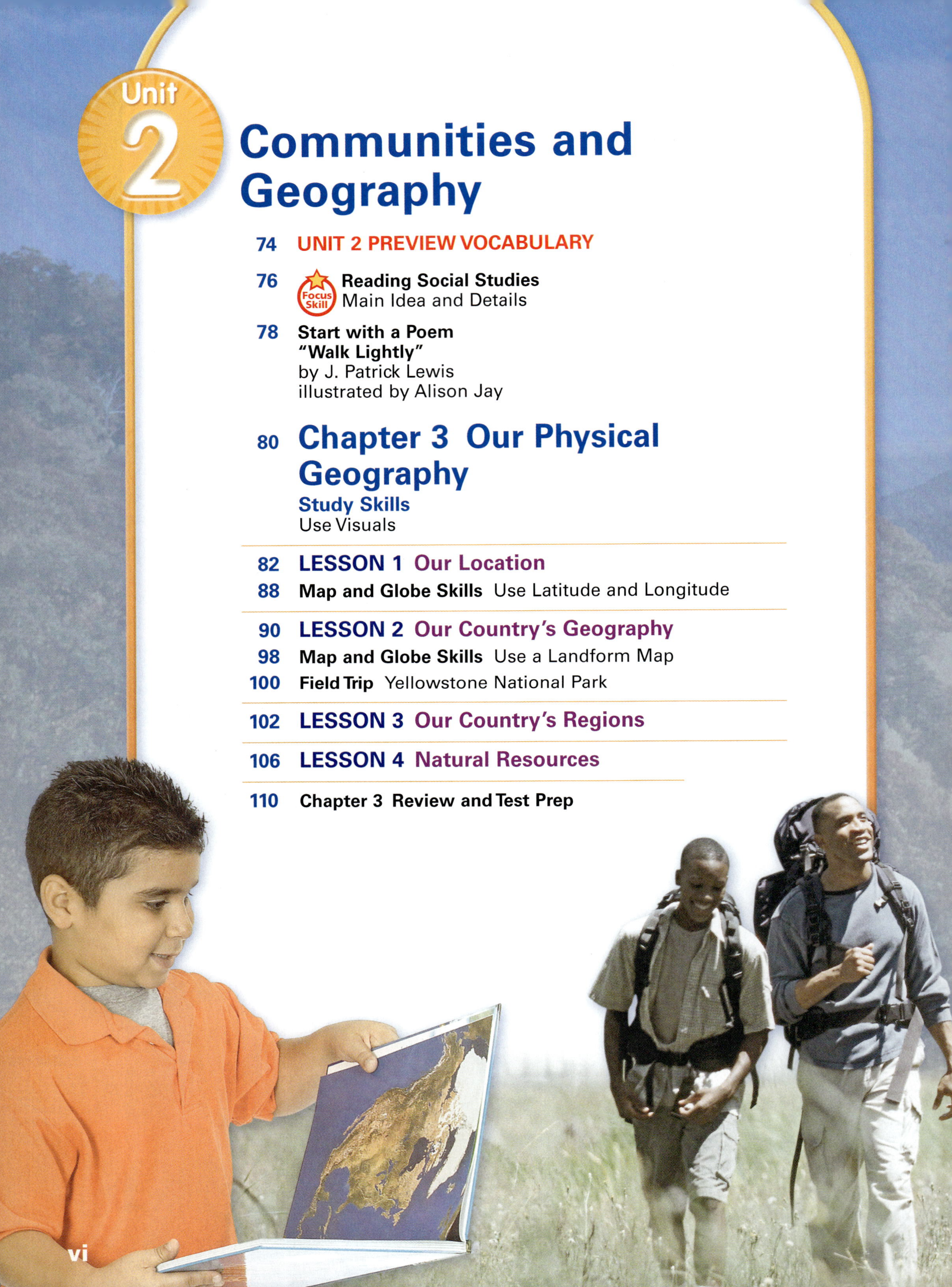

Unit 2

Communities and Geography

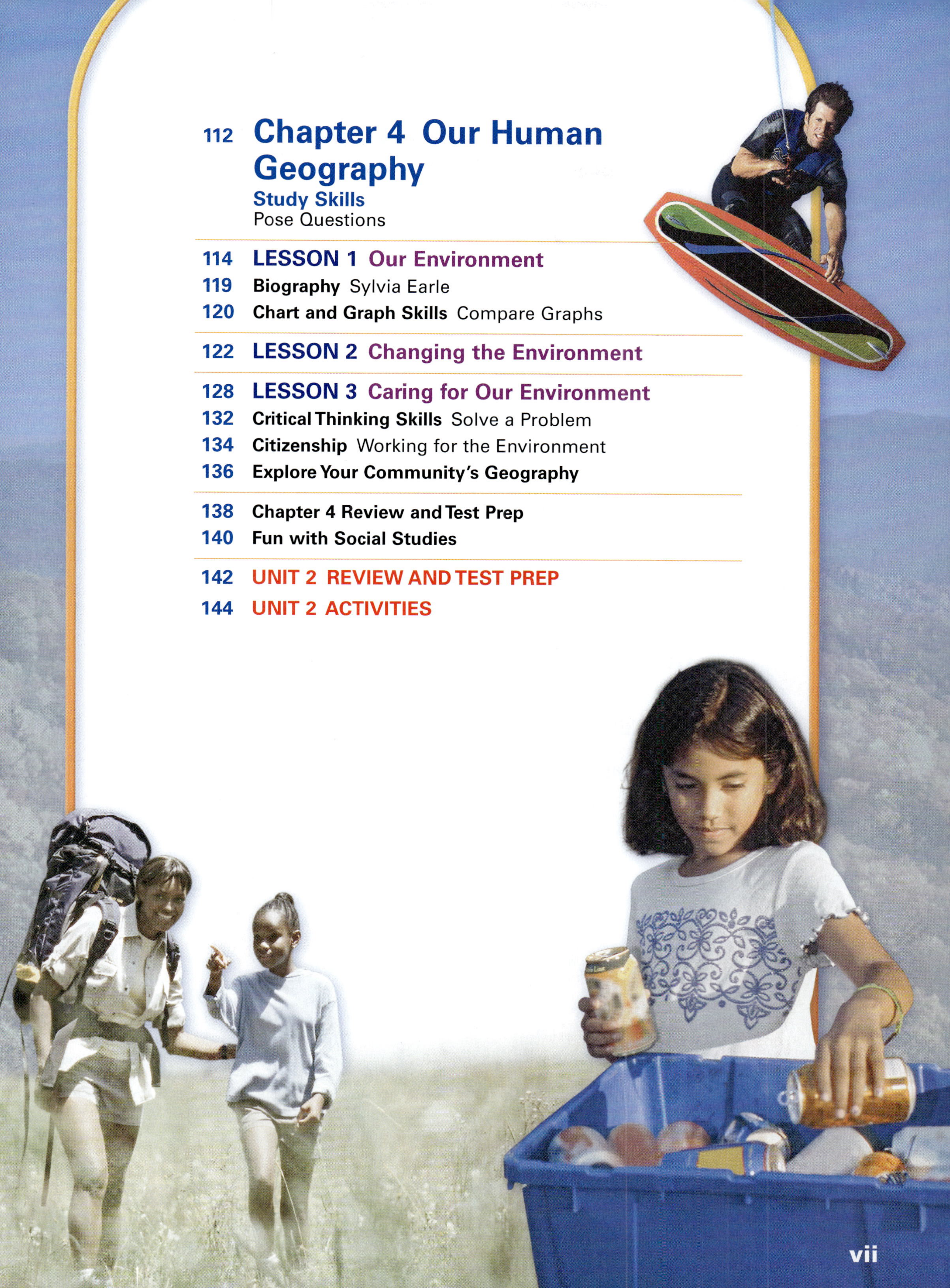

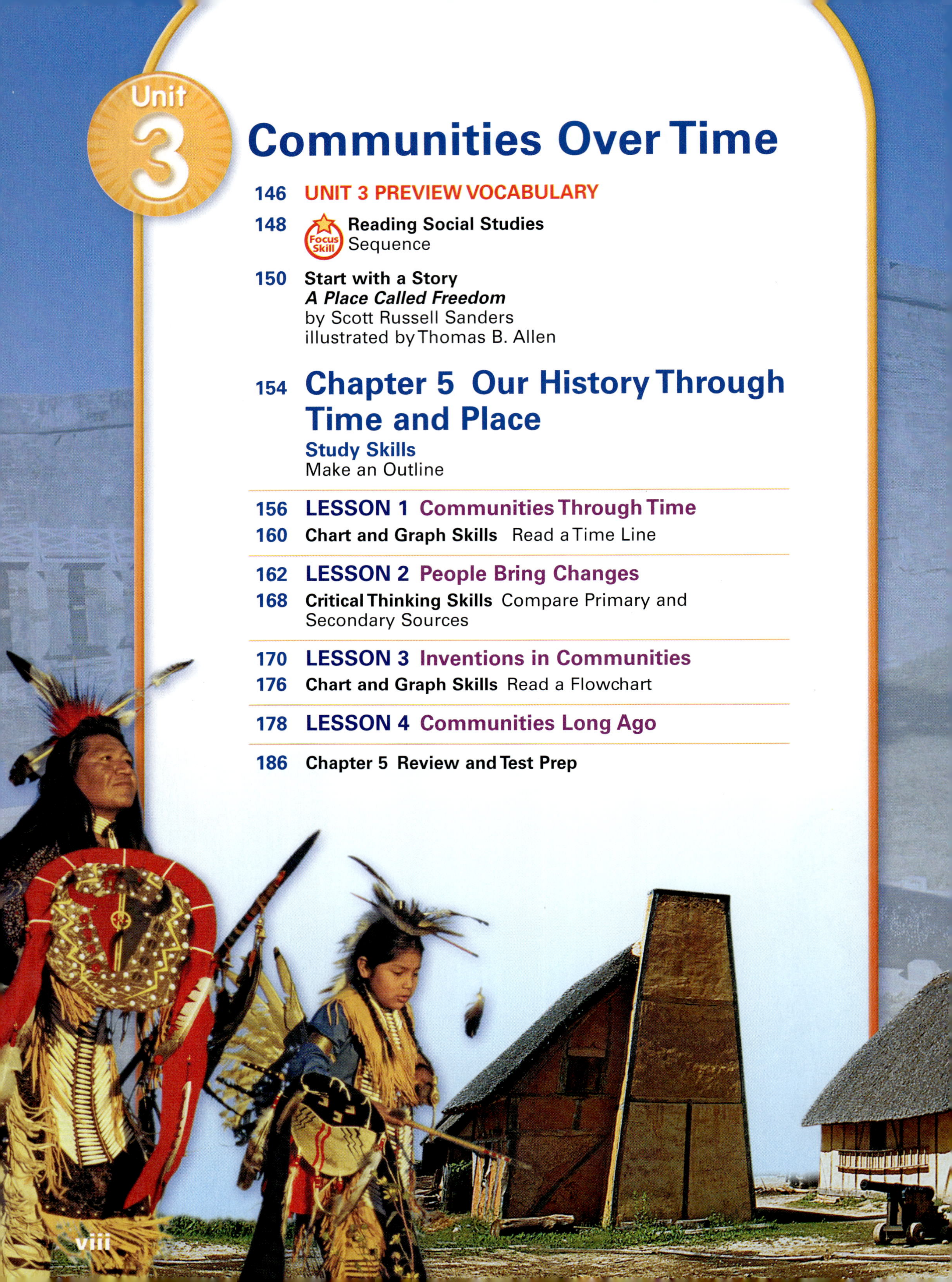

Unit 3

Communities Over Time

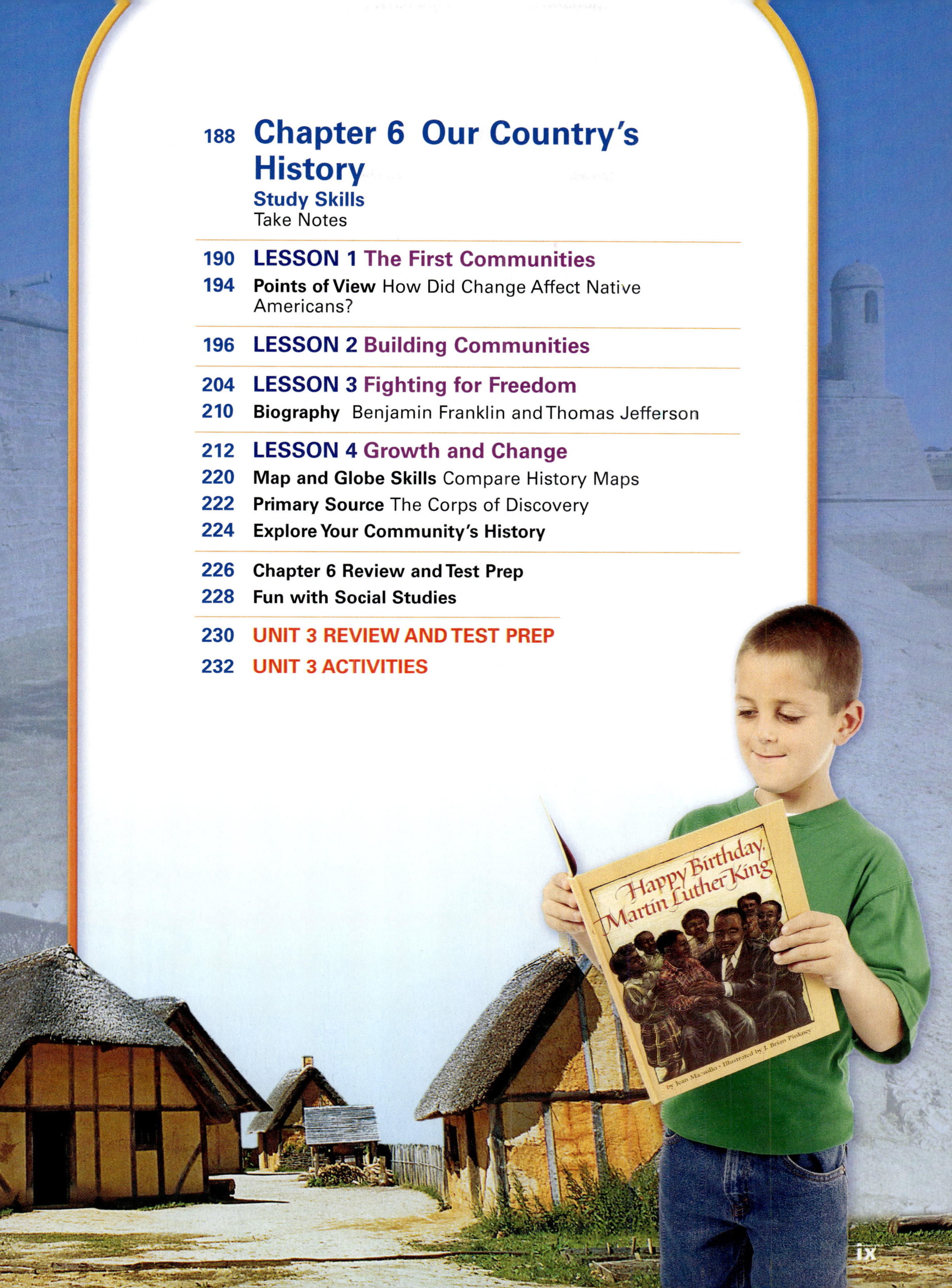
Happy Birthday, Martin Luther King
by Jean Marzollo · Illustrated by J. Brian Pinkney

Unit 4 Citizens and Government

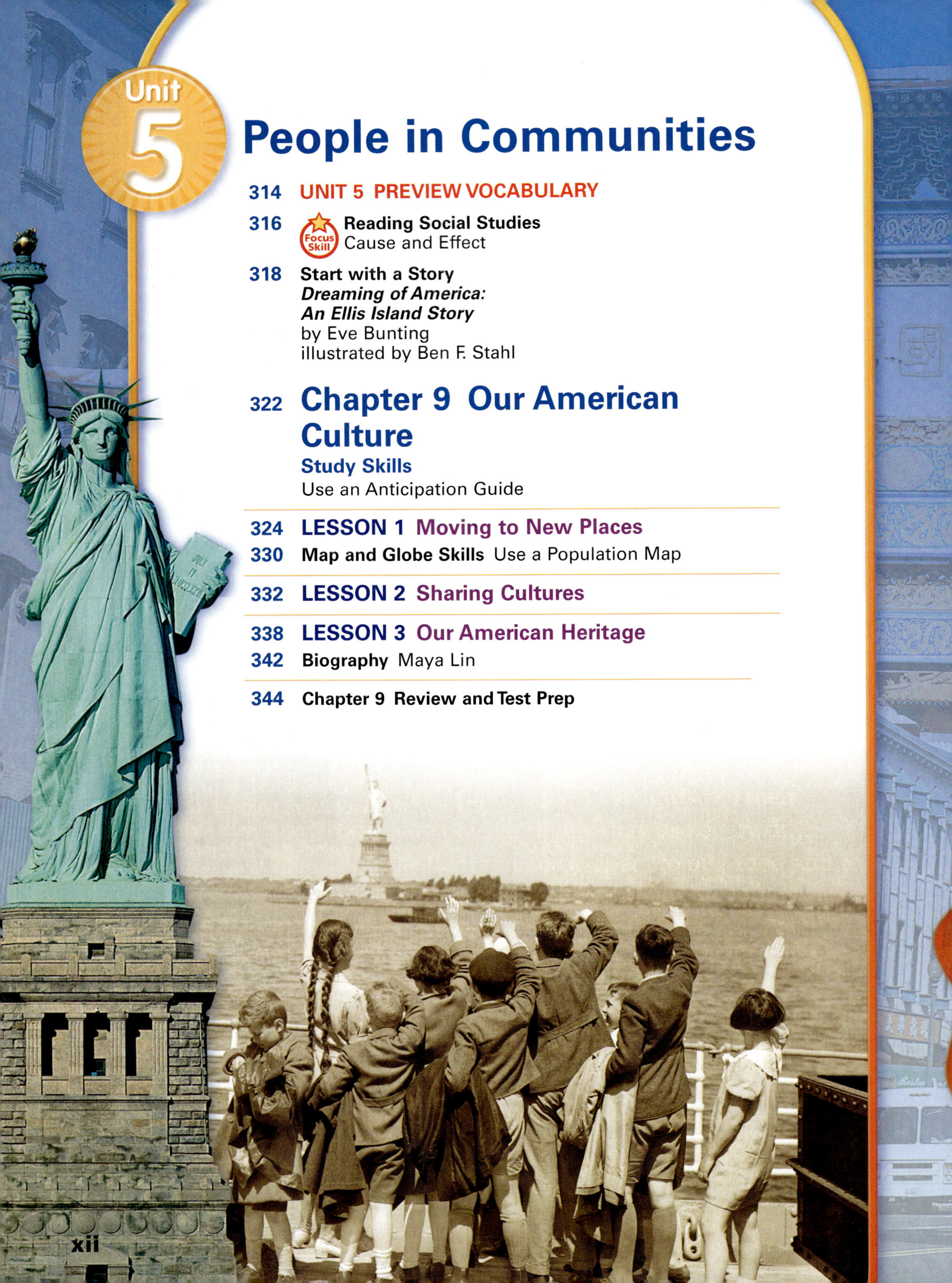

Unit 5 People in Communities

Unit 6

Working in Communities

FOR YOUR REFERENCE

Features

Skills

CHART AND GRAPH SKILLS

CITIZENSHIP SKILLS

CRITICAL THINKING SKILLS

MAP AND GLOBE SKILLS

READING SOCIAL STUDIES

STUDY SKILLS

Citizenship

Points of View

Literature and Music

Primary Sources

Documents

Biography

Children in History

Field Trip

Fun with Social Studies

Charts, Graphs, and Diagram

Maps

Time Lines

Illustrations

The Story Well Told

"The American city should be a collection of communities where every member has a right to belong."

—former President Lyndon B. Johnson

This year you will learn about different communities. You will read about what it was like to live in a different **time**. You will meet **people** from communities in other states and countries. You will visit many **places** to find out how people in different communities live.

Our Communities

The Story Is About Time, People, and Place

Every community has its own history. A **history** is the story of what has happened in a place. People who study the past are called historians. Historians study how the past and present are linked. They look for how things change over time. They look at how they stay the same.

To learn about communities long ago, historians study the objects used by people in the past. These objects are called **artifacts**.

Historians study people from the past to learn more about life long ago. They often read biographies of important people. A **biography** is the story of a person's life.

Historians also study the places where events happened. To better understand the place they are studying, historians study maps. A **map** shows a place's location. A map also tells historians about the land and the people who lived there.

Historians write the story of our past. They show us how time, people, and place are connected. You will learn to think like a historian as you study the history of your community.

Reading Your Textbook

GETTING STARTED

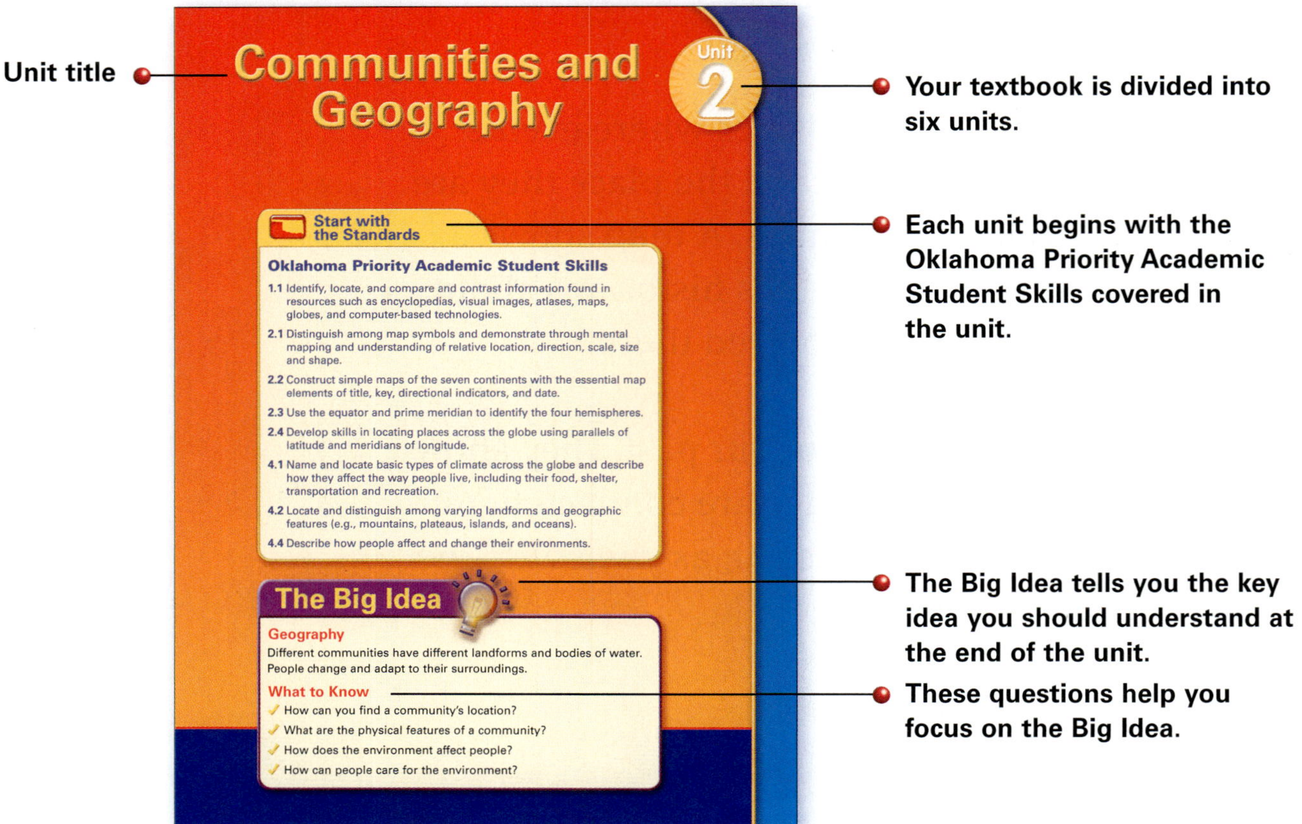

Unit title

Your textbook is divided into six units.

Each unit begins with the Oklahoma Priority Academic Student Skills covered in the unit.

The Big Idea tells you the key idea you should understand at the end of the unit.

These questions help you focus on the Big Idea.

BEGINNING A UNIT

The Reading Social Studies Focus Skill will help you better understand what you read.

You will read about these people in the unit.

Key words are introduced.

You will practice and apply the skill.

Each unit begins with a reading selection.

BEGINNING A CHAPTER

Each unit is divided into chapters, and each chapter is divided into lessons.

The Study Skill provides a strategy you can use to remember or organize what you read.

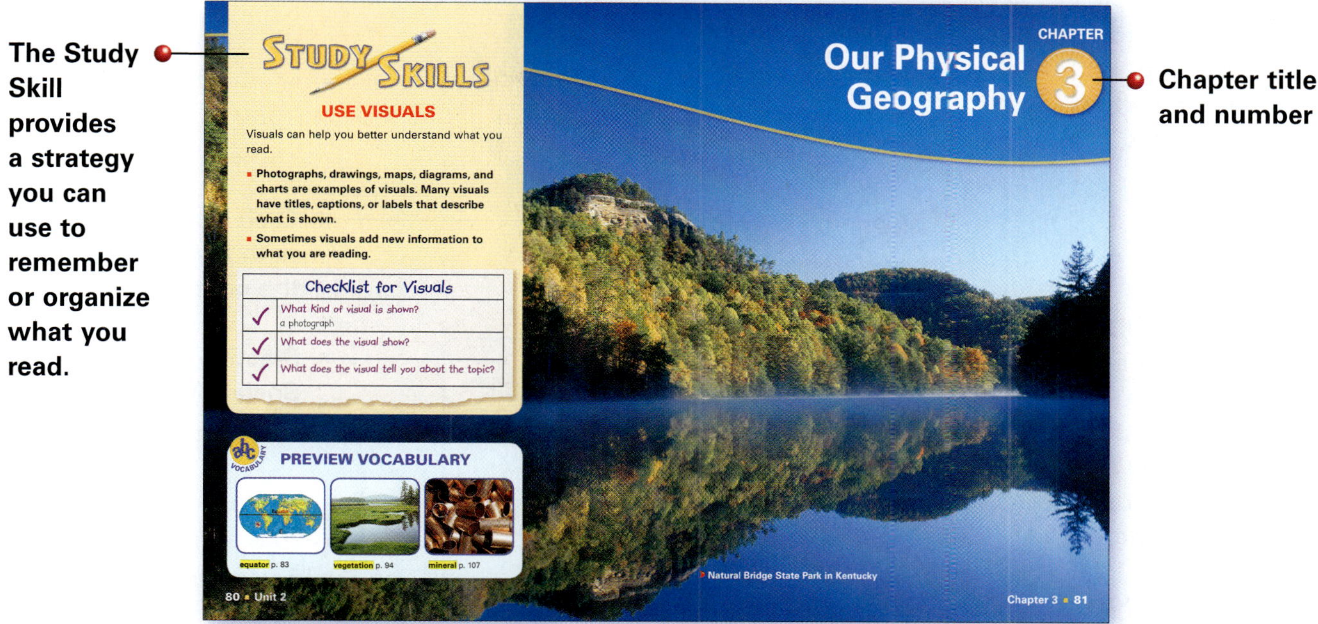

Chapter title and number

BEGINNING A LESSON

This question helps you focus on the lesson's main idea.

These are the new vocabulary terms in the lesson.

Apply the Reading Social Studies Focus Skill as you read the lesson.

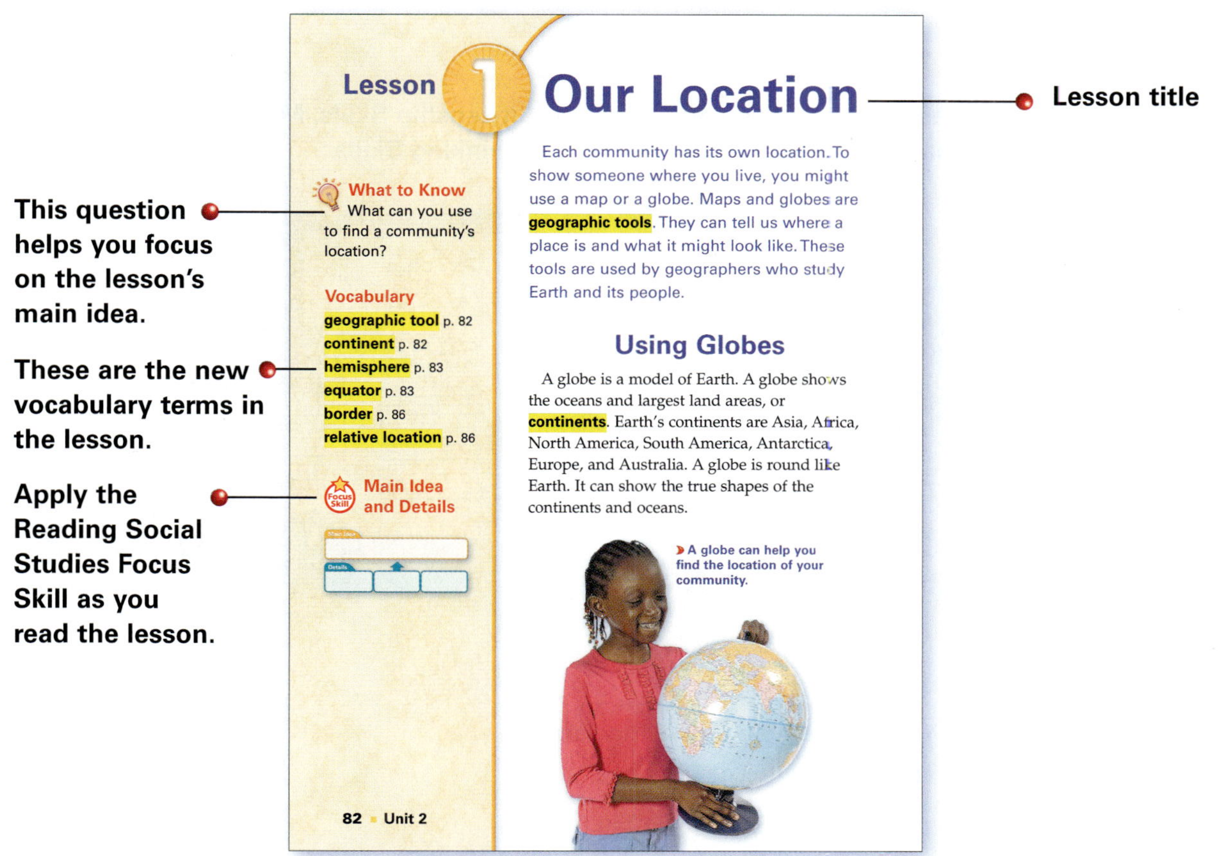

Lesson title

CONCLUDING A LESSON

Each short section ends with a **Reading Check** question, which helps you check whether you understand what you have read.

Each lesson, like each chapter and unit, ends with a review. Questions and activities help you check your understanding of the lesson.

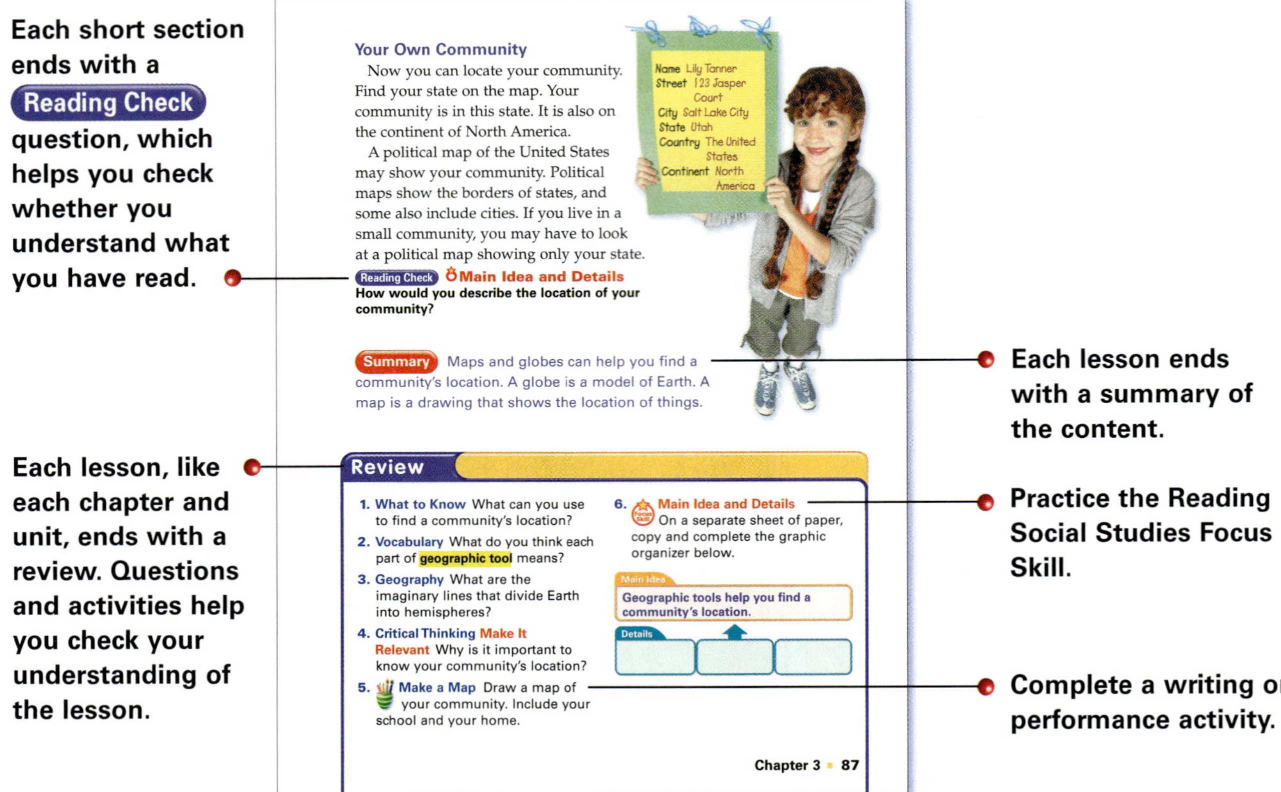

Each lesson ends with a summary of the content.

Practice the Reading Social Studies Focus Skill.

Complete a writing or performance activity.

LEARNING SOCIAL STUDIES SKILLS

Your textbook has lessons that help you build your Citizenship Skills, Map and Globe Skills, Chart and Graph Skills, and Critical Thinking Skills.

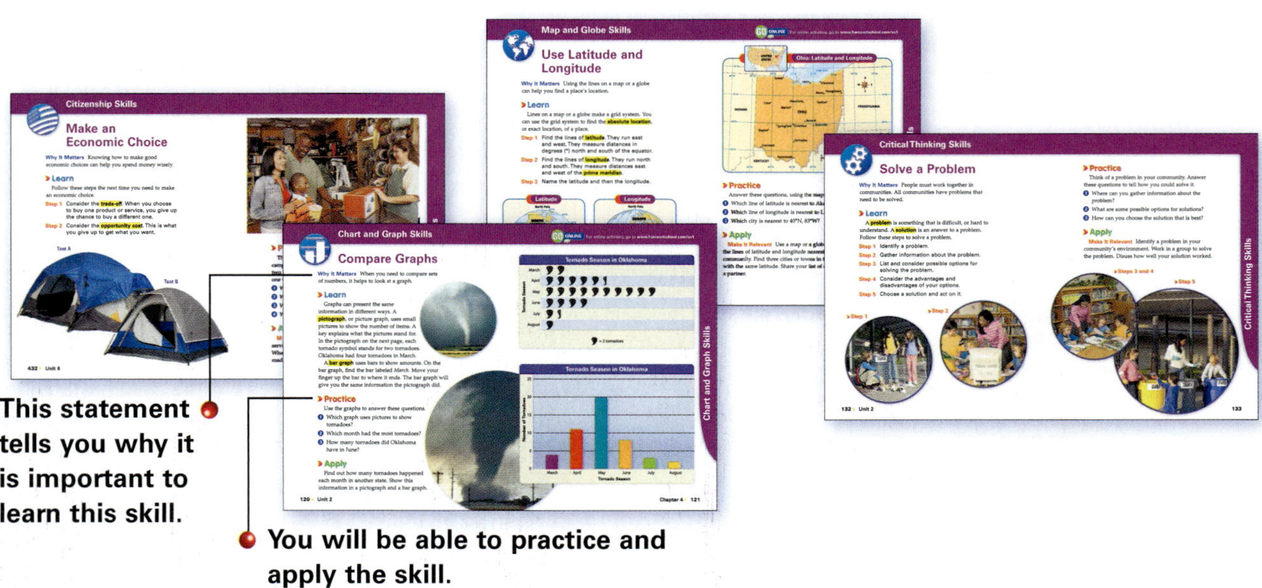

This statement tells you why it is important to learn this skill.

You will be able to practice and apply the skill.

SPECIAL FEATURES

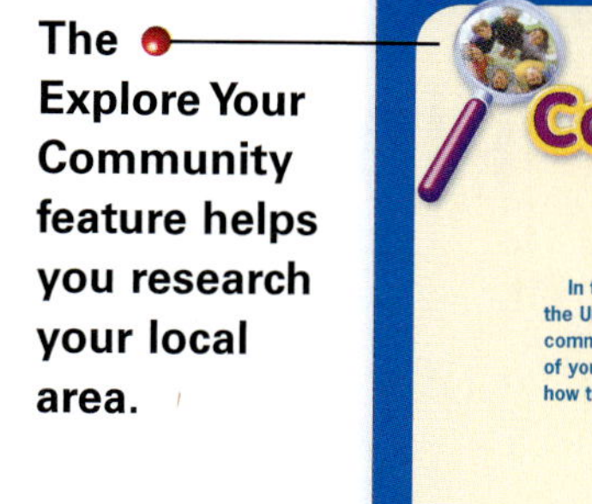

The Explore Your Community feature helps you research your local area.

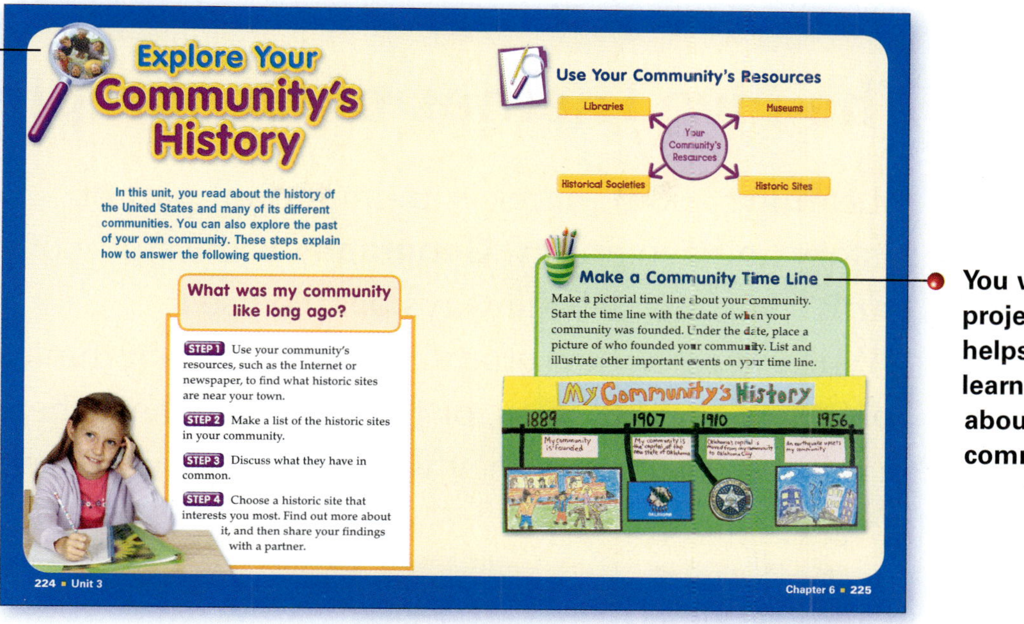

You will do a project that helps you learn more about your community.

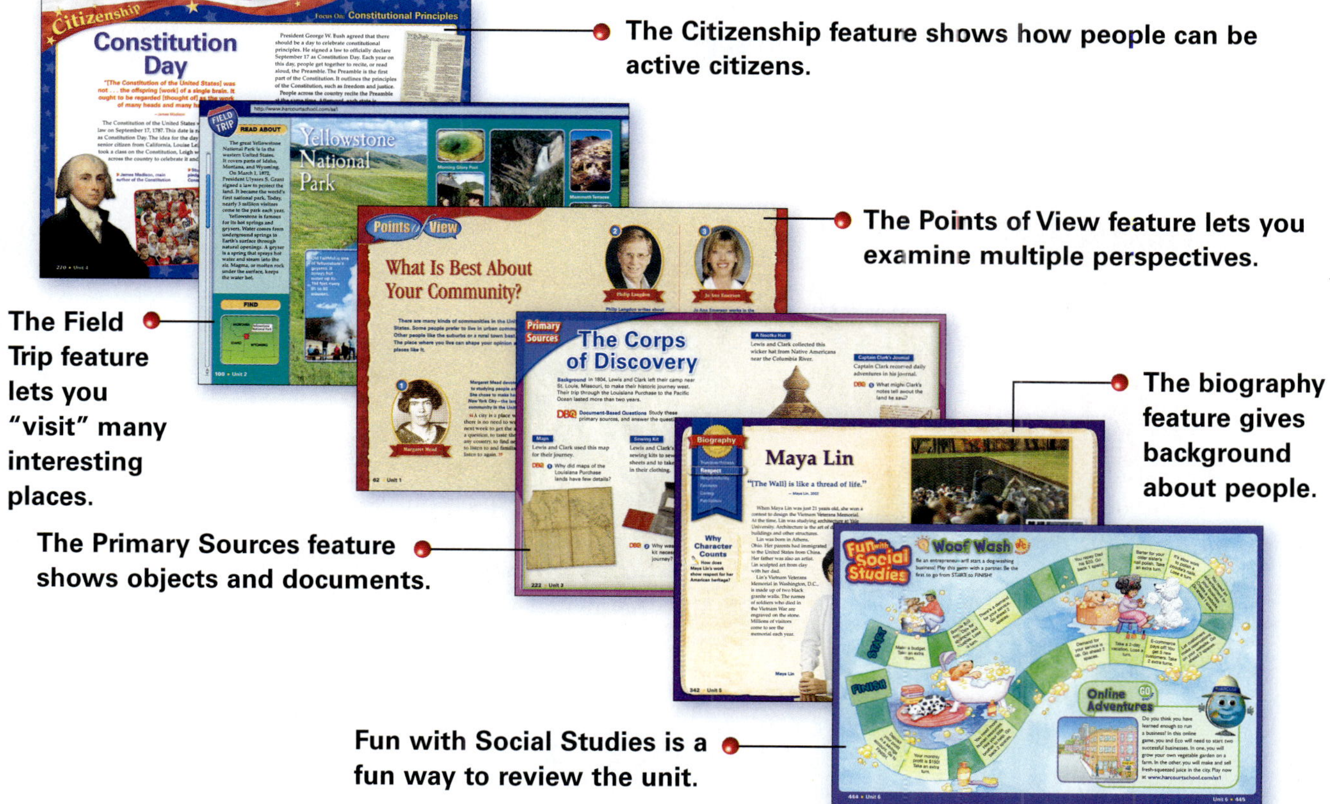

The Citizenship feature shows how people can be active citizens.

The Points of View feature lets you examine multiple perspectives.

The Field Trip feature lets you "visit" many interesting places.

The biography feature gives background about people.

The Primary Sources feature shows objects and documents.

Fun with Social Studies is a fun way to review the unit.

FOR YOUR REFERENCE

At the back of your textbook, you will find a section called For Your Reference. You can use it to look up words or to find out information about people, places, and other topics.

The Five Themes of Geography

Learning about places is an important part of history and geography. **Geography** is the study of Earth's surface and the ways people use it.

When geographers study Earth, they often think about five main themes, or topics. Keep these themes in mind as you read. They will help you think like a geographer.

Geography

Location

Everything on Earth has its own **location**—the place where it can be found.

Place

Every place has physical and human characteristics, or features, that make it different from all other places. **Physical features** are formed by nature. **Human features** are created by people.

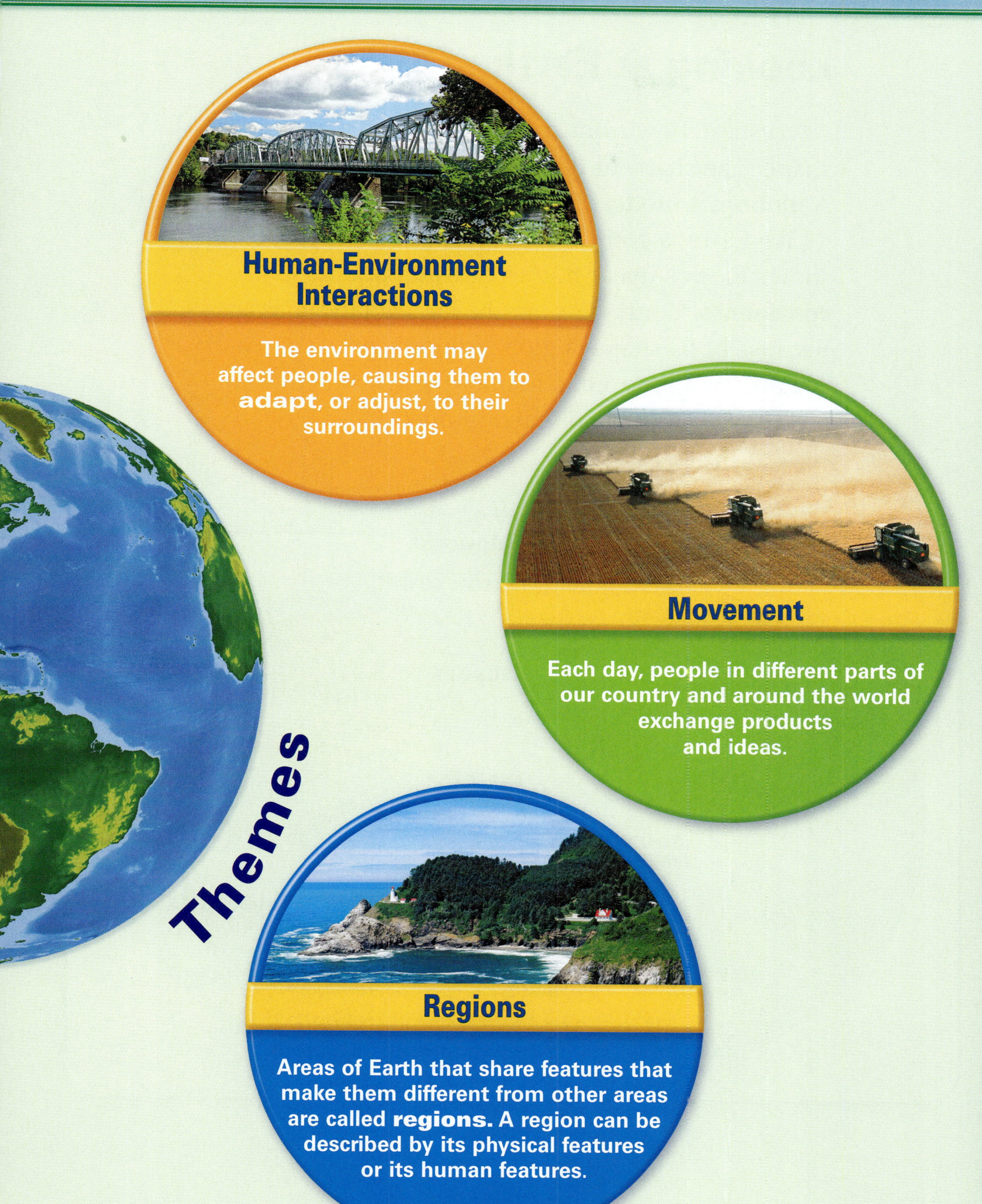
Human-Environment Interactions
The environment may affect people, causing them to **adapt**, or adjust, to their surroundings.
Movement
Each day, people in different parts of our country and around the world exchange products and ideas.
Themes
Regions
Areas of Earth that share features that make them different from other areas are called **regions.** A region can be described by its physical features or its human features.

Looking at Earth

A distant view from space shows Earth's round shape. The shape of Earth is shown best by a globe. A **globe** is a model of our planet.

Like Earth, a globe is a sphere, or ball. A globe shows Earth's major bodies of water and its **continents**. Continents are the largest land masses. Because of its shape, a globe can only show one half of Earth at a time. On a map of the world, you can see all of the land and water at once.

The World

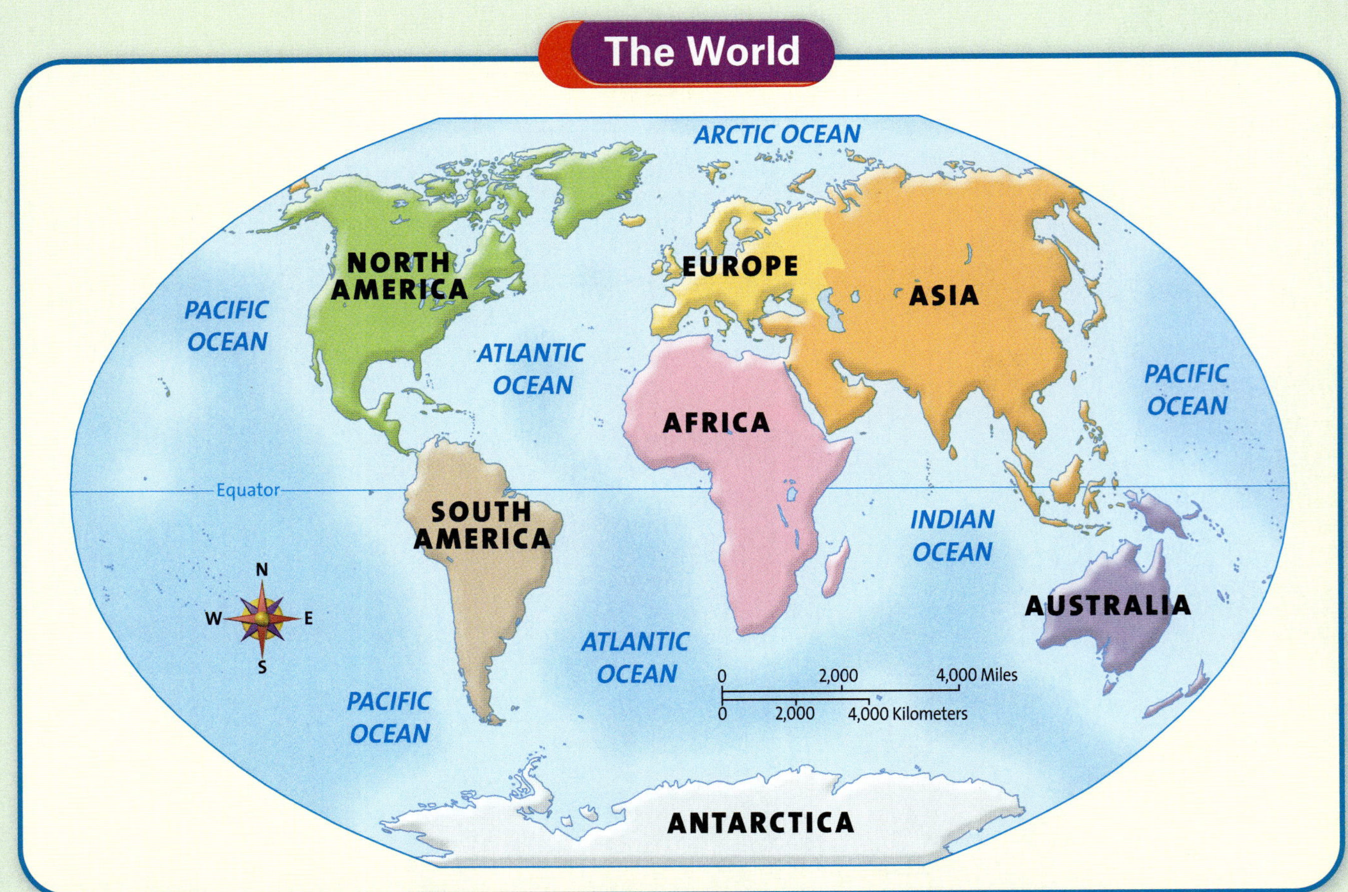

Halfway between the North and South Pole is an imaginary line called the **equator**. It divides Earth into two equal halves, or **hemispheres**. The Northern Hemisphere is north of the equator. The Southern Hemisphere is south of it.

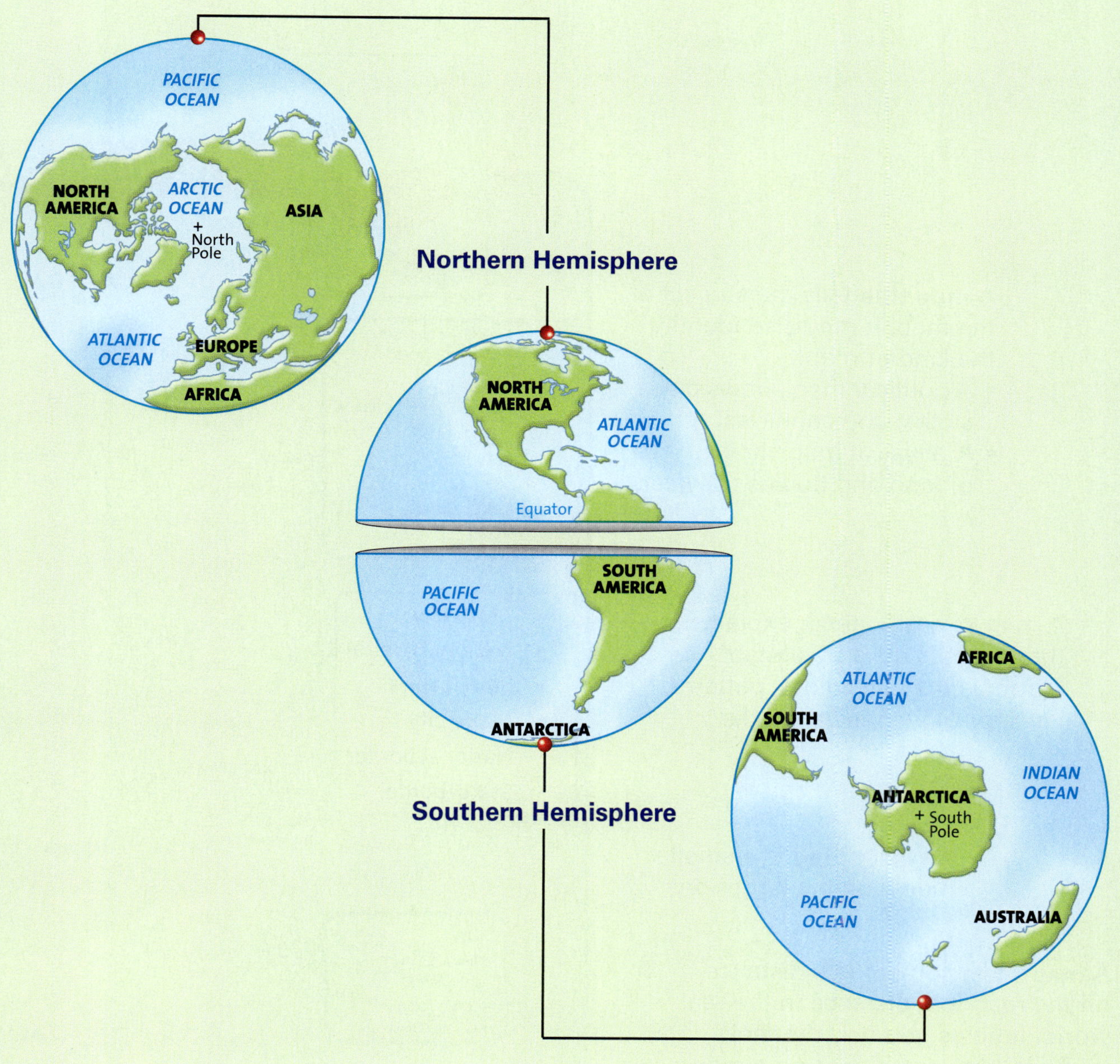

Reading Maps

Maps can provide you with many kinds of information about Earth and the world around you. To help you read maps more easily, mapmakers add certain features to most maps they draw. These features usually include a title, a map key, a compass rose, a locator, and a map scale.

A **locator** is a small map or globe that shows where the place on the main map is located within a larger area.

A **map title** tells the subject of the map. It may also identify the kind of map.

- A political map shows cities, states, and countries.
- A physical map shows kinds of land and bodies of water.

A **map key**, or legend, explains the symbols used on a map. Symbols may be colors, patterns, lines, or other special marks.

An **inset map** is a smaller map within a larger one.

A **map scale** compares a distance on the map to a distance in the real world. It helps you find the real distance between places on a map.

Mapmakers sometimes need to show places marked on a map in greater detail or places that are located beyond the area shown on the map. Find Alaska and Hawaii on the map on page R6. This map shows the location of these two states in relation to the rest of the country.

Now find Alaska and Hawaii on the map below. To show this much detail for these states and the rest of the country, the map would have to be much larger. Instead, Alaska and Hawaii are shown in separate inset maps, or a small map within a larger map.

A **compass rose**, or direction marker, shows directions.

- The **cardinal directions** are north, south, east, and west.
- The **intermediate directions**, or directions between the cardinal directions, are northeast, northwest, southeast, and southwest.

1. **desert** a large, dry area of land
2. **forest** a large area of trees
3. **gulf** a large body of ocean water that is partly surrounded by land
4. **hill** land that rises above the land around it
5. **island** a landform with water all around it
6. **lake** a body of water with land on all sides
7. **mountain** highest kind of land
8. **ocean** a body of salt water that covers a large area
9. **peninsula** a landform that is surrounded on only three sides by water
10. **plain** flat land
11. **river** a large stream of water that flows across the land
12. **valley** low land between hills or mountains

Communities Around Us

Unit 1

Start with the Standards

Oklahoma Priority Academic Student Skills

1.1 Identify, locate, and compare and contrast information found in resources such as encyclopedias, visual images, atlases, maps, globes, and computer-based technologies.

1.2 Examine and use children's literature to compare and contrast his or her own community to other United States and global communities.

2.1 Distinguish among map symbols and demonstrate through mental mapping and understanding of relative location, direction, scale, size and shape.

4.2 Locate and distinguish among varying landforms and geographic features.

5.1 Describe the difference between goods and services; explaining that, at different times and places, people are both consumers and producers of goods and services.

The Big Idea

Communities

Communities are alike and different and are found all over the world.

What to Know

- ✓ What is a community?
- ✓ How are communities different?
- ✓ How can you learn about your community?
- ✓ What are urban, suburban, and rural communities?

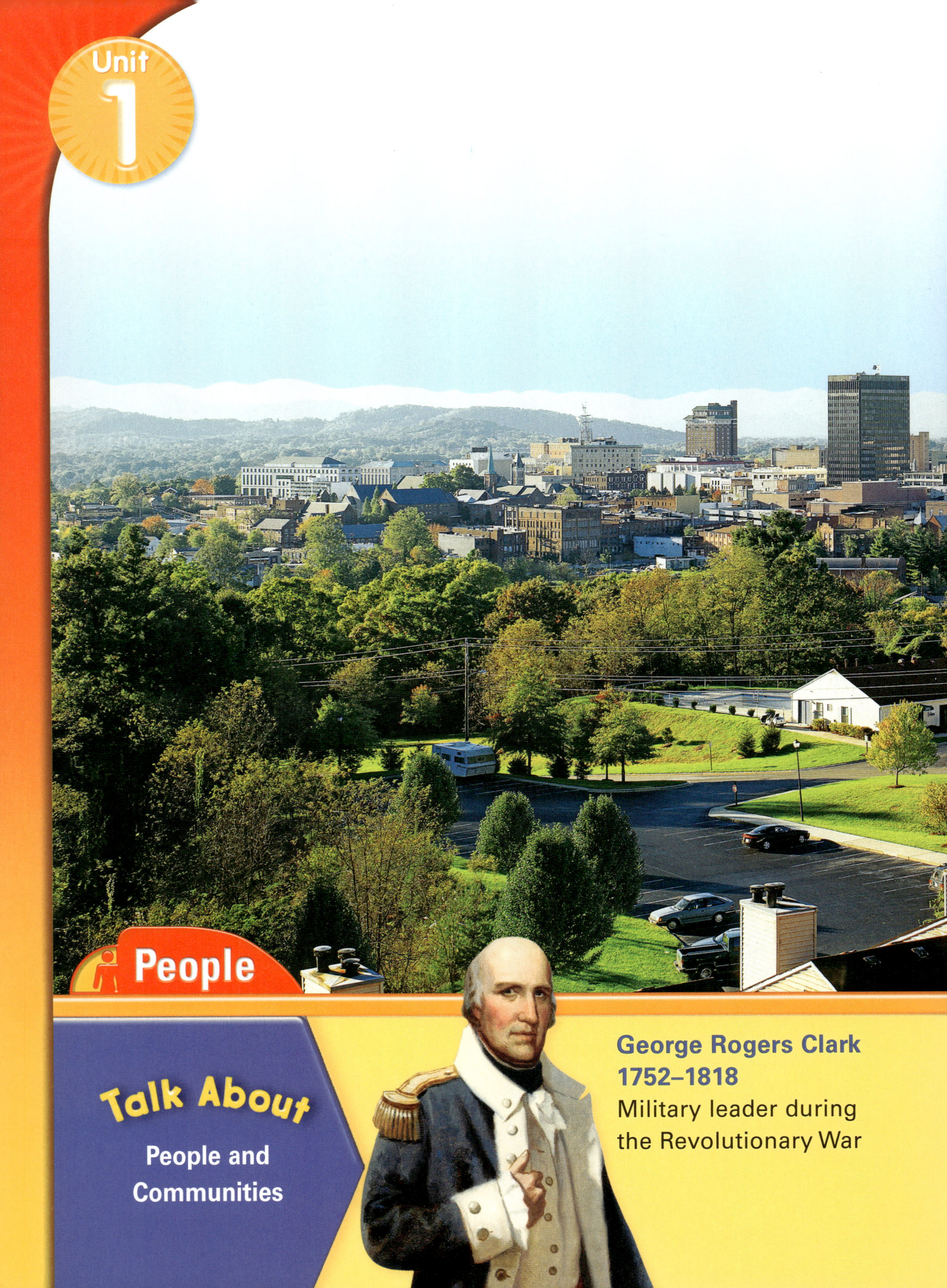

George Rogers Clark
1752–1818
Military leader during the Revolutionary War

Communities Around Us

Frederick Law Olmsted
1822–1903
Designer of several city parks, such as Central Park in New York City

Maya Angelou
1928–Present
Missouri-born poet who wrote about growing up in the South as an African American girl

Preview

Vocabulary

community A group of people who live and work in the same place. (page 14)

citizen A person who lives in and belongs to a community. (page 14)

culture A way of life shared by members of a group. (page 15)

government A group of people who make rules and solve problems for a community. (page 19)

communication The sharing of information. (page 27)

For more resources, go to **www.harcourtschool.com/ss1**

Reading Social Studies

Compare and Contrast

Why It Matters Knowing how to compare and contrast will help you understand how things, people, and ideas are alike and different.

Learn

To **compare** things is to tell how they are alike, or similar. To **contrast** things is to tell how they are different.

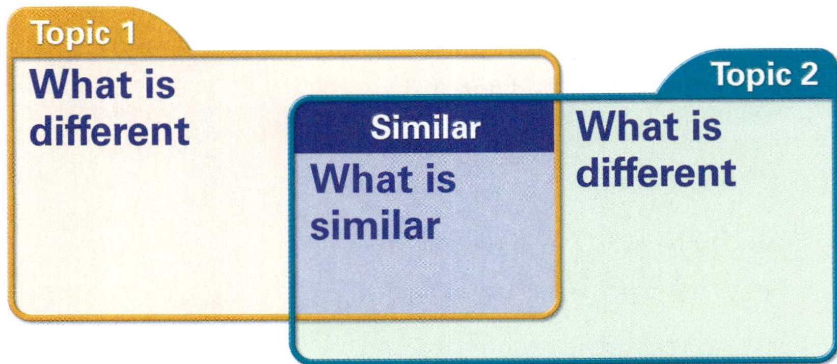

- Words and phrases, such as *the same as, like, both,* and *similar,* are clues that two things are being compared.
- Words and phrases, such as *different from, unlike, however,* and *but,* are clues that two things are being contrasted.

Practice

Read the paragraph. Then compare and contrast the cities.

Lagos is in Nigeria, Africa. Washington, D.C., is in the United States, in North America. Lagos and Washington, D.C., are both large, busy cities. However, they grew differently.

Compare

Contrast

Apply

Read the paragraphs, and answer the questions.

Lagos and Washington, D.C.

Washington, D.C., is the capital of the United States. Lagos used to be the capital of Nigeria. These cities are very different in many ways. Yet they are alike in many ways, too.

Both cities are good places to buy and sell things because they are near water. Lagos is near the Gulf of Guinea. Washington, D.C., is mainly next to the Potomac River. Boats can carry people and things to and from cities that are near water.

Washington, D.C.

The two cities grew in different ways. Lagos grew fast. It was not planned to become a large capital city. Washington, D.C., was planned to be the United States capital.

Today, Lagos and Washington, D.C., share large-city problems. Both need more homes and better ways for people to travel around the city.

Lagos

Compare and Contrast

1. How are Washington, D.C., and Lagos alike?
2. How are these cities different?
3. What problems do both cities have in common today?

Be My Neighbor

by Maya Ajmera and John D. Ivanko

Israel

A community is a group of people who live in the same place. All communities are made up of different neighborhoods. Some neighborhoods are big, but some are small.

Neighborhoods are made up of different people. These people work to make their neighborhoods nice places to live. In this story, you will learn about the ways people live in neighborhoods around the world.

United States

Canada

Your neighborhood is a special place.

A neighborhood is where you live, learn, grow up, play, and work, surrounded by your family and friends. Each and every neighborhood is a special place. Yours might be in the mountains, along a coast, or somewhere in between. It might have important historical sites, such as a monument or the home of someone famous.

Mali

It may be part of a village, town, or big city.

Neighborhoods around the world can look very different. Some neighborhoods have lots and lots of people in them, while others have only a small population, such as those on a remote island, in the country, or high up in the hills. Some neighborhoods are made up of a few buildings in a town or village, while others stretch for miles and miles and are part of a big city.

Turkey

Every neighborhood is made up of lots of different people . . .

Your neighborhood can be made up of people of all ages, interests, and backgrounds. Some members of your neighborhood may live like you and your family, and others may have different habits and customs that are celebrated in different kinds of festivals and community activities. The post office, town square, places of worship, and sports fields are places where people from your community come together.

. . . and lots of different homes.

A house can be just for your family or it can be an apartment in a large building where many families live next to one another. Houses can be made from different materials, such as wood, brick, glass, or even mud, grass, or rocks. In places where the weather is cold, houses are made to keep you warm. In warm climates houses are built to keep you cool. No matter where you live, houses are for making you and your family comfortable, dry, and safe.

Mongolia

. . . and places to buy the things you need.

Many neighborhoods have markets, restaurants, shopping malls, or grocery stores to buy what you and your family need. Some places are large with lots of different things for sale, while other stores are small, selling only specific items like bread or cheese. You can even create your own place to sell something homemade to others in your community.

France

Mexico

In your neighborhood you share responsibilities . . .

People who live in the same neighborhood often work together to make it a better place. You might join your neighbors to clean up a river or work with a youth group to plant trees in a park. Neighbors look out for one another, perhaps helping someone find a lost dog or picking up fallen branches after a big storm. There are also people in your neighborhood whose job it is to take care of you: doctors, police officers, firefighters, and mail carriers, for example.

India

United States

Your neighborhood is where you feel at home.

Neighbors have in common the place where they live. You celebrate your neighborhood because you're a part of it and it's a part of you. Your neighborhood is a place where you learn about cooperation, respect, and friendship. It's the place you call home.

Papua New Guinea

United Kingdom

Response Corner

1. Focus Skill **Compare and Contrast** How are the neighborhoods that make up communities alike? How are they different?
2. **Make It Relevant** How is your neighborhood like other places in your community?

UNDERSTAND VOCABULARY

Using a dictionary can help you learn new words as you read.

- **A dictionary shows the meanings of a word and describes where the word came from.**
- **You can use a chart to list the unknown words that you look up in a dictionary.**

community (kə•myōō´nə•tē) *n* 1: a group of people who live and work in the same place.

Word	Definition
community	A group of people who live and work in the same place.

PREVIEW VOCABULARY

business p. 16

museum p. 17

law p. 18

CHAPTER

Learning About Communities

A view of Main Street in Easton, Maryland

Lesson 1

What Is a Community?

What to Know
What is a community?

Vocabulary
community p. 14
citizen p. 14
culture p. 15
business p. 16
museum p. 17
law p. 18
government p. 19

Compare and Contrast

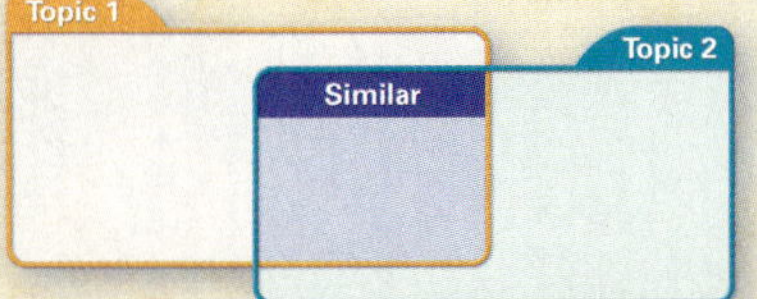

Like most people, you live in a community. A **community** is a group of people who live and work in the same place.

People live in communities all over the world. One reason they live in communities is that they like to be with others. In a community, people feel that they belong.

The people who live in and belong to a community are called **citizens**. Citizens are part of a community.

Like many communities, New York City, New York, is made up of many groups of people.

Many People, One Community

The citizens of a community may belong to different groups. They may have different cultures. A **culture** is a way of life shared by members of a group. What people eat, how they speak and dress, and what they believe in are parts of their culture.

Clothing is part of a person's culture. These girls in New Jersey dance at an Indian cultural event.

Sharing Cultures

Most communities have people from more than one culture. People often bring some of their culture to a community. They share their foods, clothing, music, and art. When a community has different cultures, people can enjoy other ways of life.

Reading Check **Compare and Contrast**
What is one way communities are alike?

Depending on One Another

People in a community depend on, or count on, one another. They depend on police and firefighters to keep them safe. People also depend on stores and other businesses. In a **business**, workers make or sell things or do work for others.

Businesses help people in communities meet their wants. A want is something that people would like to have, such as a television. Some wants are needs. Food, clothing, and a place to live are all needs.

Businesses provide jobs for people in a community. The money people earn from working can help them pay for their wants. In turn, businesses depend on the people in a community to buy what the businesses sell.

Reading Check **Generalize**
How do people in communities depend on one another?

People depend on businesses for the things they want and need.

Describing a Place

What kind of climate does your community have? Your community's climate might be hot or cold. It might change from season to season. You might live in a rainy place or in a desert. A **desert** is a place where the climate is dry.

What landforms are near your community? A **landform** is a kind of land. Your community might be on flat land, called a plain. Or you might live near mountains.

Are there any bodies of water near your community? A community might be located next to a river or a lake. People who live along the main coasts of the United States are near the Atlantic Ocean or the Pacific Ocean.

Reading Check **Compare and Contrast**
How can geography make communities different?

Burdett, Kansas

Chattanooga, Tennessee

Provincetown, Massachusetts

This movie theater in Greenbelt is built in the Art Deco style of the 1930s.

Different Pasts

Every community has its own history. Towns are started by different people and for different reasons. Some communities may be very old, while others are newer. Greenbelt, Maryland is a much newer town than Clarksville, Indiana.

Greenbelt, Maryland

By the time people began moving to Greenbelt in 1937, the whole town had already been built. The United States government planned this town. It was built for families who could not find a place to live in nearby Washington, D.C. The people of the new community made laws for the town. Greenbelt has grown and now includes new houses, new shops, and more people.

For online activities, go to **www.harcourtschool.com/ss1**

Missouri

0 50 100 Miles
0 50 100 Kilometers
N
S
E
W
IOWA
ILLINOIS
KANSAS
OKLAHOMA
ARKANSAS
KENTUCKY
TENNESSEE
MISSOURI
Maryville
St. Joseph
Chillicothe
Hannibal
Kansas City
Independence
Columbia
Jefferson City
St. Louis
Rolla
Springfield
Joplin
Cape Girardeau
Poplar Bluff
Grand River
Mississippi River
Missouri River
Osage River
St. Francis River
Mark Twain Lake
Harry S. Truman Reservoir
Stockton Lake
Table Rock Lake
Lake Wappapello

Apply

Make It Relevant Find your community on a map. Use the map scale and the compass rose to tell the distance and direction you would travel to get to a nearby community.

Lesson 4

Discover Your Community

What to Know
How can you learn about your community?

Vocabulary

reference work p. 33
ancestor p. 34
heritage p. 34
historic site p. 36
historical society p. 36

Compare and Contrast

Imagine that you are a detective. Detectives search for clues to discover the truth about events. They read books, talk to people, and visit places.

Detectives make notes about each discovery, both large and small. The clues they find are like puzzle pieces. When these pieces are put together, they form a complete picture of what happened.

Students look at old community photographs.

Libraries have many resources you can use for community research.

Become a Detective

Like a detective, you can search for facts about your own community. You can learn what life was like in your community's past. You may learn about jobs and leaders. You might also discover facts about cultures in your community.

One way to find information about your community is to visit a library. A library has many **reference works**, or sources of facts. At a library, you can study maps to learn about your community's geography. You can also look at old and new photographs of your community. Ask a librarian to help you find what you need. Take notes when you find something useful.

Reading Check **Compare and Contrast**
How is researching your community like being a detective?

Interview Other Citizens

Interviewing, or asking questions, is another good way to learn about your community. There are many people you can interview. You can ask business owners about jobs in your community. You can also talk to community members about different cultures found in your community.

Older family members are also good sources of information. They can tell you about your ancestors. An **ancestor** is someone in a person's family who lived long ago.

An older person can also tell you about your heritage. A **heritage** is the set of values and ways of life handed down from people who lived long ago.

Students interview a person in their community of Nashville, Tennessee.

Plan the Interview

- Decide what the interview will be about.
- Write or call to ask for an interview.
- Tell the person who you are and why you would like to interview him or her.
- Set a time and a place to meet.

Before the Interview

- Find facts about your topic and the person.
- Make a list of questions to ask.

During the Interview

- If you want to use a digital video camera or tape recorder, ask the person first.
- Listen carefully, and do not interrupt.
- Take notes as you talk with the person. Write down some of his or her exact words.

After the Interview

- Before you leave, thank the person.
- Write the person a thank-you note.

Reading Check **Sequence**
What steps should you take before interviewing someone?

Write to or Visit Places

To get information about your community's history, you can write to or visit museums and historic sites. A **historic site** is a place where an important event took place.

Another source of information is your community's historical society. A **historical society** is an organization of community members who are interested in their community's history.

You can get more information about your community from other places, too. Businesses, parks, schools, and government offices are some of these places.

How to Write for Information

You can write a letter or send an e-mail to ask for information. Follow these steps.

- Write neatly, or use a computer.
- Tell who you are and why you are writing.
- Tell exactly what you want to know.

The Maxton Historical Society in Maxton, North Carolina, keeps old photographs, diaries, and newspapers.

How to Ask Questions During a Visit

If you visit a museum, historical society, or historic site, be sure to do these things.

- Take along a list of questions to ask.
- Tell who you are and why you are visiting.
- Listen carefully, and take notes.
- Take any information that the place offers.
- Before you leave, thank the person you spoke with.

Reading Check **Compare and Contrast**
How are historical societies and historic sites different?

A historian at the Maxton Historical Society studies his community.

Summary You can be a detective in your own community. To gather facts, you can visit a library, interview people, and write to or visit special places.

Review

1. **What to Know** How can you learn about your community?
2. **Vocabulary** What might you find at a **historic site**?
3. **Your Community** Whom can you interview to find out about your own community?
4. **Critical Thinking** How are museums and historical societies alike? How are they important to a community?
5. **Make a Web Page** Make a web page to show places where you can get information about your community.
6. **Compare and Contrast** On a separate sheet of paper, copy and complete the graphic organizer below.

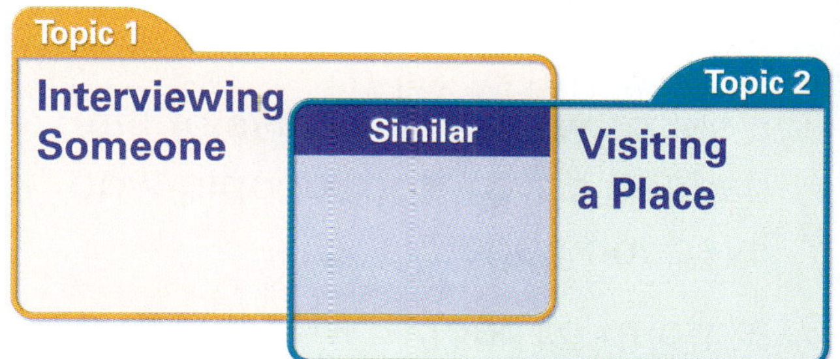

Chapter 1 Review

Visual Summary

Communities are places where people live and work.

Summarize the Chapter

Compare and Contrast Complete this graphic organizer to compare and contrast communities.

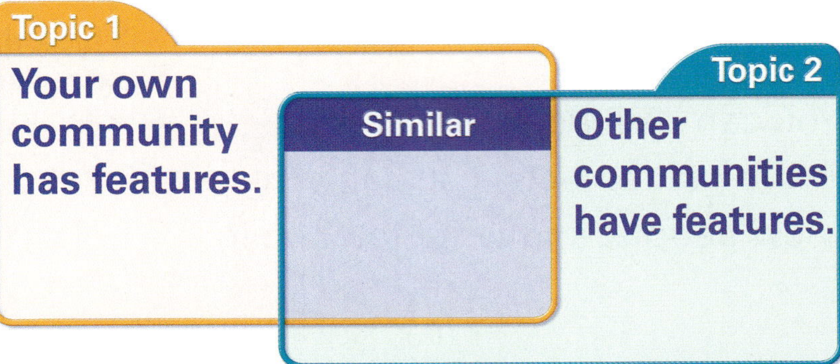

Identify the term from the word bank that correctly matches each definition.

1. a group of people that makes laws for a community, a state, or a country
2. a set of values and ways of life handed down from people who lived long ago
3. a group of people who live and work in the same place
4. the weather a place has over a long period of time
5. an area of land with its own people and laws

Word Bank

community p. 14
government p. 19
climate p. 20
nation p. 26
heritage p. 34

Communities are similar and different in many ways.

People can learn about their communities.

Facts and Main Ideas

Answer these questions.

6. What do people from different cultures share with others in their community?
7. What could you talk about to describe a community's geography?
8. How can people communicate with others who live far away?

Write the letter of the best choice.

9. Which of the following is a landform?
   A mountain
   B climate
   C region
   D weather
10. Which of the following is a place where an important event happened?
   A library
   B museum
   C historic site
   D historical society

Critical Thinking

11. **Make It Relevant** If your community chose a sister city, what might you learn from that city?
12. **Make It Relevant** What would your community be like without its businesses?

Skills

Find Directions and Distances
Use the map on page 31 to answer the question.

13. In what direction would you travel to go from Maryville to Hannibal? How far is it between the two cities?

writing

Write an Article Write an article telling how libraries can help you learn about the past.

Write a Poem Make a list of words about your community. Use the words to write a poem.

PREVIEW AND QUESTION

Previewing a lesson helps you identify main ideas. Asking questions about these ideas can help you find important information.

- **Reading the lesson titles and section titles gives clues about the main topic. Think of any questions you have about the topic.**
- **Read to find the answers to your questions.**
- **Finally, review what you have read.**

Communities of Different Sizes			
Preview	Questions	Read	Review
Lesson 1 A city is an urban community.	What is it like to live in an urban community?	✓	✓
Lesson 2			

PREVIEW VOCABULARY

urban p. 43

suburban p. 52

rural p. 56

CHAPTER 2

Communities of Different Sizes

Navy Pier and Chicago's skyline

Lesson 1

Urban Communities

What to Know
What is an urban community?

Vocabulary

region p. 42
population p. 42
urban p. 43
harbor p. 45
transportation p. 46

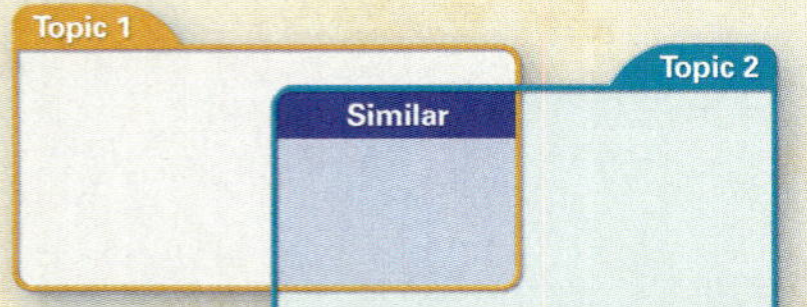

Compare and Contrast (Focus Skill)

Communities are different. They have different people, jobs, and histories. They also may be located in different regions. A **region** is an area with at least one feature that makes it different from other areas.

The features of a community might include its landforms or climate. Another feature that makes a region different from others is its population. The **population** of a place is the number of people living there.

The skyline of Chicago, Illinois

Communities Large and Small

How would you describe the population of your own community? It may be large, small, or in between. Your community may have a lot of people or just a few.

Urban Regions

Most people in the United States live in or near **urban**, or city, regions. A city is the largest kind of community.

A city has busy streets, many people, and tall buildings. Cities need more schools and businesses than smaller communities do. In a city, crowded buses and trains carry people from place to place.

Reading Check **Compare and Contrast**
How is an urban community different from other communities?

State Street in Chicago

Baltimore, an Urban Community

Kelsey lives in a row house building in Baltimore, Maryland. On her way to school, Kelsey sees people opening businesses for the day. Other people are catching buses to their jobs.

A Picture of Kelsey's City

The city of Baltimore is located on the Patapsco (puh•TAP•skoh) River. More than half a million people live in the city. Long ago, Baltimore began as a place where goods were loaded and unloaded onto ships. Over time, it grew into the city it is today.

Kelsey's area of Baltimore has people of many cultures. Living in Baltimore allows Kelsey to learn about these cultures.

Kelsey leaves her Baltimore home to go to elementary school.

The Inner Harbor is located near downtown Baltimore, along the waterfront.

Living in Baltimore

Kelsey's parents moved to Baltimore to work there. Her mother rides the subway, or underground train, to her job at a local hospital. Baltimore also has a lightrail system. A lightrail is like a train. It rides on a rail and carries people. Kelsey's father works in a skyscraper, a very tall building. The building is in downtown Baltimore, the city's main business district. A business district is where many businesses are located.

On the weekends, Kelsey and her family visit many places in Baltimore. At the Inner Harbor, they go to museums and watch boats on the river. A **harbor** is a protected place with deep water that allows ships to come close to shore.

Reading Check **Main Idea and Details**
What makes Baltimore an urban area?

Other Urban Communities

Baltimore is at the center of one of many urban regions in the United States. Some other cities are even larger than Baltimore. New York City, New York, is the nation's largest city. It is located near a harbor on the Atlantic Ocean.

Cities are often located near harbors and rivers because this location makes transportation easier. **Transportation** is the movement of people and goods.

People in New York City have many ways to get around. They ride the bus or the subway to get from place to place. Many people choose to walk or ride bikes.

Chicago, Illinois, the nation's third-largest city, sits in the middle of the country near Lake Michigan. Like Baltimore and New York City, Chicago has many businesses and people. People in Chicago ride elevated trains that circle the city.

New Yorkers use MetroCards to ride the subway.

The subway in New York City is mostly underground. In some places, however, the tracks are above ground.

Cities with Different Cultures

Los Angeles, the nation's second-largest city, is near the Pacific coast in southern California. As in other cities, many of its citizens came from different parts of the United States or from other countries. They moved to Los Angeles to work at jobs, go to school, and make new lives. In Los Angeles, you can find neighborhoods in which people of many different cultures live together.

Reading Check **Compare and Contrast**
How is New York City different from Chicago?

Many people celebrate Hispanic culture in Los Angeles.

Summary A city is the largest kind of community. Urban regions are filled with people, buildings, jobs, and different forms of transportation.

Review

1. **What to Know** What is an urban community?
2. **Vocabulary** Write a sentence about **population**, using the term **urban**.
3. **Geography** Why are many cities located near bodies of water?
4. **Critical Thinking** **Make It Relevant** Do you think your community is in an urban area? Why or why not?
5. **Create a Postcard** Create a picture postcard of an urban community. Write about what makes this community special.
6. Focus Skill **Compare and Contrast** On a separate sheet of paper, copy and complete the graphic organizer below.

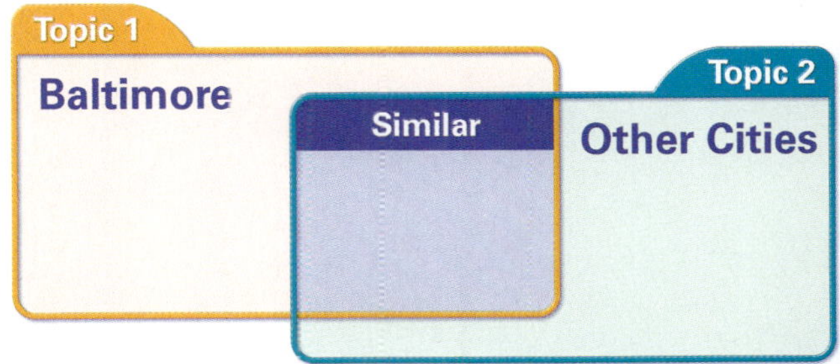

Use a Map Grid

Why It Matters Sometimes you need to find the exact location of a park, a school, or a road.

Learn

To find the exact location of a place, you can use a map that has a grid system. A **grid system** is a set of lines the same distance apart that cross one another to form boxes. The grid on this page shows rows and columns of boxes. The rows are labeled with letters, and the columns are labeled with numbers. Follow these steps to use a map grid.

Step 1 Put a finger on the red box. Slide your finger to the left, to the letter D.

Step 2 Now put a finger on the red box again. Slide your finger to the top, to the number 3. The exact location of the red box is D-3, or row D, column 3.

Grid system

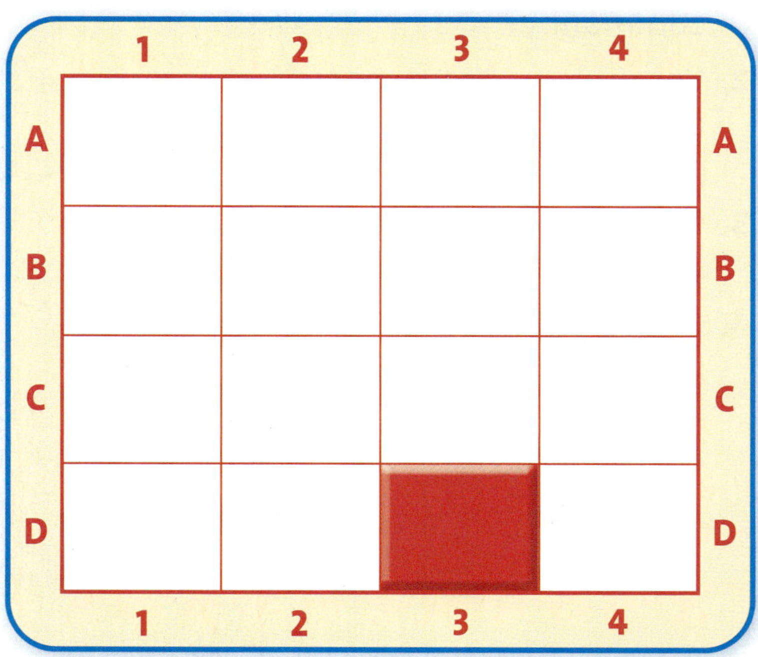

For online activities, go to **www.harcourtschool.com/ss1**

Mount Vernon in Baltimore, Maryland

Map Key
- Point of interest
- Lightrail train line

Practice

Use this map and its grid system to answer the questions. Give exact locations by using a letter and a number.

1. Where is the Contemporary Museum?
2. What point of interest do you see in the box at D-5?
3. Where is the Maryland General Hospital?

Apply

Make It Relevant Draw a map of your school, house, or community. Add a grid, and label places on your map. Then share your map with classmates.

Frederick Law Olmsted

"An artist, he paints with lakes and wooded slopes; . . . with mountain sides and ocean views."

— Architect Daniel Burnham on Frederick Law Olmsted

Why Character Counts

How did Frederick Law Olmsted show caring for people in urban communities?

Frederick Law Olmsted designed many of our country's famous urban parks. He wanted people in urban communities to enjoy nature.

Olmsted grew up on a farm in Connecticut. Early in his life, he began reading books about natural landscapes.

As a young man, Olmsted spent time traveling throughout Europe. During his travels, he studied parks and landscapes.

Frederick Law Olmsted

Central Park in New York City

FREDERICK LAW OLMSTED
33
USA
LANDSCAPE ARCHITECT

This stamp shows Olmsted and Central Park.

Olmsted worked as the supervisor for planning Central Park in New York City. In 1858, the city held a contest to choose a new park design. Olmsted worked with Calvert Vaux, another parks designer, on a plan. Their design won the contest.

Olmsted then spent nearly 40 years planning and creating parks in communities across the United States. One of his last projects was the Emerald Necklace, a 7-mile system of parks around Boston, Massachusetts.

Frederick Law Olmsted is remembered for his landscaping. Landscaping is the use of natural materials, such as plants and rocks, to create outdoor spaces. His landscape designs have improved many urban areas.

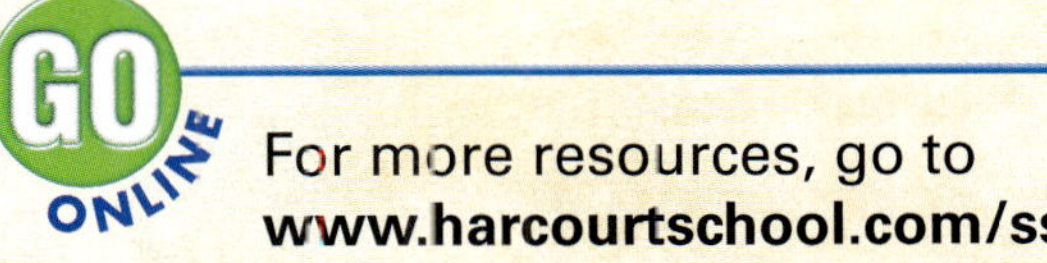

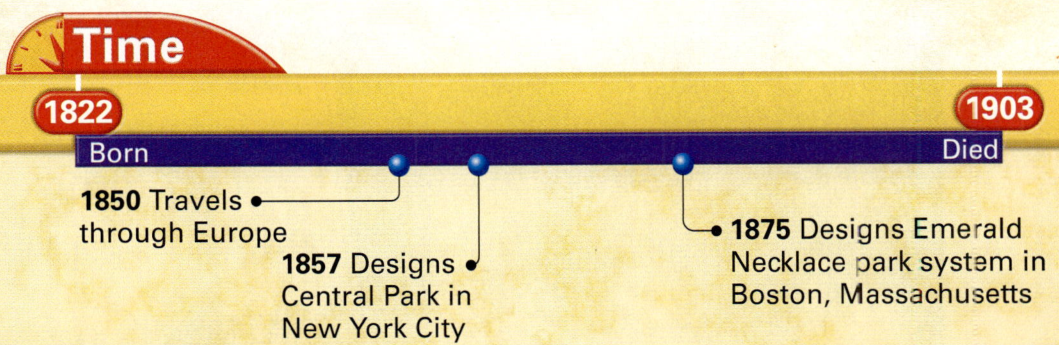

Lesson 2

Suburban Communities

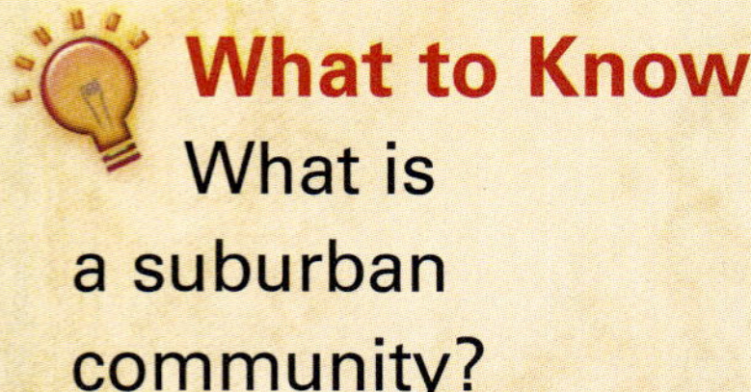

What to Know
What is a suburban community?

Vocabulary
suburb p. 52
suburban p. 52

Compare and Contrast

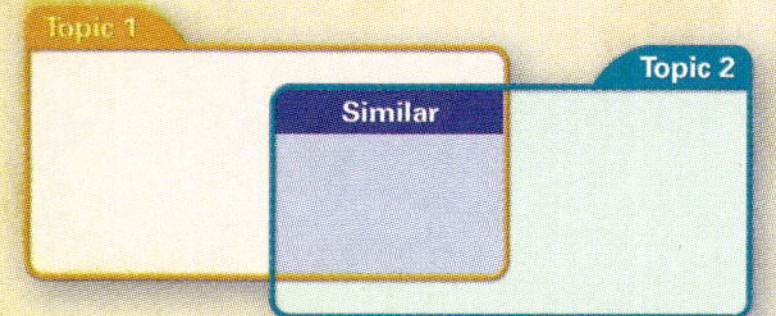

Many large cities have smaller communities around them. A smaller city or town built near a large city is called a **suburb** (suh•berb).

Maplewood, a Suburban Community

Maplewood, New Jersey, is a suburb of New York City. It is one of hundreds of suburbs around New York City. This suburban region includes communities in New York, New Jersey, Pennsylvania, and Connecticut. A **suburban** region is made up of all the suburbs around a large city.

Living in Maplewood

Years ago, John's parents lived in a New York City apartment. After John was born, they decided to move to Maplewood, just 18 miles away. Now, they live in a house with a large yard on a tree-lined street. They have more space for their growing family.

Like many suburbs, Maplewood has its own government and its own businesses. John and his family shop at the local supermarket, at small stores in downtown Maplewood, and at shopping centers at the edge of town. They also enjoy the town's parks and movie theater.

John attends one of the elementary schools in Maplewood. Every school day, his parents drive him to school. Then they ride the train into New York City, where they work.

Reading Check **Compare and Contrast**
How is life in a suburb different from life in a city?

People in this suburban community enjoy spending time with their neighbors.

John likes to play soccer in his front yard in Maplewood, New Jersey.

Urban Connections

Top Five Ways Suburban Workers Travel to New York City
1. By subway
2. By train
3. By car
4. By bus
5. By ferry

Table How do most workers travel to New York City?

Long ago, communities were often built near railroad stations. As people moved from large cities to these communities, the communities grew into suburbs. As more and more people began driving cars, more suburbs were built near roads and highways. Today, people in suburbs travel on trains, subways, and highways to nearby cities.

Maplewood is its own town, but it is closely connected to New York City. Like John's parents, many people in Maplewood work in New York City.

Suburban citizens also travel to urban areas to visit interesting places. Many suburbs have their own theaters and museums, but nearby cities offer people more choices. John and his family visit New York City to see his favorite sports teams compete.

Many people drive to and from the suburbs and New York City.

Suburbs Grow

Today, more and more people are living in suburban regions. Businesses are moving to the suburbs. This allows them to be closer to people's homes. It also costs less to run a business in the suburbs.

Museums and other cultural sites are also being built in the suburbs. In many suburbs, people attend music concerts and other events. Though still connected to cities, these suburbs are their own communities.

Most suburban communities have parks.

Reading Check **Main Idea and Details**
How are suburban and urban areas connected?

Summary Suburban communities are smaller communities near urban areas. They are connected to cities through transportation and jobs.

Review

1. **What to Know** What is a suburban community?
2. **Vocabulary** Write a description of a **suburban** area.
3. **History** Where did many suburban areas start?
4. **Critical Thinking** Why do you think people live in suburbs?
5. **Make a Flyer** Make a flyer about a suburban community. Describe what it is like to live there.
6. Focus Skill **Compare and Contrast** On a separate sheet of paper, copy and complete the graphic organizer below.

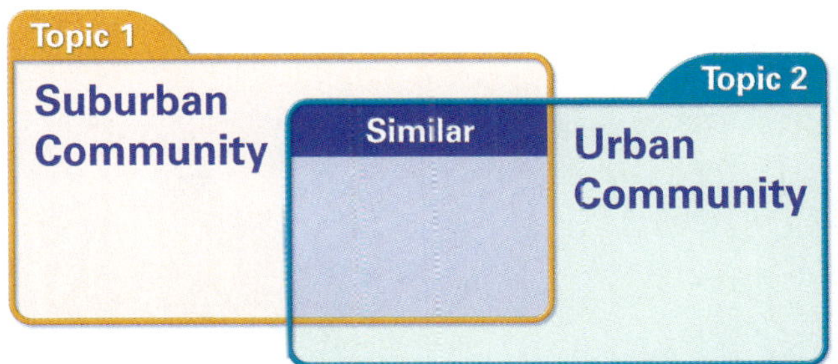

Lesson 3

Rural Communities

What to Know
What is a rural community?

Vocabulary
rural p. 56
agriculture p. 60
economy p. 60

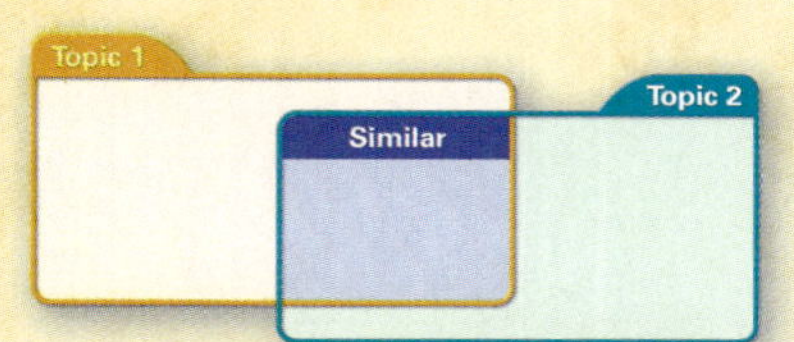

Many people live in urban and suburban communities in the United States. Other people live in small towns far away from these areas.

Searcy, a Rural Community

A **rural** region is in the countryside, away from cities and large towns. Small towns, farms, fields, and woods make up rural regions. Searcy (SER•see) is a rural community in Arkansas.

Corn and other crops are grown near Searcy, Arkansas.

Small Town Life

Mallory lives in a small house in Searcy. Her father works at a store in the town. Her mother works at the community's newspaper. The newspaper provides important local information to the citizens of Searcy.

Mallory attends one of the elementary schools in Searcy. She enjoys playing soccer with her friends at a nearby soccer field. She also spends time at the community center, where people play basketball, tennis, and other sports.

In the fall, Mallory visits the county fair. She enjoys looking at the many animals that are brought to the fair from the surrounding countryside. She also enjoys the rides and games at the carnival.

The White County Fair in Searcy

Reading Check **Compare and Contrast**
How is Searcy different from a large city?

Mallory lives in Searcy, a rural community.

Urban and Suburban Connections

Rural, urban, and suburban communities may all be different, but they are important to each other. Colleges in each kind of area provide education for students from the other areas. Many rural areas grow and produce food for other communities.

People in rural areas sometimes travel long distances to visit cities. Some cities have more choices in stores and more choices of doctors to visit.

Sherwood and Little Rock, Arkansas

Little Rock, Arkansas, is the large city nearest to Searcy. It is located 50 miles from the town. Little Rock is an urban community and the center of the state's government. A few miles south is Sherwood, a suburb of Little Rock. Many people in Sherwood work in Little Rock. People in Searcy sometimes drive to Little Rock to visit hospitals or shop at stores.

Reading Check Summarize
How are all types of communities connected?

This farmer grows cotton in Arkansas.

Communities in Arkansas

Suburban Community

Sherwood

MAP SKILL **Location** Searcy, Sherwood, and Little Rock are communities of different sizes. Along which river is Little Rock located?

In Stillwater, many people attend and work at Oklahoma State University.

Other Rural Communities

Many people in Searcy work in agriculture. **Agriculture** is the raising of farm animals and the growing of crops for sale. Not all rural communities have farms and ranches.

A College Town

Stillwater is a town in Oklahoma. The economy of Stillwater is based on the university there. An **economy** is the way a community or country makes and uses goods and services.

Many people who live in Stillwater work or take classes at Oklahoma State University. The university is important to Stillwater. When the school grows, so does the town. Students who go to the university live in Stillwater's apartments and houses. Students also eat at restaurants in Stillwater. The town's businesses hire students.

Children in History

Maya Angelou

Writer Maya Angelou (AN•juh•loh) lived in a rural community in Arkansas in the 1930s. Angelou helped at a store her grandmother owned.

She later wrote her memories in a book about her life. She wrote, "Customers could find food staples [common foods], a good variety of colored thread . . . corn for chickens, coal oil for lamps, light bulbs for the wealthy, shoestrings, hair dressing, balloons, and flower seeds."

Make It Relevant What businesses in your community sell these goods?

Outdoor Activities and Historic Towns

Rural areas offer outdoor activities, such as fishing, skiing, and hiking. Some towns have historic sites. Michigan's Mackinac (MA•kuh•naw) Island offers both. Visitors fish and go boating on Lake Michigan. They explore history at Fort Mackinac. This site has the oldest buildings in Michigan.

Reading Check **Compare and Contrast**
How can rural communities be different from each other?

Summary Rural areas are far from cities. Urban, suburban, and rural communities all depend on each other.

Fast Fact

In the 1920s, Mackinac Island no longer allowed automobiles on the island. Horses and bikes are now the main kinds of transportation.

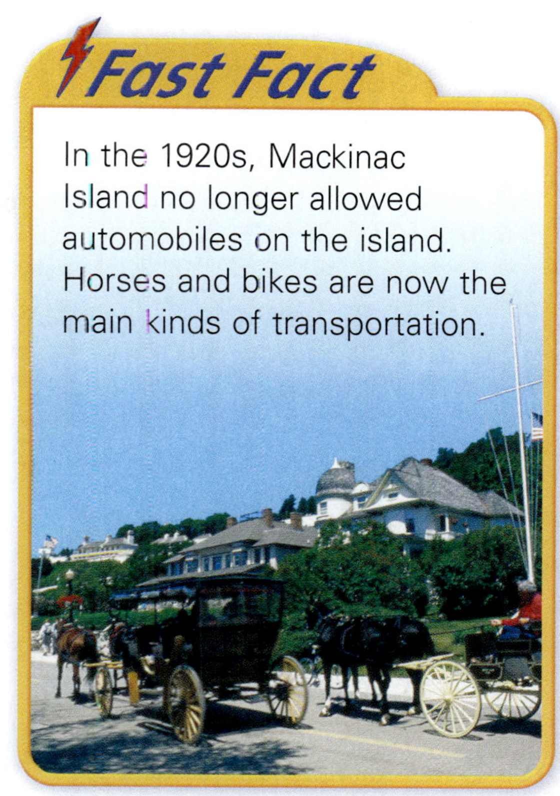

Review

1. **What to Know** What is a rural community?
2. **Vocabulary** Use the terms **agriculture** and **rural** in a sentence.
3. **Your Community** How is your own community connected to rural, suburban, or urban areas?
4. **Critical Thinking** Why are rural communities important?
5. **Write a Diary Entry** Write a diary entry about the type of community you live in. What makes your community different from other communities?
6. Focus Skill **Compare and Contrast** On a separate sheet of paper, copy and complete the graphic organizer below.

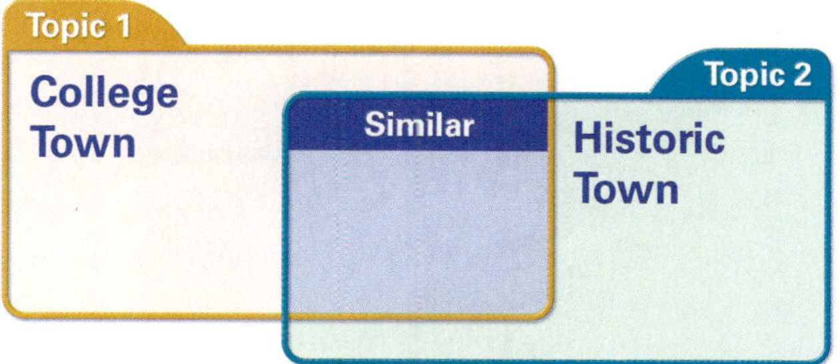

What Is Best About Your Community?

There are many kinds of communities in the United States. Some people prefer to live in urban communities. Other people like the suburbs or a rural town best. The place where you live can shape your opinion about places like it.

Margaret Mead devoted her life to studying people and places. She chose to make her home in New York City—the largest urban community in the United States.

"A city is a place where there is no need to wait for next week to get the answer to a question, to taste the food of any country, to find new voices to listen to and familiar ones to listen to again."

Philip Langdon

Philip Langdon writes about communities and design. In one book, he describes what he likes about East Aurora, an older suburban community in New York.

"Stores, churches, restaurants, offices, and civic buildings were strung along a pleasant, maple-shaded Main Street. . . . Nearly everything the inhabitants [community members] needed . . . was close to home."

Jo Ann Emerson

Jo Ann Emerson works in the government. Each year, she tours southern Missouri to learn about rural communities.

"Many Americans who live in urban or suburban areas may not realize just how important our rural communities are to them and to America. Our farming and ranching neighbors feed the country."

It's Your Turn

Compare Points of View Review each point of view, and answer the questions.

1. Who would most likely want to live in a rural area?
2. What words in Margaret Mead's quote tell about the different cultures in a city?
3. What does Philip Langdon like about East Aurora?

Make It Relevant Why might people have different points of view about the size of a community?

Explore Your Community

In this unit, you learned about the different features of a community. There are resources in your community to help you learn about those features.

Libraries

Museums

Find Out About Your Community

- What are some different features in your community?
- Where can people come together in your community?
- Do you live in a rural, a suburban, or an urban community?
- What is your community's population?

Create a Community Collage

Make a collage of your community. Gather pictures from magazines or newspapers that show its different features. Include pictures of climate, landforms, businesses, transportation, and places where people come together.

Chapter 2 Review

Visual Summary

Many people in the United States live in urban regions.

Summarize the Chapter

Compare and Contrast Complete this graphic organizer to compare and contrast two different kinds of communities.

Topic 1	Similar	Topic 2
Maplewood, New Jersey, is a suburban community.		Searcy, Arkansas, is a rural community.

Vocabulary

Write the correct term from the list to complete each sentence.

1. Cities are located in ______ regions.
2. The way a community makes and uses goods and services is its ____________.
3. A smaller city or town near a larger city is a ________.
4. The ________ of a place is the number of people living there.
5. ____________ is the movement of people, and goods.
6. A ____________ community is in the countryside, away from large cities.

Word Bank

population p. 42
suburb p. 52
urban p. 43
rural p. 56
transportation p. 46
economy p. 60

Suburban communities are connected to urban communities.

Rural regions are made up of small towns, farms, and woods.

Facts and Main Ideas

Answer these questions.

7. What kinds of transportation do people use in urban areas?
8. What makes up a suburban region?
9. How do rural communities help other communities?

Write the letter of the best choice.

10. Which of the following best describes an urban area?
    - **A** agricultural community
    - **B** small community
    - **C** community near a city
    - **D** city with many people
11. Which community is rural?
    - **A** Stillwater, Oklahoma
    - **B** Chicago, Illinois
    - **C** Maplewood, New Jersey
    - **D** Baltimore, Maryland
12. What is a feature of Stillwater, Oklahoma?
    - **A** skyscrapers
    - **B** agriculture
    - **C** college
    - **D** subway

Critical Thinking

13. How do urban, suburban, and rural regions depend on each other?
14. **Make It Relevant** Is your community in an urban, suburban, or rural region? Why?

Skills

Use a Map Grid
Use the map on page 49 to answer the question.

15. Where do Madison Street and the lightrail train line meet?

writing

Write a Story Imagine living in a different kind of community. Write a story about a day in this community.

Write an Invitation Invite a friend to your community. In the invitation tell about your community, including its population and economy.

Postcard Mania

	1	2	3	4	5
A	a	b	c	d	e
B	f	g	h	i	j
C	k	l	m	n	o
D	p	q	r	s	t
E	u	v	w	x	y

Use the grid to find the missing words in the postcards. Then decide what kind of region each person has moved to—urban, rural, or suburban.

Hi All!
We're here!
There are [E-3, C-5, C-5, A-4, D-4] near our house. I can't wait for the [B-1, A-1, B-4, D-3]! There will be a lot of [A-1, C-4, B-4, C-3, A-1, C-2, D-4].
Your buddy,
Josh

Dear Grace,
We're here!
Our house has a huge [E-5, A-1, D-3, A-4], so now I can have a [A-4, C-5, B-2].
Dad drops me off at [D-4, A-3, B-3, C-5, C-5, C-2].
Bye for now,
Stacie

Dear Grandpa Joe,
We're here!
There are so many [D-1, A-5, C-5, D-1, C-2, A-5]. Mom likes all the [D-3, A-5, D-4, D-5, A-1, E-1, D-3, A-1, C-4, D-5, D-4] and [D-4, D-5, C-5, D-3, A-5, D-4].
This place is fun!
Love,
Terry

Each book in the historical society's library has a mixed-up word in its title. Fix it. Then find the book that doesn't belong in the library.

Online Adventures

GO ONLINE

Join Eco to play a game in this online community. A scavenger hunt is taking place in town today. You'll need to explore the police station, the grocery store, the town hall, and other buildings. If you can find all the items in time, you win! Play now at **www.harcourtschool.com/ss1**

Review and Test Prep

The Big Idea

Communities Communities are alike and different and are found all over the world.

Chattanooga, Tennessee

Reading Comprehension and Vocabulary

Communities Around Us

People live in communities all over the world. Citizens in these communities follow laws, depend on one another, and have their own cultures. They stay connected to others through communication.

Communities are different in many ways. They have different landforms, climates, histories, and jobs. Communities are also different sizes, depending on their populations. Urban, suburban, and rural communities depend on each other.

Read the summary above. Then answer the questions that follow.

1. Which of the following is a citizen?
   A a school
   B a place to find resources
   C a person living in a community
   D a business

2. Which of the following is a form of communication?
   A the Internet
   B a train
   C farming
   D a library

3. What makes each community different?
   A landforms
   B climate
   C history
   D all of the above

4. How would you describe the population of an urban community?
   A few people
   B few cultures
   C many people
   D few businesses

Facts and Main Ideas

Answer these questions.

5. How do communities around the world communicate?
6. What resources can you use to learn about a community?
7. What are some different kinds of communities?

Write the letter of the best choice.

8. Which of the following jobs would likely be found in a community near water?
   A tree farmer
   B fisher
   C dairy farmer
   D mountain-climbing guide
9. Which of the following is not a good?
   A a television
   B a fruit
   C a doctor's visit
   D a computer
10. Which of the following groups depend on each other?
    A businesses and workers
    B citizens in the same community
    C urban and rural communities
    D all of the above

Critical Thinking

11. What do you think a community would be like if its people did not share their culture with others?
12. **Make It Relevant** What is one feature in your community that makes it different from another community?

Skills

Find Directions and Distances

Use the map below to answer the following questions.

13. Which is closer to Stillwater—Enid or Durant? Find the distances.
14. Name a town northwest of Stillwater.

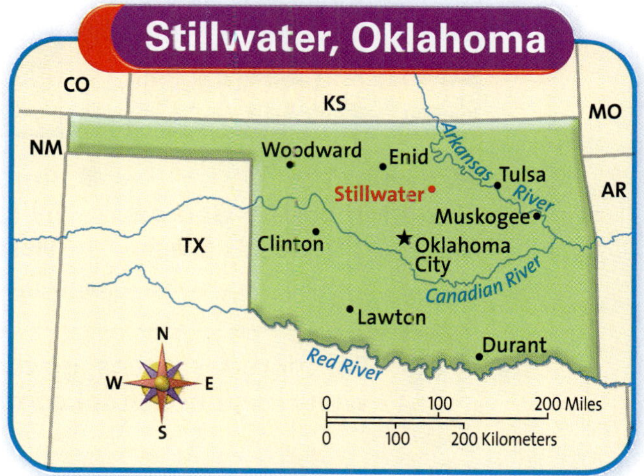

Unit 1

Activities

Show What You Know

Unit Writing Activity

Write an Article Write an article about two communities.

- Research two communities.
- Compare and contrast facts about the communities.
- Explain how people live, work, and play in each community.

Unit Project

Community Catalog Create a catalog of the resources in your community.

- List the resources, and tell where they can be found.
- Explain what each resource can tell about your community.

Read More

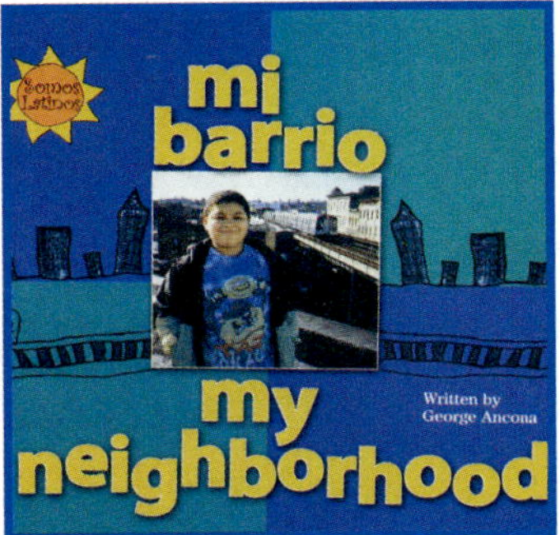

- *Mi Barrio/My Neighborhood* by George Ancona. Children's Press.

- *America Is . . .* by Louise Borden. Margaret K. McElderry.

- *If the World Were a Village* by David J. Smith. Kids Can Press.

GO ONLINE For more resources, go to **www.harcourtschool.com/ss1**

Communities and Geography

Unit 2

Start with the Standards

Oklahoma Priority Academic Student Skills

1.1 Identify, locate, and compare and contrast information found in resources such as encyclopedias, visual images, atlases, maps, globes, and computer-based technologies.

2.1 Distinguish among map symbols and demonstrate through mental mapping and understanding of relative location, direction, scale, size and shape.

2.2 Construct simple maps of the seven continents with the essential map elements of title, key, directional indicators, and date.

2.3 Use the equator and prime meridian to identify the four hemispheres.

2.4 Develop skills in locating places across the globe using parallels of latitude and meridians of longitude.

4.1 Name and locate basic types of climate across the globe and describe how they affect the way people live, including their food, shelter, transportation and recreation.

4.2 Locate and distinguish among varying landforms and geographic features (e.g., mountains, plateaus, islands, and oceans).

4.4 Describe how people affect and change their environments.

The Big Idea

Geography

Different communities have different landforms and bodies of water. People change and adapt to their surroundings.

What to Know

- ✓ How can you find a community's location?
- ✓ What are the physical features of a community?
- ✓ How does the environment affect people?
- ✓ How can people care for the environment?

Unit
2
People
Talk About
People and
Geography
John Muir
1838–1914
Naturalist and writer
who helped protect
our national parks

Communities and Geography

Sylvia Earle
1935–Present
Scientist who studies and protects ocean life

Wangari Maathai
1940–Present
Founder of a group that planted 30 million trees in Kenya

Unit 2

Preview

Vocabulary

physical feature A feature found in nature, such as weather, plant life, water, or land. (page 90)

natural resource An item from nature that people can use, such as trees, water, or soil. (page 106)

environment The physical and human features of a place. (page 114)

human feature A feature such as a building, bridge, or road, that people add to a landscape. (page 114)

conservation The saving of resources to make them last longer. (page 130)

For more resources, go to **www.harcourtschool.com/ss1**

Reading Social Studies

Focus Skill Main Idea and Details

Why It Matters Knowing the main idea helps you better understand what you've read.

Learn

The **main idea** is the most important idea of a paragraph or passage. The main idea is often in the first sentence of a passage. **Details** give more information about the main idea.

Main Idea
The most important idea

Details

Facts about the main idea	Facts about the main idea	Facts about the main idea

Practice

Read the paragraph. Find the main idea. Then find the supporting details.

Main Idea / Details

The Great Lakes are so big that they have an effect on the weather, known as the lake efect. Tiny drops of lake water enter the air. In winter, the wet air is picked up by west winds and blown toward the east, causing heavy snowfall there.

Read the paragraphs, and answer the questions.

The Great Lakes

The Great Lakes are the world's largest group of freshwater lakes. They begin at the northwestern corner of Wisconsin. They end at the northwestern corner of New York. Most of the lakes are located in both the United States and Canada.

Lakes Superior, Michigan, and Huron are the largest Great Lakes. At 350 miles long and 160 miles wide, Lake Superior is the largest lake on Earth. East of Lake Superior is Lake Michigan. It is 307 miles long and 118 miles wide. Farther east is Lake Huron, the second-largest Great Lake. It is 206 miles long and up to 183 miles wide.

Lakes Erie and Ontario are the smallest Great Lakes. At 241 miles long and 57 miles wide, Lake Erie is the fourth-largest Great Lake. It flows into Lake Ontario, the smallest Great Lake. Lake Ontario is 193 miles long and up to 53 miles wide.

Focus Skill Main Idea and Details

1. What is the main idea of this selection?
2. What are the names of the Great Lakes?
3. Which Great Lake is the largest?

Start with a Poem

Walk Lightly

Geographic Travels in Verse and Rhyme

by J. Patrick Lewis
illustrated by Alison Jay

Author J. Patrick Lewis likes to travel and write poetry for children. In this poem, he suggests how to think about some of the places he has visited.

Make the Earth your companion.
Walk lightly on it, as other creatures do.
Let the Sky paint her beauty—she is always
watching over you.

Learn from the Sea how to face harsh forces.
Let the River remind you that everything will pass.
Let the Lake instruct you in stillness.
Let the Mountain teach you grandeur.
Make the Woodland your house of peace.
Make the Rainforest your house of hope.
Meet the Wetland on twilight ground.
Save some small piece of Grassland for a red kite
on a windy day.
Watch the Icecaps glisten with crystal majesty.
Hear the Desert whisper hush to eternity.
Let the Town bring you togetherness.
Make the Earth your companion.
Walk lightly on it, as other creatures do.

Response Corner

1. Focus Skill **Main Idea and Details** What do you think is the main idea of the poem?
2. **Make It Relevant** What is the geography of your community like?

USE VISUALS

Visuals can help you better understand what you read.

- **Photographs, drawings, maps, diagrams, and charts are examples of visuals. Many visuals have titles, captions, or labels that describe what is shown.**
- **Sometimes visuals add new information to what you are reading.**

Checklist for Visuals	
✓	What kind of visual is shown? a photograph
✓	What does the visual show?
✓	What does the visual tell you about the topic?

PREVIEW VOCABULARY

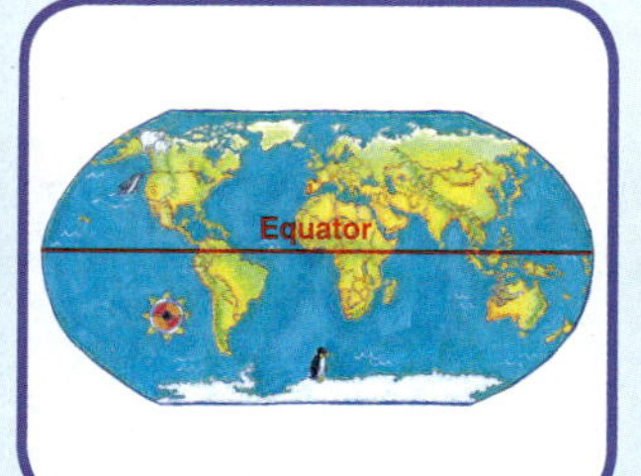

equator p. 83

vegetation p. 94

mineral p. 107

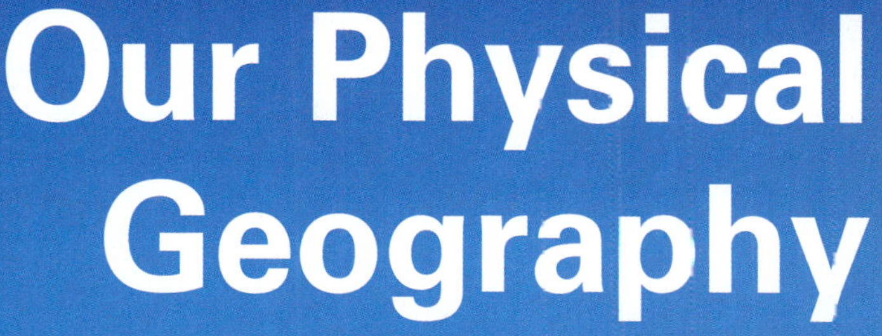

Our Physical Geography

Natural Bridge State Park in Kentucky

Lesson 1 Our Location

What to Know
What can you use to find a community's location?

Vocabulary
geographic tool p. 82
continent p. 82
hemisphere p. 83
equator p. 83
border p. 86
relative location p. 86

Main Idea and Details

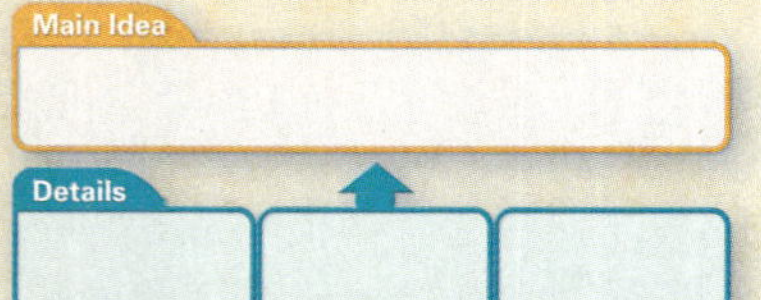

Each community has its own location. To show someone where you live, you might use a map or a globe. Maps and globes are **geographic tools**. They can tell us where a place is and what it might look like. These tools are used by geographers who study Earth and its people.

Using Globes

A globe is a model of Earth. A globe shows the oceans and largest land areas, or **continents**. Earth's continents are Asia, Africa, North America, South America, Antarctica, Europe, and Australia. A globe is round like Earth. It can show the true shapes of the continents and oceans.

A globe can help you find the location of your community.

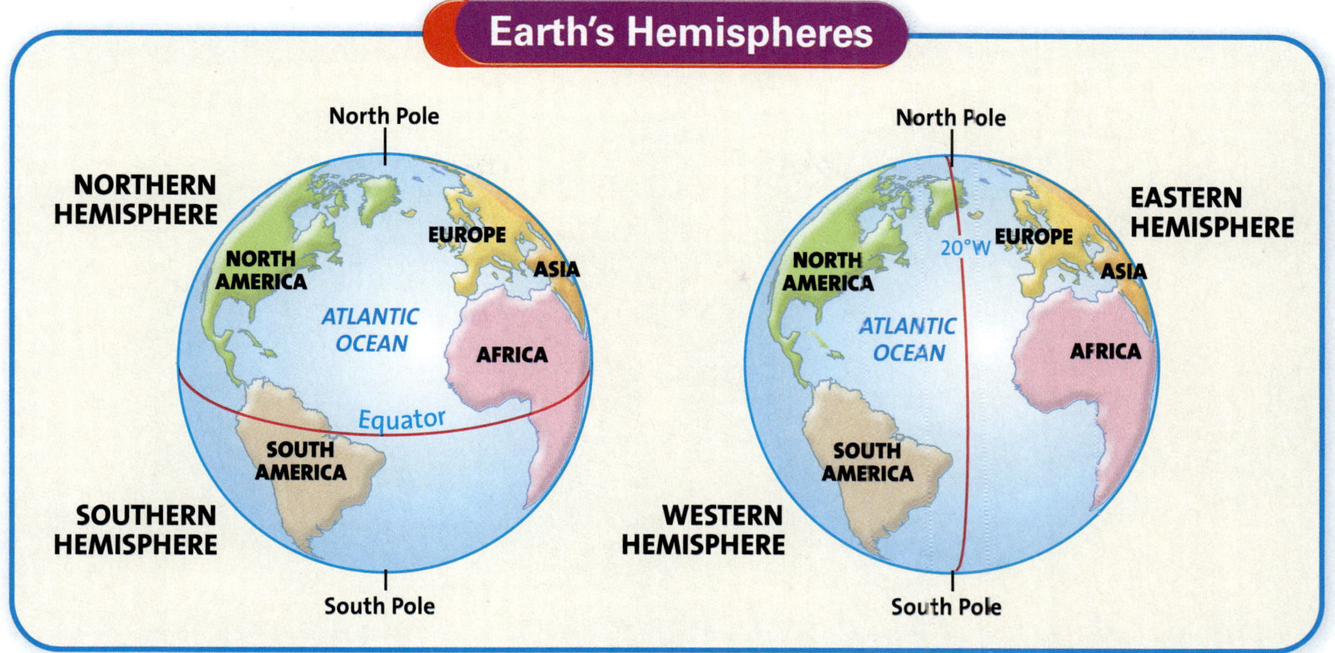

MAP SKILL **Location In which two hemispheres is Asia located?**

Hemispheres

On a globe, Earth can be divided into halves. A half of Earth is called a **hemisphere** (HEH•muh•sfeer). One way to divide Earth in half is to use the equator. The **equator** is an imaginary line that is halfway between the North Pole and the South Pole. It divides Earth into a Northern Hemisphere and a Southern Hemisphere.

Another imaginary line runs from the North Pole to the South Pole. It is often used to divide Earth into a Western Hemisphere and an Eastern Hemisphere.

Every place on Earth is in two hemispheres. North America, for example, is in the Northern Hemisphere and also in the Western Hemisphere.

Reading Check **Main Idea and Details**
In which two hemispheres is North America located?

MAP SKILL **Location The aerial photo and the map above show the same location—Salt Lake City, Utah. Which features do you see in both?**

Using Maps

While a globe is round, a map is flat. A map is a drawing that shows the location of places.

An Aerial View

Looking at a map of a community is like seeing it from an airplane. A map shows an aerial (AIR•ee•uhl) view of the location of a place. An aerial view is the view from above. Aerial photographs, or photographs taken from above, also show what a community looks like from the air.

The World

ARCTIC OCEAN
NORTH AMERICA
EUROPE
ASIA
PACIFIC OCEAN
ATLANTIC OCEAN
AFRICA
PACIFIC OCEAN
Equator
SOUTH AMERICA
INDIAN OCEAN
N
W
E
S
AUSTRALIA
ATLANTIC OCEAN
0 2,000 4,000 Miles
0 2,000 4,000 Kilometers
PACIFIC OCEAN
ANTARCTICA

MAP SKILL **Location What are the four oceans on this map?**

Maps

Unlike photographs, maps use colors, drawings, and symbols to show places on Earth. Because a map is flat, it is easy for people to carry. Maps can also give more information about a place.

A map can show the whole Earth or just a small part of it. Unlike a globe, however, a map cannot show the true shapes of oceans and continents.

Reading Check **Compare and Contrast**
How are maps and aerial photographs alike?

Finding Your Location

A **border** is a line that shows where a state or a country ends. The map on this page shows the borders of the countries in North America. You can also see the borders of all 50 states.

The compass rose on the map will help you find the **relative location**, or the location of a place in relation to another place. For example, Mexico's location relative to the United States is south.

MAP SKILL **Place** With what country does Alaska share a border?

Your Own Community

Now you can locate your community. Find your state on the map. Your community is in this state. It is also on the continent of North America.

A political map of the United States may show your community. Political maps show the borders of states, and some also include cities. If you live in a small community, you may have to look at a political map showing only your state.

Reading Check **Main Idea and Details**
How would you describe the location of your community?

Summary Maps and globes can help you find a community's location. A globe is a model of Earth. A map is a drawing that shows the location of things.

Review

1. **What to Know** What can you use to find a community's location?
2. **Vocabulary** What do you think each part of **geographic tool** means?
3. **Geography** What are the imaginary lines that divide Earth into hemispheres?
4. **Critical Thinking Make It Relevant** Why is it important to know your community's location?
5. **Make a Map** Draw a map of your community. Include your school and your home.
6. **Main Idea and Details** On a separate sheet of paper, copy and complete the graphic organizer below.

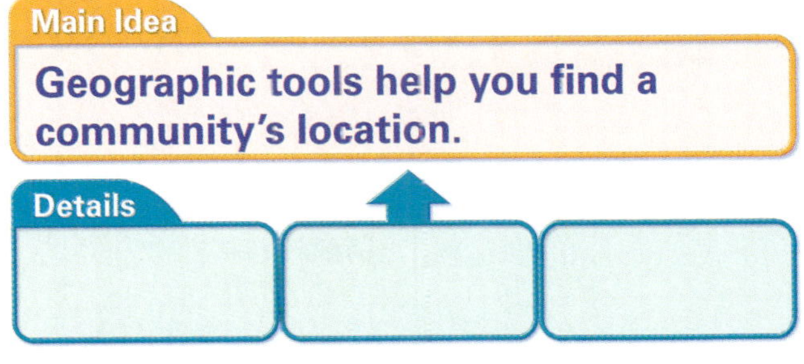

Map and Globe Skills

Use Latitude and Longitude

Why It Matters Using the lines on a map or a globe can help you find a place's location.

Learn

Lines on a map or a globe make a grid system. You can use the grid system to find the **absolute location**, or exact location, of a place.

Step 1 Find the lines of **latitude**. They run east and west. They measure distances in degrees (°) north and south of the equator.

Step 2 Find the lines of **longitude**. They run north and south. They measure distances east and west of the **prime meridian**.

Step 3 Name the latitude and then the longitude.

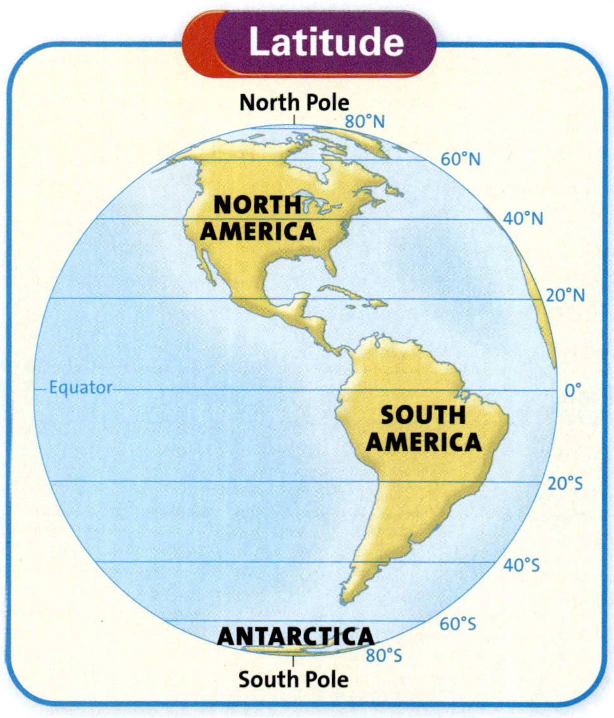

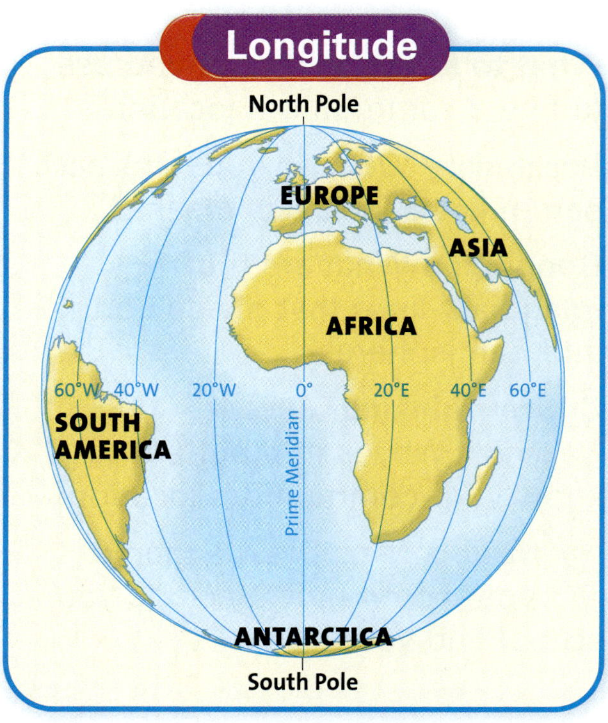

For online activities, go to **www.harcourtschool.com/ss1**

Ohio: Latitude and Longitude

Practice

Answer these questions, using the map.

1. Which line of latitude is nearest to Akron?
2. Which line of longitude is nearest to Lima?
3. Which city is nearest to 40°N, 83°W?

Apply

Make It Relevant Use a map or a globe to find the lines of latitude and longitude nearest your community. Find three cities or towns in the world with the same latitude. Share your list of cities with a partner.

Lesson 2

Our Country's Geography

What to Know
What are the physical features of a community?

Vocabulary

physical feature p. 90
mountain range p. 91
valley p. 91
plateau p. 91
vegetation p. 94
growing season p. 94
erosion p. 96
ecosystem p. 97

Main Idea and Details

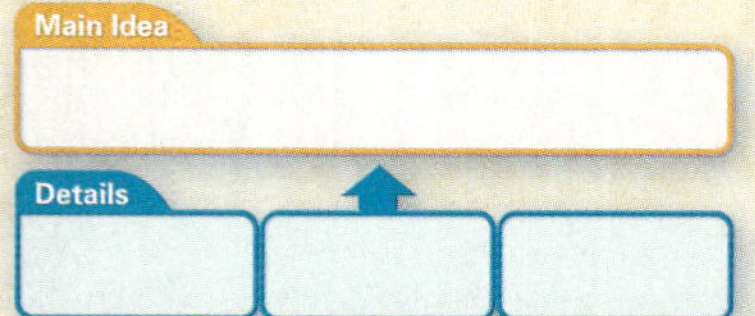

All places on Earth have features that make them special. Some of these are physical features. **Physical features** include land, water, climate, and plant life.

Land Features

You can describe a place by listing its physical features. Many communities have both land and water features.

The Appalachian Mountains are a mountain range in the eastern United States.

Changes in Ecosystems

Physical processes affect ecosystems every day. An **ecosystem** is made up of the plants, animals, land, water, and climate that make up an area.

Plants and animals in an ecosystem need each other to survive. Trees in a forest provide food and shelter for animals. In turn, the animals spread the seeds of the trees. Trees also provide shade for other plants.

Reading Check **Main Idea and Details**
What makes up an ecosystem?

The Everglades in Florida is an example of an ecosystem.

Summary Every place has physical features. Land, water, climate, and weather are different in different places. Physical processes are always changing Earth.

Review

1. **What to Know** What are the physical features of a community?
2. **Vocabulary** Write one or two sentences about **ecosystems**, using the word **vegetation**.
3. **Your Community** What is the climate like in the area where your community is located?
4. **Critical Thinking** **Make It Relevant** How do the physical features of your community affect the way you live?
5. **Write a Description** Write a paragraph that describes the physical features of your community.
6. **Main Idea and Details** On a separate sheet of paper, copy and complete the graphic organizer below.

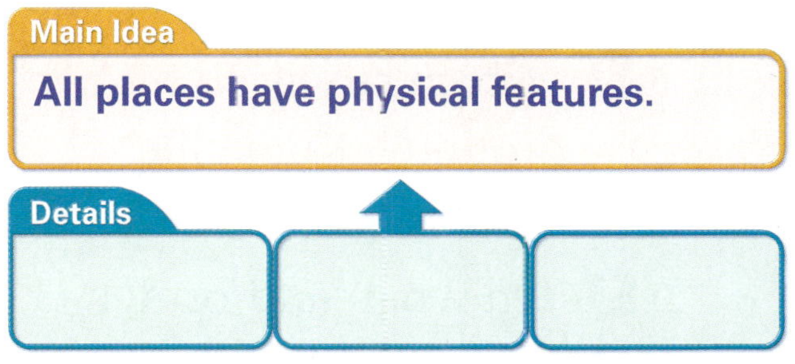

Use a Landform Map

Why It Matters Physical maps show what the land and water of Earth look like.

Learn

A **landform map** shows a place's main physical features. People use this kind of map to learn about the geography of a place. A landform map uses a different color or pattern for each kind of physical feature.

Step 1 Look at the map key.

Step 2 Find examples of each landform on the map.

Step 3 Look back at the key to remember which color or pattern matches a physical feature.

Practice

Use the landform map to answer these questions.

1. What body of water is found near Minneapolis?
2. Which city is on higher ground—Knoxville or Chicago?
3. On what landform is Oklahoma City built?

For online activities, go to **www.harcourtschool.com/ss1**

Apply

Make It Relevant On the landform map, find your state. What landforms does it have? Write a paragraph to describe the landforms of your state.

Landform Map of the United States

CANADA
ROCKY MOUNTAINS
GREAT PLAINS
INTERIOR PLAINS
BLACK HILLS
Missouri River
Mississippi
Lake Superior
Lake Michigan
Lake Huron
Lake Ontario
Lake Erie
Boise
Salt Lake City
Minneapolis
Chicago
Detroit
Columbus
Boston
Washington, D.C.
Ohio River
Mississippi River
St. Louis
Frankfort
Knoxville
Charlotte
APPALACHIAN MOUNTAINS
COASTAL PLAIN
Phoenix
Oklahoma City
Little Rock
Atlanta
ATLANTIC OCEAN
Dallas
Mississippi River
COASTAL PLAIN
New Orleans
Orlando
MEXICO
Gulf of Mexico
N
W
E
S
0 200 400 Miles
0 200 400 Kilometers

Yellowstone National Park

READ ABOUT

The great Yellowstone National Park is in the western United States. It covers parts of Idaho, Montana, and Wyoming.

On March 1, 1872, President Ulysses S. Grant signed a law to protect the land. It became the world's first national park. Today, nearly 3 million visitors come to the park each year.

Yellowstone is famous for its hot springs and geysers. Water comes from underground springs to Earth's surface through natural openings. A geyser is a spring that sprays hot water and steam into the air. Magma, or molten rock under the surface, keeps the water hot.

FIND

Old Faithful is one of Yellowstone's geysers. It sprays hot water up to 184 feet every 65 to 90 minutes.

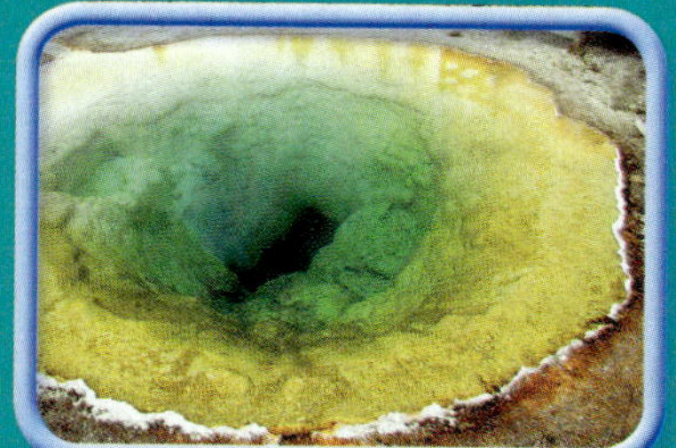
Morning Glory Pool

A park ranger

The Lower Falls of the Yellowstone River

Mammoth Terraces

A bald eagle

A VIRTUAL TOUR

GO ONLINE For more resources, go to www.harcourtschool.com/ss1

Lesson 3

Our Country's Regions

What to Know
What are our country's regions?

Vocabulary
preserve p. 104

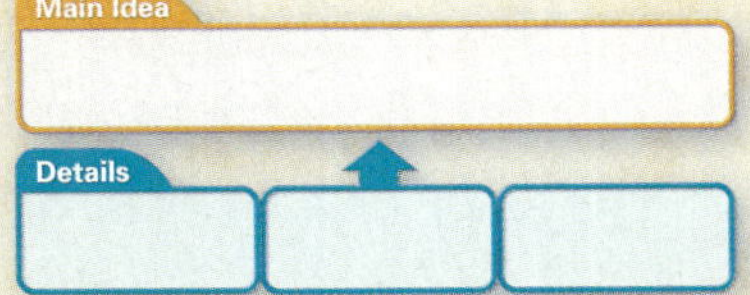

Main Idea and Details

Geographers sometimes divide countries and states into regions. A region is an area with at least one feature that makes it different from other areas. The parts of a region may share many features, such as location, landforms, culture, or economy.

The Regions

The United States is often divided into five large regions. These regions are the Northeast, the Southeast, the Midwest, the Southwest, and the West. The states in each region share a relative location in the country.

Reading Check **Main Idea and Details**
What are the five regions of the United States?

West

Southwest

Regions of the United States

Map Key
- Northeast
- Southeast
- Midwest
- Southwest
- West

AK WA OR ID MT WY CA NV UT CO AZ NM TX OK ND SD NE KS MN IA MO WI IL MI IN OH AR LA MS AL TN KY GA FL SC NC VA WV ME VT NH MA RI CT NY PA NJ DE MD HI

Canada
Mexico
Cuba
Pacific Ocean
Atlantic Ocean
Gulf of Mexico
N S E W

Regions In which region is your state located?

Midwest

Southeast

Northeast

Other Regions

Geographers can study a region based on any of its features. The features of a region include its culture and economics.

This business district is in Lexington's urban region.

One Community, Many Regions

A community can be part of more than one kind of region. Lexington, Kentucky, is part of the Southeast region of the United States. Lexington is also closely connected with Appalachia, the region in and around the Appalachian Mountains.

In the past, the people of Appalachia were separated from the rest of the United States by the Appalachian Mountains. They developed their own culture, which includes music and storytelling. Today, the people of Lexington work to **preserve**, or save, Appalachian culture.

Lexington, Kentucky

Diagram In which region of the United States is Lexington?

Lexington
Kentucky
The Southeast
The United States

Lexington is also part of an economic region that depends on horses. The region has grasses that are good food for horses. Today, many businesses in Lexington are connected with raising horses.

Reading Check **Main Idea and Details**
With what cultural region is Lexington closely connected?

Summary Regions in the United States include the Northeast, Southeast, Midwest, Southwest, and West. A community can be part of more than one kind of region.

Lexington's Appalachian Heritage Festival

Lexington is known as The Horse Capital of the World.

Review

1. **What to Know** What are our country's regions?
2. **Vocabulary** Use the term **preserve** in a paragraph about the Appalachian culture.
3. **Your Community** What regions is your community a part of?
4. **Critical Thinking** **Make It Relevant** What are some physical features of your region of the country?
5. **Write a Travel Brochure** Write about the different types of features of your region. Include things visitors can see and do.
6. Focus Skill **Main Idea and Details** On a separate sheet of paper, copy and complete the graphic organizer below.

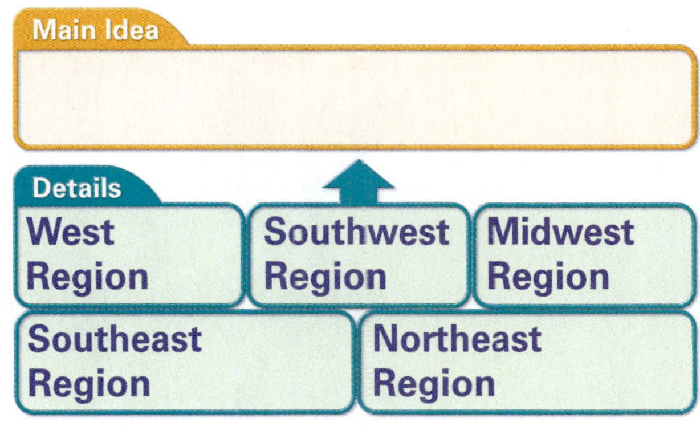

Lesson 4

Natural Resources

What to Know

What are natural resources?

Vocabulary

natural resource p. 106

mineral p. 107

renewable p. 108

nonrenewable p. 108

fuel p. 108

Main Idea and Details

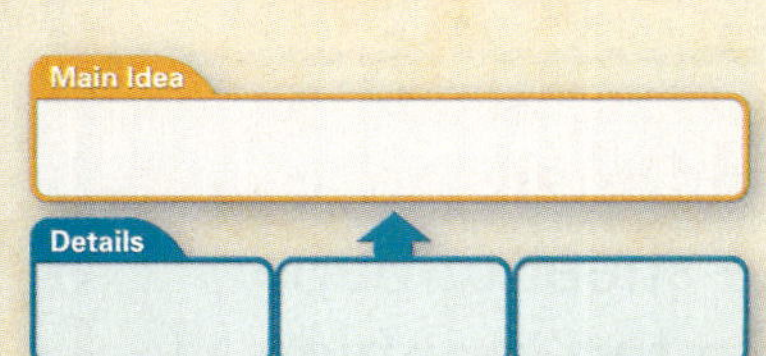

The naturalist John Muir wrote, "So extraordinary [amazing] is Nature with her choicest [best] treasures." The treasures Muir wrote about can still be found today. They are Earth's natural resources. A **natural resource** is something from nature that people can use, such as trees, water, and soil. Many of Earth's "choicest treasures" are found here in the United States.

Our Resources

Forests cover a lot of land in the United States. Trees, a natural resource, are used to build houses, to make furniture and paper, and to burn for heat.

Another natural resource is the land itself. The soil of many states in the United States is rich. Rich soil allows people to grow many crops. For example, cotton is grown to make clothing. Cows, chickens, and other animals are also raised on farmland.

Water is another natural resource. People use water for drinking, watering crops, and fishing.

Other natural resources are found underground. These are called **minerals**. Gold, iron, copper, and salt are some of Earth's many minerals.

Reading Check **Main Idea and Details**
How is land a natural resource?

On farms, land is used for growing crops, such as corn, and for raising animals, such as cows.

Types of Resources

There are different types of natural resources. Some can be replaced quickly, but others cannot.

Third graders plant trees, an important renewable resource.

Renewable and Nonrenewable Resources

A **renewable** resource is one that can be made again by nature or people. Trees and other plants are renewable resources. When trees are cut down, new trees can be planted. Wild animals, such as fish, are also renewable. People just have to let the fish populations stay steady by not fishing too much.

A **nonrenewable** resource cannot be made again quickly by nature or people. Minerals are nonrenewable. It might take thousands of years for Earth to replace a mineral that has been used. Many fuels, such as coal and oil, are also nonrenewable. A **fuel** is a natural resource that is burned to make heat or energy.

Pine trees are grown on a tree farm.

Living and Nonliving Resources

Natural resources can also be living or nonliving. Plants, trees, and wild animals are all examples of living resources. Nonliving resources include water, metals, soil, and minerals.

Reading Check **Main Idea and Details**
What are some nonrenewable resources?

Oil is a nonliving resource found deep underground. Wells are drilled to get to the oil.

Summary Natural resources are materials from nature that people use. Renewable resources can be replaced, but nonrenewable resources cannot.

Review

1. **What to Know** What are natural resources?
2. **Vocabulary** Write a sentence that includes the terms **fuel** and **nonrenewable**.
3. **Economics** Why might a resource that is nonrenewable, such as gold, cost a lot of money?
4. **Critical Thinking** What might happen if a nonrenewable resource, such as oil, were used up?
5. **Draw a Picture** Draw a picture that shows some natural resources in your community.
6. **Main Idea and Details** On a separate sheet of paper, copy and complete the graphic organizer below.

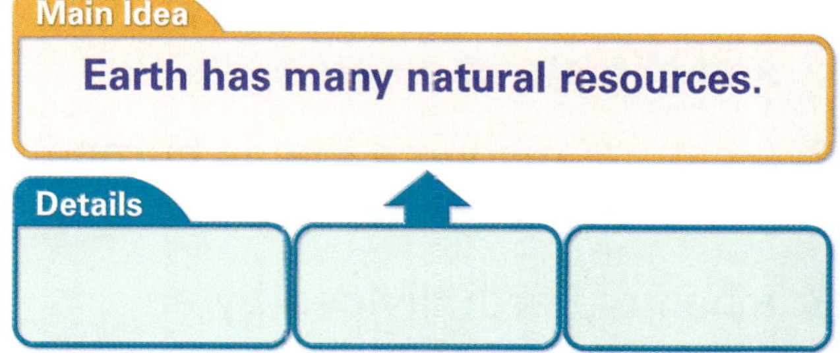

Chapter 3 Review

Visual Summary

Our country's geography has many physical features.

Summarize the Chapter

Main Idea and Details Complete the graphic organizer to show that you understand the important main idea and details about our country's geography.

Main Idea

Our country's geography has many special features.

Details

Our country has different physical features.		Our country has many regions.

Vocabulary

Identify the term from the word bank that correctly matches each definition.

1. the plants, animals, land, water, and climate of an area
2. a natural resource that is burned to make heat or energy
3. a half of Earth divided by an imaginary line
4. to save
5. one of Earth's largest land areas
6. a natural resource found underground.

Word Bank

continent p. 82
hemisphere p. 83
ecosystem p. 97
preserve p. 104
mineral p. 107
fuel p. 108

A community can be part of more than one region.

Communities have many natural resources.

Facts and Main Ideas

Answer these questions.

7. What are some causes of erosion?
8. What three regions is Lexington, Kentucky, part of?
9. Where are minerals found?

Write the letter of the best choice.

10. How are maps and globes similar?
    - **A** They show the true shapes of oceans and continents.
    - **B** They are flat.
    - **C** They show locations.
    - **D** They are round.
11. Which natural resource do people use to make paper?
    - **A** trees
    - **B** animals
    - **C** land
    - **D** minerals

Critical Thinking

12. **Make It Relevant** How might your community be different if it had a different climate?
13. **Make It Relevant** How might physical processes affect you?

Use Latitude and Longitude

Use the map on page 89 to answer the question.

14. Near which lines of latitude and longitude is Zanesville, Ohio?

Use a Landform Map

Use the map on pages 98 and 99 to answer the question.

15. What landforms are found in southeastern Oklahoma?

writing

Write a Postcard Describe a physical feature in a postcard to a friend.

Write a Paragraph Write a paragraph about why people use maps.

POSE QUESTIONS

Asking questions as you read can help you understand what you are learning.

- **Ask questions about events and ideas as you read.**
- **Look for the answers to your questions as you read.**

Our Human Geography	
Questions	Answers
How can people use land?	They may use land to farm.
How can we protect the environment?	

PREVIEW VOCABULARY

canal p. 123

irrigation p. 124

recycle p. 130

People and Disasters

Environments are always changing. People adapt their ways of living to these changes. When change happens quickly, however, it can be hard for people to adapt.

Earth's Big Events

Hurricanes, tornadoes, earthquakes, and forest fires all cause quick changes. These events are known as natural disasters. A **natural disaster** is an event in nature that causes great harm to people and damages their property. Earthquakes can damage buildings and roadways. Tornadoes can knock down trees and damage houses. Hurricanes can also destroy houses, cause flooding, and knock down trees and power lines.

Floods affected many communities after Hurricane Katrina in 2005.

Preparing for Disasters

People can prepare for the natural disasters that happen where they live. In Oklahoma, the time between March and August is when tornadoes are most likely to happen. People there store food and water and plan safe places to go to during dangerous weather.

Reading Check **Main Idea and Details**
What are some kinds of natural disasters?

Extra supplies can help in a natural disaster.

Summary Communities are affected by the features of their environment. People have ways of adapting to their environments. One way they do this is by preparing for natural disasters.

Review

1. **What to Know** What are some ways in which the environment affects people?
2. **Vocabulary** What do you think each word part of **natural disaster** means?
3. **Your Community** How is your community most affected by its environment?
4. **Critical Thinking** How might new tools help people better adapt to their environment?
5. **Write a Story** Write a story about a family who must adapt to a new environment.
6. **Focus Skill** **Main Idea and Details** On a separate sheet of paper, copy and complete the graphic organizer below.

Main Idea
People adapt their ways of life to fit their environments.

Sylvia Earle

Trustworthiness
Respect
Responsibility
Fairness
Caring
Patriotism

"I wasn't shown frogs with the attitude 'yuk,' but rather my mother would show my brothers and me how beautiful they are."

—Sylvia Earle, 1992

Sylvia Earle has spent more than 6,000 hours underwater in the world's oceans. Earle is an oceanographer (oh•shuh•NAH•gruh•fer). She studies ocean plants and animals.

Earle was born in 1935 in New Jersey. In 1948, her family moved to the west coast of Florida. There, she learned about marine, or sea, life in the Gulf of Mexico.

Earle wanted to study the ocean depths. She and her husband designed the *Deep Rover*. This ship carries scientists 3,000 feet below the water's surface.

Earle has written many books about the oceans. In *Sea Change: A Message of the Oceans*, she explains our responsibility to protect the ocean environment.

Why Character Counts

How does Sylvia Earle show a sense of responsibility toward the ocean environment?

For more resources, go to **www.harcourtschool.com/ss1**

Sylvia Earle

Time

1935 Born

Present

1948 Moves to Florida from New Jersey

1981 Designs the *Deep Rover*

1995 *Sea Change: A Message of the Oceans* is published

Compare Graphs

Why It Matters When you need to compare sets of numbers, it helps to look at a graph.

Learn

Graphs can present the same information in different ways. A **pictograph**, or picture graph, uses small pictures to show the number of items. A key explains what the pictures stand for. In the pictograph on the next page, each tornado symbol stands for two tornadoes. Oklahoma had four tornadoes in March.

A **bar graph** uses bars to show amounts. On the bar graph, find the bar labeled *March*. Move your finger up the bar to where it ends. The bar graph will give you the same information the pictograph did.

Practice

Use the graphs to answer these questions.

1. Which graph uses pictures to show tornadoes?
2. Which month had the most tornadoes?
3. How many tornadoes did Oklahoma have in June?

Apply

Find out how many tornadoes happened each month in another state. Show this information in a pictograph and a bar graph.

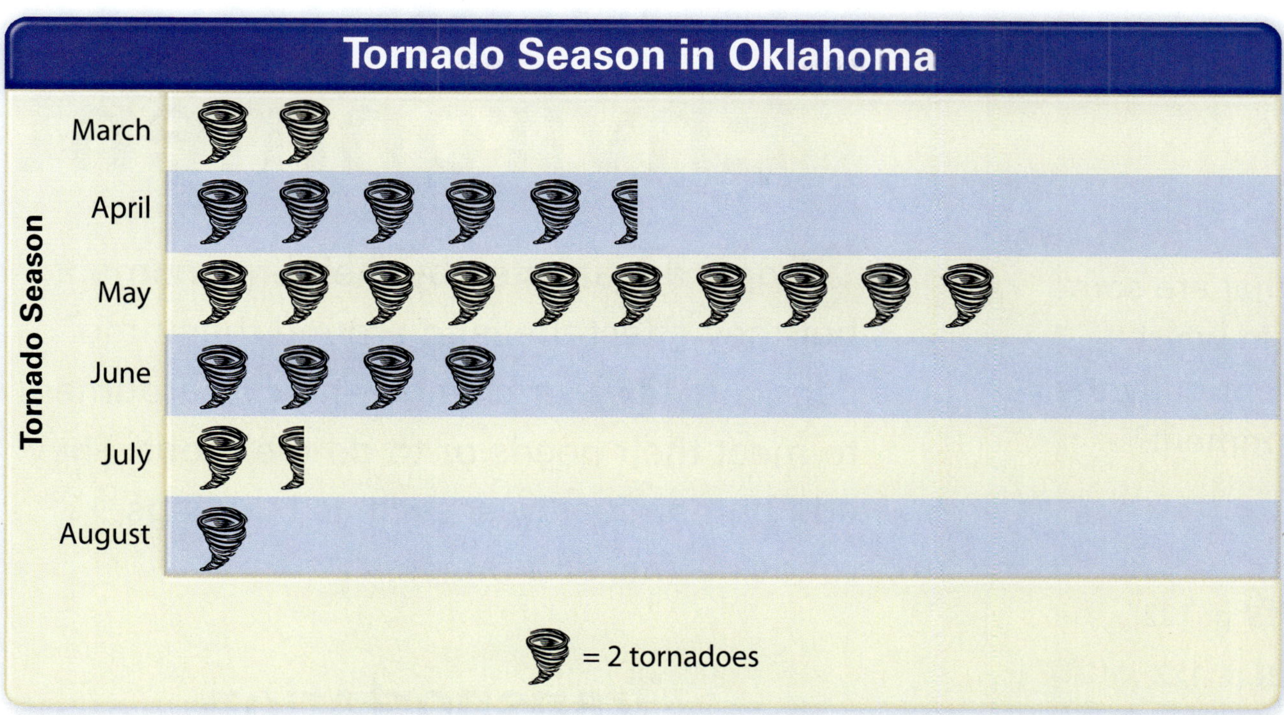

Tornado Season in Oklahoma

Number of Tornadoes

25
20
15
10
5
0

March April May June July August

Tornado Season

Lesson 2

Changing the Environment

What to Know
What are some ways in which people modify their environment?

Vocabulary
modify p. 122
tunnel p. 123
canal p. 123
terrace p. 124
irrigation p. 124
dam p. 126
reservoir p. 126

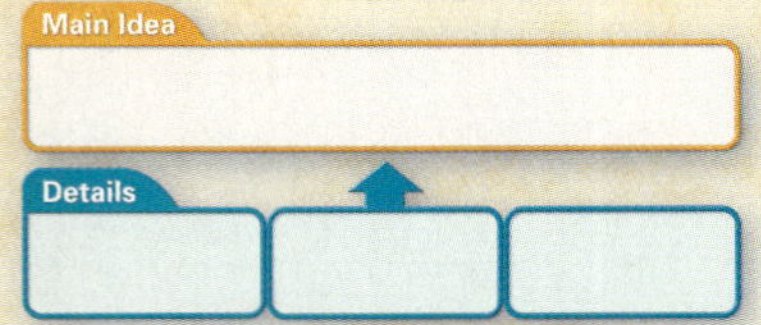

People are affected by their environment, but they affect the land around them, too. People **modify**, or change, their environment to meet their needs or to do their jobs. They add human features, such as buildings, roads, farms, and mines.

Transportation

Today much of Earth is covered with roads, highways, bridges, and railroads. People add these features to the environment for transportation. Building a new road or bridge is a huge project. It takes many workers and a lot of money and time.

Digging tunnels is one way to speed up transportation. A **tunnel** is a path that runs under something. The Channel Tunnel, or "Chunnel," lets high-speed trains travel under the waterway between Britain and France. The trip takes only 20 to 35 minutes!

Building canals is another way to speed up transportation. A **canal** is a waterway dug across land. The Panama Canal cuts across the narrow strip of land that connects North America and South America. The canal was built to let ships travel a shorter distance between the Atlantic Ocean and Pacific Ocean. The canal trip takes 8 to 10 hours, but this is much faster than sailing around South America.

Reading Check **Main Idea and Details**
How do people modify the environment to speed up transportation?

A ship enters a lock on the Panama Canal. The water in the lock will be raised or lowered to bring the ship to the next level of the canal.

Panama Canal under construction

Farms and Mines

People modify the land to use natural resources. Farming and mining can greatly change the way the environment looks.

▶ Irrigation is used to water these crops.

Farming

To grow crops, farmers clear land. Then they plow, or turn over the soil, to plant seeds. They might also build fences for raising animals.

All over the world, people modify their environments for farming. Long ago in Peru, people of the Inca culture found a way to farm on the sides of mountains. They built **terraces,** which look like giant stairs cut into hillsides. Crops are still grown on terraces today.

People have also found ways to farm dry land or to water their crops during dry weather. They use irrigation to water their crops. **Irrigation** is the moving of water to dry areas.

▶ Many communities in Asia use terraces to grow rice.

An open pit mine in Kentucky

Mining

People create mines to get minerals from beneath Earth's surface. These mines can be either deep tunnels dug into the ground or open pit mines. Open pit mines are carved into the surface by earth-moving machines.

Open pit mines are also used to get stone from the land. Stone is used for making buildings and roads. Small stones, called gravel, are spread over roads before they are paved. People use a type of stone called limestone to make other building supplies, such as cement.

Reading Check **Main Idea and Details**
How do people modify the land to use resources?

A miner who works underground

Water and Electricity

Communities modify the environment to control the flow of water. They also change the land to get electricity.

Water

In some areas, people dig wells to bring up underground water. In other places, they build dams across rivers. **Dams** are huge structures built to hold back water.

Bagnell Dam in Missouri was built in 1929. The dam created a large **reservoir** (REH•zuh•vwar), or human-made lake used for collecting and storing water. Called the Lake of the Ozarks, it is a place where people enjoy fishing and water sports.

Dams also control the flow of rivers to prevent flooding. Some communities near rivers build walls called levees to keep back floodwaters.

Reservoirs provide places for water sports, such as wakeboarding.

Bagnell Dam at Lake of the Ozarks in Missouri

Electricity

People also build dams to use waterpower. Water falling through the dam turns machines that produce electricity. This is called hydroelectric power. *Hydro* means "water."

People also get energy from wind. The wind's power turns thousands of windmills, called wind turbines, to produce electricity.

Reading Check **Main Idea and Details**
How do people modify the water around them?

Turbines at a wind farm

Summary People modify, or make changes to, their environment. They add many human features to both land and water.

Review

1. **What to Know** What are some ways in which people modify their environment?
2. **Vocabulary** Write a sentence using the words **dam** and **reservoir**.
3. **Geography** Why do people build canals?
4. **Critical Thinking** **Make It Relevant** What have people done to modify landforms and bodies of water in your community?
5. **Draw a Picture** Draw a picture showing an example of how people modify the environment.
6. **Main Idea and Details** On a separate sheet of paper, copy and complete the graphic organizer below.

Main Idea

People modify the land to improve transportation.

Details

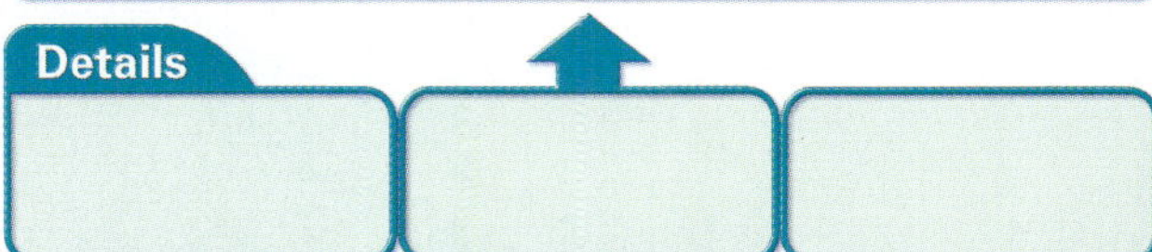

Lesson 3

Caring for Our Environment

What to Know
What are some things people can do to care for the environment?

Vocabulary

pollution p. 128
conservation p. 130
recycle p. 130

Main Idea and Details

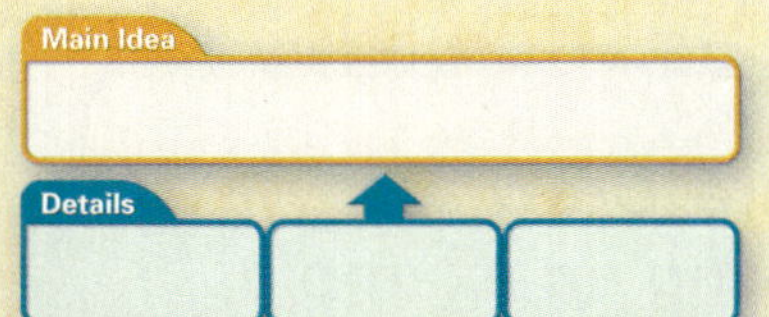

People make changes to the environment every day. Some of the changes people make can cause problems. We can care for the environment by protecting our natural resources.

Controlling Pollution

One way people change the environment is by creating pollution. **Pollution** is anything that makes a natural resource dirty or unsafe to use. For example, water that is polluted is not safe to drink.

San Diego, California and other cities have worked to keep the air clean.

Causes of Pollution

Trash and other kinds of waste can cause pollution. Some people throw trash onto the ground or into bodies of water. Because of this, trash collects on the land and in waterways. This can make soil and water unsafe for plants, animals, and people.

Factories and cars can cause air pollution. Smoke in the air can mix with fog. This kind of pollution is called smog. Breathing polluted air can lead to health problems.

Reducing Pollution

Many communities have made changes to cut down on pollution. Some carmakers now make hybrid cars that have both a gasoline engine and an electric motor with a battery. By burning less gasoline, hybrids cause less air pollution.

Reading Check **Main Idea and Details**
How does pollution harm the environment?

Fast Fact

Hybrid cars save gas in several ways. Besides their efficient engines, they also have smoother shapes and lighter weight than regular cars.

Conserving Our Resources

Recycling is a way to conserve our resources.

People protect natural resources through conservation. **Conservation** is the saving of resources to make them last longer. One form of conservation is to set aside lands for special protection. The use of the resources in these lands is limited.

Reusing Resources

Another way people conserve is by recycling. When people **recycle**, they use resources over again. Newspapers and cardboard, many plastics, glass from bottles and jars, and aluminum from cans can be reused. By recycling, people do not add as much trash to landfills. Landfills are places where trash is dumped.

Children in History

The First Earth Day

On April 22, 1970, more than 20 million people showed their support across the country for conservation. Nearly half of them were schoolchildren and college students.

In Washington, D.C., schoolchildren gathered at the Washington Monument to hear music and a speech. In New York City, thousands of people marched in the streets to encourage conservation. Today, Earth Day is a yearly event at many schools.

Make It Relevant **How does your school celebrate Earth Day?**

A Plan for the Future

Not everybody agrees on the best ways to care for the environment. However, changes people make now will improve the environment in the future. A plan to care for the environment can make sure these changes are good ones.

Reading Check **Summarize**
What are some resources that people can recycle?

A school in Maryland built a bog. This wetland's ecosystem helps keep the school's environment clean.

Summary Waste from trash, cars, and factories causes pollution. People can reduce pollution by caring for the environment. Conservation and recycling help protect our natural resources.

Review

1. **What to Know** What are some things people can do to care for the environment?
2. **Vocabulary** Compare and contrast the meaning of the words **pollution** and **conservation**.
3. **Your Community** What are some ways in which people in your community help protect the environment?
4. **Critical Thinking** How might recycling help protect the environment?
5. **Write a Persuasive Letter** Write a letter that persuades people in your community to help protect the environment.
6. Focus Skill **Main Idea and Details** On a separate sheet of paper, copy and complete the graphic organizer below.

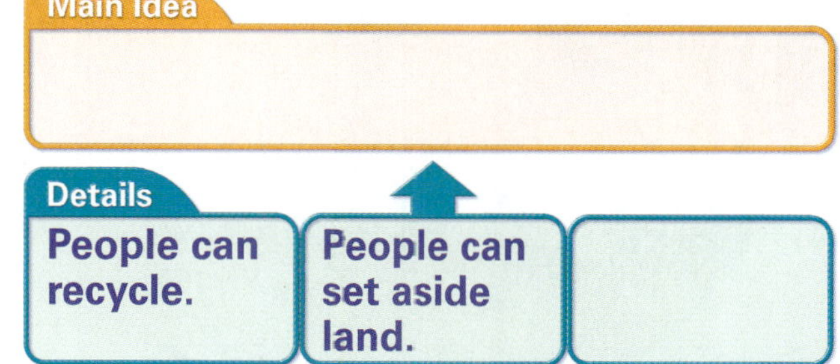

Solve a Problem

Why It Matters People must work together in communities. All communities have problems that need to be solved.

Learn

A **problem** is something that is difficult, or hard to understand. A **solution** is an answer to a problem. Follow these steps to solve a problem.

Step 1 Identify a problem.

Step 2 Gather information about the problem.

Step 3 List and consider possible options for solving the problem.

Step 4 Consider the advantages and disadvantages of your options.

Step 5 Choose a solution and act on it.

Step 1

Step 2

Use Your Community's Resources

Your Community's Resources

- Libraries
- Museums
- Nature Centers
- Internet

Make a Mural of Your Environment

Make a mural that shows your community's environment. On a posterboard, draw or add pictures of its landforms, bodies of water, climate, and vegetation. Also include some human features, such as buildings, roads, and bridges. Label each feature as a physical or human feature.

Chapter 4 Review

Visual Summary

People are affected by their environment.

Summarize the Chapter

Main Idea and Details Complete the graphic organizer to show that you understand the important idea and details about changing the environment.

Main Idea

People modify their environment.

Details

Vocabulary

Write the correct term from the list to complete each sentence.

1. People ______ their environment to meet their needs.
2. A _______ is a path that runs under something.
3. We _______ when we use resources over again.
4. The _______ is the physical and human features of a place.
5. A human-made lake used to store or collect water is a ______.
6. ______ is anything that makes a natural resource dirty.

Word Bank

environment p. 114
modify p. 122
tunnel p. 123
reservoir p.126
pollution p.128
recycle p. 130

People modify the environment around them.

People should care for their environment.

Facts and Main Ideas

Answer these questions.

7. Why is a road a human feature of an environment?
8. How do people modify the environment for transportation?
9. What happens when trash collects on the land and in waterways?

Write the letter of the best choice.

10. Which is hardest for people to adapt to?
    - **A** a wet climate
    - **B** a mountain
    - **C** a hurricane
    - **D** a warm climate
11. How do people modify the environment when they mine?
    - **A** They build terraces on mountains.
    - **B** They dig deep tunnels.
    - **C** They use irrigation.
    - **D** They build dams.

Critical Thinking

12. What would happen if we did not care for the environment?
13. **Make It Relevant** How has your family adapted to your environment?

Skills

Compare Graphs
Use the graphs on page 121 to answer the question.

14. Which month has the fewest tornadoes?

Solve a Problem
Use the steps on page 132 to answer the question.

15. What do you do after identifying a problem?

writing

Write a Letter Write a letter explaining ways your school can help protect the environment.

Write a Narrative Suppose you are on a trip. Write a narrative about the human features you see along the way.

What's Wrong with This Map?

Landforms of the United States

Mexico

Atlantic Ocean

Pacific Ocean

Gulf of Mexico

Canada

E

W

N

S

Map Key

Northeast

Southeast

Midwest

Southwest

West

Figure It Out

Use the rebus to figure out each two-word term.

VOCABULARY

+ location = ?

growing +  = ?

 + range = ?

Online Adventures

GO ONLINE

Get ready to race! Join Eco on the online landform road race to see how far you can travel. In this game, you'll explore mountains, plains, rivers, and oceans. There is a special surprise waiting for you at the end. Play now at **www.harcourtschool.com/ss1**

Review and Test Prep

The Big Idea

Geography Different communities have different landforms and bodies of water. People change and adapt to their surroundings.

Reading Comprehension and Vocabulary

Communities and Geography

Earth is covered by many physical features. People can find the locations of these features by using geographic tools, such as maps and globes. People use natural resources, such as trees, water, soil, and minerals. People must adapt to their environment. They modify their environment to meet their needs. They build human features such as terraces, mines, and dams. People in all communities should conserve and protect natural resources.

Read the summary above. Then answer the questions that follow.

1. What are physical features?
   A aerial photographs
   B maps and globes
   C land, water, climate, plants
   D mines

2. How can people find the locations of physical features?
   A by protecting natural resources
   B by building dams
   C by using geographic tools
   D by modifying their environment

3. What does natural resources mean in the passage above?
   A human features
   B pollution
   C the time when plants grow
   D something from nature people can use

4. Why do people build human features?
   A to change the climate
   B to prevent pollution
   C to look at maps and globes
   D to meet their needs

Facts and Main Ideas

Answer these questions.

5. What are the imaginary lines that divide Earth into four hemispheres?
6. What are some renewable resources?
7. What are some causes of pollution?

Write the letter of the best choice.

8. Which of the following has the hottest climate?
   - **A** a city in the Western Hemisphere
   - **B** a community with a short growing season
   - **C** a place near the equator
   - **D** a town in the mountains
9. Which human feature can help produce electricity?
   - **A** tunnel
   - **B** dam
   - **C** canal
   - **D** mine
10. How does recycling help the environment?
   - **A** It cleans smog from the air.
   - **B** It adds less trash to landfills.
   - **C** It uses less gas.
   - **D** It cleans polluted water.

Critical Thinking

11. **Make It Relevant** How do you use relative location to locate places that are near your community? Give examples.
12. **Make It Relevant** How can your community prepare for a natural disaster?

Skills

Use Latitude and Longitude

Use the map below to answer the following questions.

13. Which line of longitude is closest to the western tip of North Carolina?
14. Which line of latitude runs through southeastern North Carolina?

Unit 2

Activities

Show What You Know

Unit Writing Activity

Write a Story Write a story about a community that worked to protect its environment.

- Talk about the community's environment or resources.
- Tell why and how the community saved its natural treasures.

Unit Project

Community Nature Center Exhibit Create a nature exhibit that tells about your community.

- Describe the climate, land, water, vegetation, and natural resources.
- Show information on posters.

Read More

- ***Mapping Penny's World*** **by Loreen Leedy. Owlet.**

- ***High as a Hawk*** **by T. A. Barron. Philomel.**

- ***Rachel: The Story of Rachel Carson*** **by Amy Ehrlich. Silver Whistle.**

GO ONLINE

For more resources, go to **www.harcourtschool.com/ss1**

Communities Over Time

Unit 3

Start with the Standards

Oklahoma Priority Academic Student Skills

1.1 Identify, locate, and compare and contrast information found in resources such as encyclopedias, visual images, atlases, maps, globes, and computer-based technologies.

1.2 Examine and use children's literature to compare and contrast his or her own community to other United States and global communities.

3.1 Investigate through children's literature the cultural similarities and differences among people in different regions, and how they have changed over time.

4.4 Describe how people affect and change their environments.

The Big Idea

History

Every community has a unique history. Some features of a community change, while others stay the same, over time.

What to Know

- ✓ How do communities change and stay the same?
- ✓ How have people changed communities?
- ✓ Who formed the first communities in North America?
- ✓ How did the United States grow and change?

Sacagawea
1786?–1812
Guide to Meriwether Lewis and William Clark on their journey west

Communities Over Time

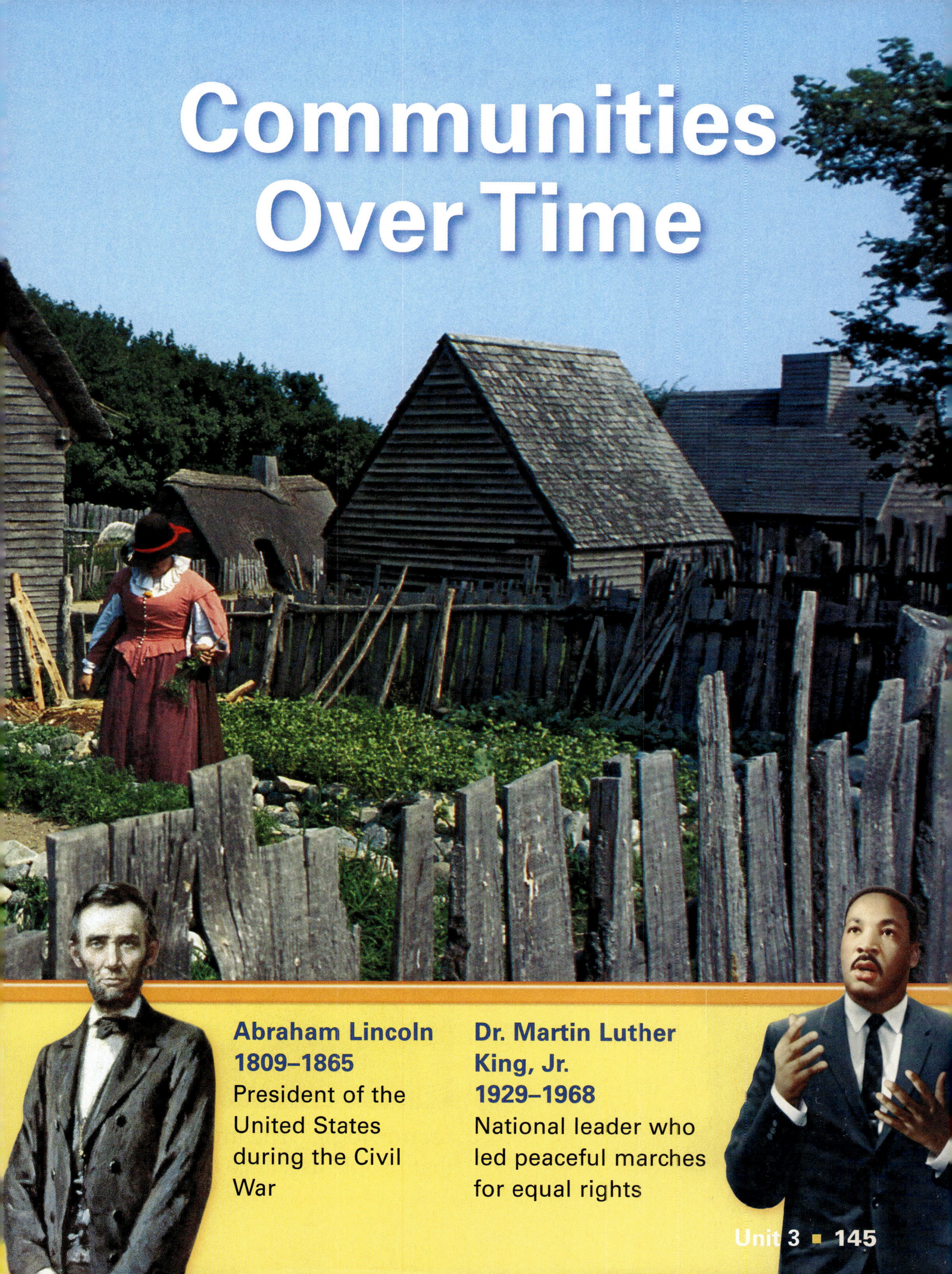

Abraham Lincoln
1809–1865
President of the United States during the Civil War

Dr. Martin Luther King, Jr.
1929–1968
National leader who led peaceful marches for equal rights

Unit 3

Preview

Vocabulary

invention An object that has been made for the first time. (page 162)

technology The inventions that people use. (page 170)

explorer A person who goes to find out about a place. (page 196)

settlement A new community. (page 197)

colony A place that is ruled by another country. (page 204)

For more resources, go to www.harcourtschool.com/ss1

Unit 3

Reading Social Studies

Focus Skill Sequence

Why It Matters Identifying the order in which events happen helps you understand what you read.

Learn

Sequence is the order in which events happen.

- Words, such as *first, next, then, last, after,* and *finally,* are sequence clues.
- Sometimes events are not listed in the order in which they happened.

Practice

Read the paragraph. Look for sequence clues.

Sequence

At first, Memphis was a small city. When Memphis was built, it had only 50 people and was just four blocks wide. Then its harbor on the Mississippi River made it important. Ships brought and took away people and goods, causing the city to grow. Today, Memphis has more than 650,000 people.

Apply

Read the paragraphs, and answer the questions.

The Story of Memphis, Tennessee

The city of Memphis, in southwestern Tennessee, has a long history. It was not always a city. In 1541, Hernando de Soto (er•NAHN•doh day SOH•toh), from Spain, explored the area. Next, Europeans came to live there. Before then, however, Native Americans, the Chickasaw, lived in the area.

In 1818, the United States government forced the Chickasaw to give up their land. Memphis was founded there in 1819. It was named after Memphis, Egypt, because both cities sit by large rivers.

Later, during the 1900s, Memphis became a center for blues music. Blues was a new style of music that began in the region. Musicians, such as Muddy Waters and B. B. King, played at clubs on Beale Street. They helped create the style of music known as Memphis blues.

Today, Memphis is Tennessee's largest city. People visit from all over the world to hear Memphis blues.

Sequence

1. What word clue tells you Europeans arrived after the Chickasaw?
2. What happened before Memphis was founded in 1819?
3. Which paragraph tells about Memphis today?

Start with a Story

A PLACE CALLED FREEDOM

by Scott Russell Sanders

illustrated by Thomas B. Allen

In this story, James Starman, his parents, and his sister, Lettie, were once enslaved. In this story, they leave their home in Tennessee and move to Indiana. They help start the community of Freedom. The Starman family want a place to begin a new life after they become free.

At last one morning, just after sunrise, we came to the Ohio River. A fisherman with a face as wrinkled as an old boot carried us over the water in his boat. On the far shore we set our feet on the free soil of Indiana. White flowers covered the hills that day like feathers on a goose.

By and by we met a Quaker family who took us into their house, gave us seed, and loaned us a mule and a plow, all because they believed that slavery was a sin. We helped on their farm, working shoulder to shoulder, and we planted our own crops.

That first year Papa raised enough corn and wheat for us to buy some land beside the Wabash River, where the dirt was as black as my skin. Papa could grow anything, he could handle horses, and he could build a barn or a bed.

Before winter, Papa and Mama built us a sturdy cabin. Every night we sat by the fire and Papa told stories that made the shadows dance. Every morning Mama held school for Lettie and me. Mama knew how to read and write from helping with lessons for the master's children. She could sew clothes that fit you like the wind, and her cooking made your tongue glad.

While the ground was still frozen, Papa rode south through the cold nights, down to the plantation in Tennessee. We fretted until he showed up again at our door, leading two of my aunts, two uncles, and five cousins. They stayed with us until they could buy land near ours and build their own cabins.

Again and again Papa went back to Tennessee, and each time he came home with more of the folks we loved.

Hearing about our settlement, black people arrived from all over the South, some of them freed like us, some of them runaways. There were carpenters and blacksmiths, basket weavers and barrel makers.

Soon we had a church, then a store, then a stable, then a mill to grind our grain. For the first time in our lives, we had money, just enough to get by, and we watched every penny.

After a few years, the railroad decided to run tracks through our village, because so many people had gathered here. If our place was going to be on the map, it needed a name. At a meeting, folks said we should call it Starman, in honor of Mama and Papa. But Mama and Papa said, "No, let's name it Freedom."

And that's how we came to live in a place called Freedom.

Response Corner

1. Focus Skill **Sequence** What happened after the Quakers took the family into their home?
2. **Make It Relevant** This story is about how a community started. Do you know how your community started?

MAKE AN OUTLINE

An outline organizes topics, main ideas, and details.

- **Topics are shown by Roman numerals.**
- **Main ideas about each topic are shown by capital letters.**
- **Details about each main idea are shown by numbers.**

Our History Through Time and Place

I. Communities Through Time
  A. Communities change in some ways over time.
    1. Many old buildings are replaced with new ones.
    2.
  B. Communities stay the same in some ways.
    1. The kind of work some people do can stay the same.
    2.

PREVIEW VOCABULARY

equality p. 166

primary source p. 168

civilization p. 178

CHAPTER 5

Our History Through Time and Place

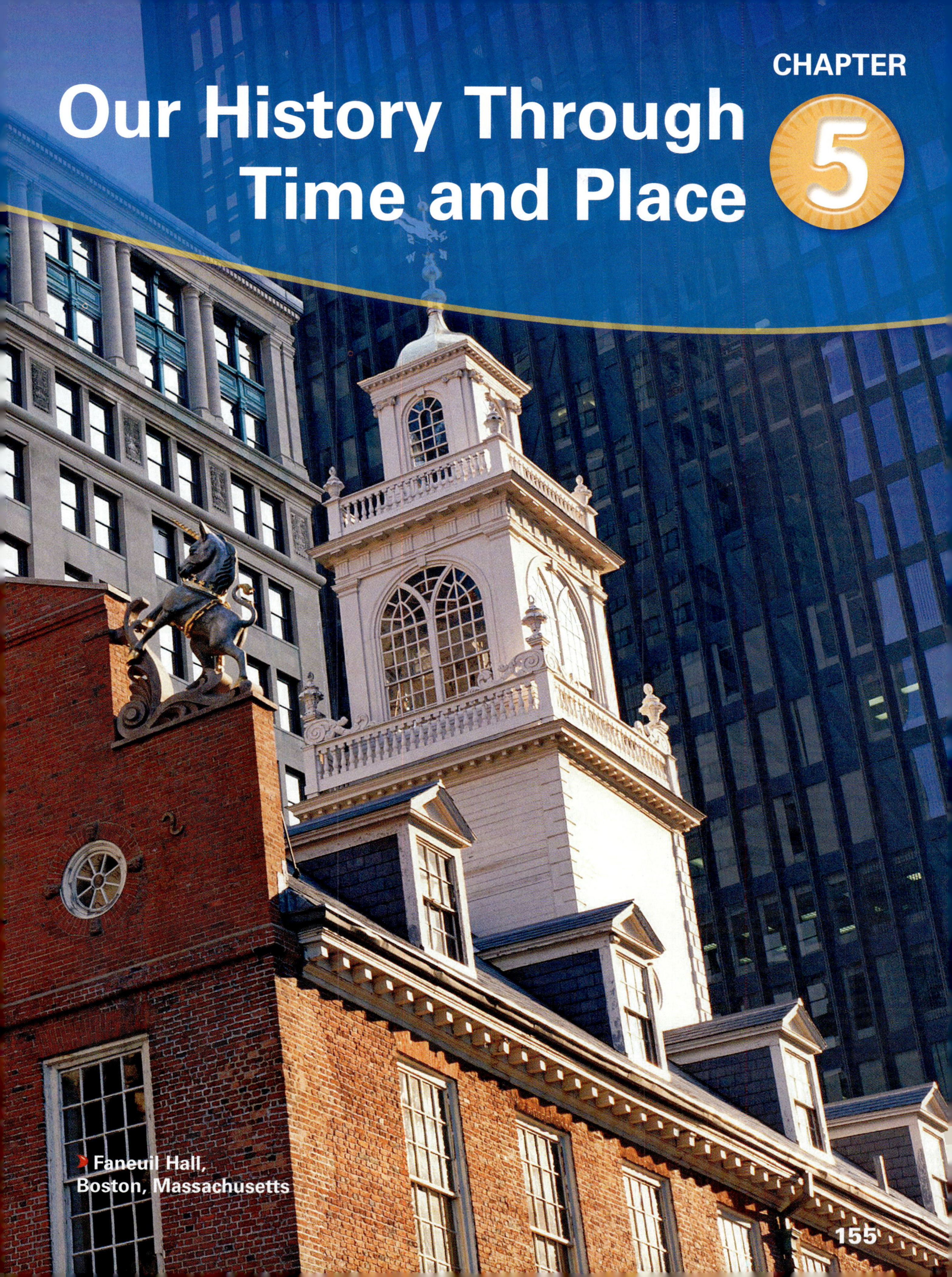

Faneuil Hall, Boston, Massachusetts

Lesson 1 Communities Through Time

What to Know
How do communities both change and stay the same?

Vocabulary
decade p. 156
century p. 156
continuity p. 157

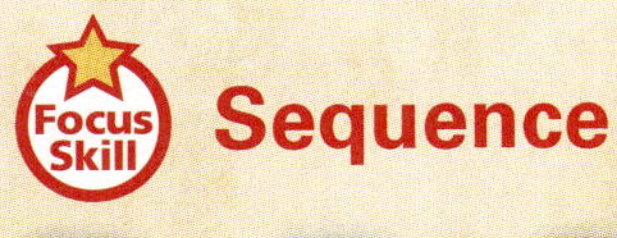

Events that happened long ago often affect communities today, or in the present. What happens today will affect communities in the future, or in the time still to come.

Changes Over Time

All communities change in some ways and stay the same in other ways. Change may take place in a day, a week, a month, a year, a decade, or a century. A **decade** is 10 years. A **century** is 100 years.

You can use old and new photographs to see change. The photos on these pages show Chicago, Illinois. What changes can you see in this community?

The skyline of Chicago today

Continuity in a Community

You can also use the same photographs to see continuity (kahn•tuhn•OO•uh•tee) in Chicago. **Continuity** is continuing without changing.

In communities everywhere, some things stay the same. Many old buildings in Chicago are still used today. They just have new things in them, such as computers. Some kinds of work in the community can stay the same, but the work may be done in new ways.

Reading Check **Sequence**
Which is longer—a decade or a century?

Built in 1869, the Chicago Water Tower still stands today. The tower shows continuity, while the area around it has changed.

Long Ago

Today

This painting shows the Great Chicago Fire.

This photograph shows Chicago's streets after the Great Chicago Fire.

Fast Changes

Changes in communities usually happen slowly. A community may grow larger as more people move there. New roads may be built, and old roads may be made wider. People may start new businesses. They may tear down old buildings.

The Great Chicago Fire

Some changes happen very fast. In October 1871, a fire started in a barn in Chicago. Some people believe that a cow kicked over a lighted lantern.

At that time, most of Chicago's buildings were made of wood. The buildings burned easily. When the fire was finally put out more than a day later, thousands of homes and businesses had burned down. Chicago was rebuilt after that terrible fire. It is now one of the country's largest cities.

Jerome, Arizona

Some changes can cause a community to grow fast and then nearly disappear. In the 1870s, Jerome, Arizona, grew from a few tents into a town of almost 15,000. People came to mine the copper that had been found there. By 1953, the mines had closed. Soon, only 50 people lived there.

Today, people visit Jerome to see what it was like to live in a mining town. Because of the visitors, more people now work in Jerome than when the mines closed.

Reading Check **Sequence**
What happened after the mines closed in Jerome?

Summary Communities both change and stay the same. Sometimes, changes are fast and unplanned.

Jerome, Arizona

Review

1. **What to Know** How do communities both change and stay the same?
2. **Vocabulary** Write the meaning of the term **continuity**.
3. **History** How has Chicago, Illinois, changed and stayed the same?
4. **Critical Thinking Make It Relevant** What are some ways in which your community has changed over time?
5. **Make a Brochure** Make an illustrated brochure that shows both change and continuity in your community.
6. Focus Skill **Sequence** On a separate sheet of paper, copy and complete the graphic organizer below.

Chart and Graph Skills

Read a Time Line

Why It Matters Knowing the order of events helps you understand history. Knowing how time is measured is also helpful.

Learn

A **time line** is a diagram that shows when and in what order events took place. You read a time line from left to right. The events on the left happened first. The events on the right happened later.

Time lines are divided into equal time periods. A time period can be any length. It can be a year, a decade, a century, or a millennium (muh•LEH•nee•uhm). A **millennium** is 1,000 years.

Chicago's Early History

1801 | 1811 | 1821 | 1831 | 1841 | 1851

1803 The United States adds its first fort to the area

1818 Illinois becomes a state

1837 Chicago becomes an official city

1848 Galena and Chicago Union Railroad is built

Fort Dearborn

Galena and Chicago Union Station

Working for Suffrage

People also use ideas to change communities. Many have worked to make sure that everyone has the same **rights**, or freedoms.

United States citizens have the right to vote. To **vote** is to make a choice that gets counted. In the early 1900s, women could not vote. Susan B. Anthony believed this should change. In the mid-1800s, she and Elizabeth Cady Stanton set up groups of people to work for woman's suffrage. **Suffrage** is the right to vote.

People printed **slogans**, or short sayings, on buttons and signs to tell their message. They held meetings and talked to people about the importance of giving suffrage to women. Finally, in 1920, women won the right to vote.

Reading Check **Main Idea and Details**
When did women win the right to vote?

Susan B. Anthony (below left) and others worked for woman's suffrage.

Gandhi was a leader for equality in India.

Working for Equality

In the 1900s, many worked for **equality**, or equal treatment, for all people. Both Mohandas Gandhi (moh•HAHN•dahs GAHN•dee) and Dr. Martin Luther King, Jr., believed that everyone should have the same rights.

Mohandas Gandhi

Gandhi wanted people in India to have freedom. At the time, India was ruled by Britain. Britain's leaders made the laws for India. Many people were not treated fairly or equally.

Instead of fighting, Gandhi used peaceful actions to work for equality. He did not want people to hurt others. He led marches and refused to follow laws that he felt were wrong.

In 1947, India became its own country. Gandhi had helped the people of India become free.

Dr. Martin Luther King, Jr.

Dr. Martin Luther King, Jr., believed that laws should treat all people equally. The rights to be treated equally are called **civil rights**. In Dr. King's lifetime, laws in the United States separated people. For example, African Americans could not go to the same schools as white people.

Dr. King led peaceful marches and spoke against unfair laws. In the 1960s, laws were passed to support equality.

Reading Check **Compare and Contrast**
What did Gandhi and Dr. King both do?

Dr. Martin Luther King, Jr., agreed with Gandhi about using peaceful actions to work for equality.

Summary People cause change all over the world. They help communities grow. They also work for equality.

Review

1. **What to Know** How have people changed their communities?
2. **Vocabulary** Use the term **slogan** in a sentence about **suffrage**.
3. **Your Community** How has a person or group changed your community?
4. **Critical Thinking** How did Gandhi help change the way people around the world work for change?
5. **Write a Paragraph** Write a paragraph about a person in this lesson who has brought change to many communities.
6. Focus Skill **Sequence** On a separate sheet of paper, copy and complete the graphic organizer below.

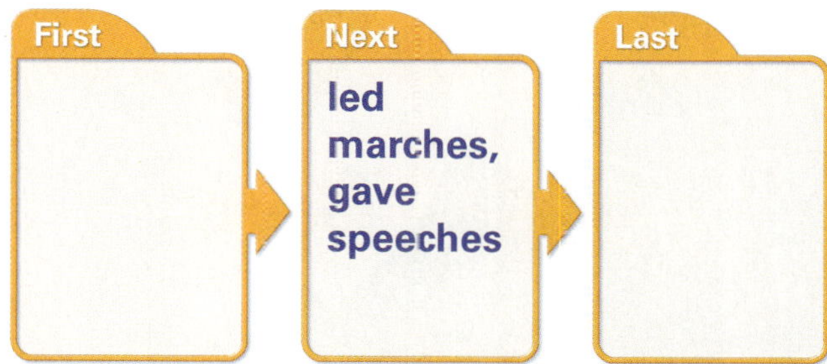

Compare Primary and Secondary Sources

Why It Matters People use both primary sources and secondary sources to learn about history.

Learn

A **primary source** is a record made by people who saw or took part in an event. A letter, diary entry, photo, or film can be a primary source.

A **secondary source** is a record of an event that was made by a person who was not there. An encyclopedia article is an example of a secondary source.

The record below is part of the "I Have a Dream" speech made by Dr. Martin Luther King, Jr. The photo below shows him making this speech.

Primary sources about Dr. King include

1. a photograph of him
2. a speech
3. a Nobel Peace Prize, which he won in 1964.

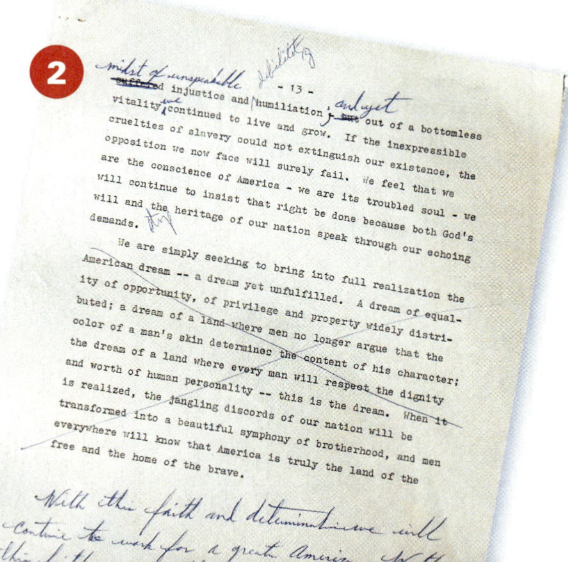

- 13 -

d injustice and humiliation, out of a bottomless vitality continued to live and grow. If the inexpressible cruelties of slavery could not extinguish our existence, the opposition we now face will surely fail. We feel that we are the conscience of America - we are its troubled soul - we will continue to insist that right be done because both God's will and the heritage of our nation speak through our echoing demands.

We are simply seeking to bring into full realization the American dream -- a dream yet unfulfilled. A dream of equality of opportunity, of privilege and property widely distributed; a dream of a land where men no longer argue that the color of a man's skin determines the content of his character; the dream of a land where every man will respect the dignity and worth of human personality -- this is the dream. When it is realized, the jangling discords of our nation will be transformed into a beautiful symphony of brotherhood, and men everywhere will know that America is truly the land of the free and the home of the brave.

Practice

Use the primary and secondary sources on these pages to answer these questions.

1. Which images show primary sources?
2. Which images show secondary sources?
3. How is a primary source different from a secondary source?

Apply

Make It Relevant Find one primary source and one secondary source about an event or a person in your community. Share these sources with your class.

Secondary sources about Dr. King include 4 websites and 5 reference books.

Lesson 3

Inventions in Communities

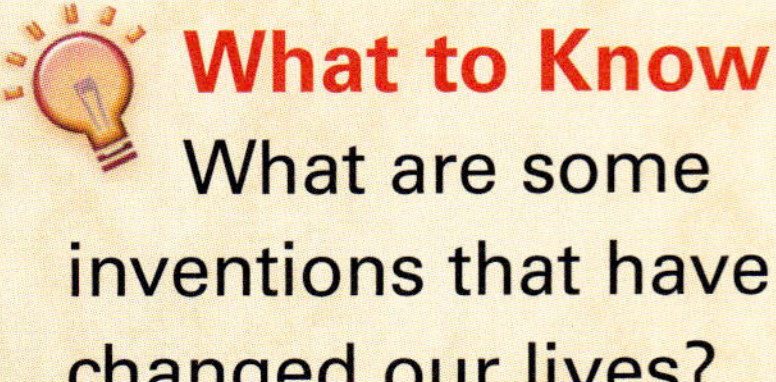

What to Know
What are some inventions that have changed our lives?

Vocabulary
technology p. 170

Sequence

New inventions add to **technology**, or all of the tools people can use every day. Changes in technology change the ways people live and work.

Changes in Communication

Long ago, people did not have many ways to communicate with others who were far away. Most messages were sent by mail, but a letter could take days or weeks to arrive. In the 1800s, new inventions made it faster and easier to communicate.

The Pony Express made mail delivery faster. This painting by Frederic Remington is called *Coming and Going of the Pony Express.*

Samuel Morse invented the telegraph.

Alexander Graham Bell's telephone was one of the first of many designs.

Samuel Morse and the Telegraph

Samuel Morse was a painter, but he had many ideas for inventions. In 1840, Morse invented the telegraph. This machine used a code of dots and dashes to send messages over wires. Before long, telegraph wires were strung across the country. People could now get news quickly from far away.

Alexander Graham Bell and the Telephone

Alexander Graham Bell also changed the way people communicated. Bell had improved the telegraph. In 1876, he built a telephone. The next year, he started the first telephone company. For the first time, people could speak to and hear others who were far away.

Reading Check **Sequence**
Which was invented first—the telegraph or the telephone?

Changes in Transportation

Canals and then railroads had made travel faster and easier. However, the invention of the automobile in the late 1800s made it possible for people to travel on their own.

Henry Ford with his Model T

Henry Ford and the Automobile

At first, cars cost a lot of money. In 1908, Henry Ford made a car that more people could buy. It was called the Model T. Because all Model Ts were the same, they could be made faster and at a lower cost.

As more people bought them, cars became the main form of transportation. People could now live outside of cities and drive to work. The automobile also led to the building of highways all across the country.

The Wright Brothers and the Airplane

Airplanes also changed transportation. In 1903, Orville Wright made a 12-second flight in an airplane. He and his brother, Wilbur, had built the plane. They had been building and improving airplanes for several years.

Later, airplane companies used the Wright brothers' ideas to build larger airplanes. Today, airplanes carry both people and goods around the world.

Reading Check **Sequence**
What happened after the Wright brothers made an airplane that could fly?

Orville Wright and the Model A Flyer

The Model T was the first car in the United States that many people could afford to buy.

Inventions such as the vacuum cleaner and the television changed daily life.

Edison (top) and Latimer (bottom) invented the first practical lightbulb.

Changes in the Home

Homes are filled with inventions. Toasters, vacuum cleaners, and lightbulbs are all inventions that make life easier. These inventions have changed the way people live.

Thomas Edison, Lewis Latimer, and the Lightbulb

Many inventors worked together to bring electricity to homes. In the 1880s, Thomas Edison and Lewis Latimer invented the first practical electric lightbulbs. Before the lightbulb, people used candles, oil lamps, and gas lamps for light.

The lightbulb let people light their homes without the danger of causing a fire. Because of the lightbulb, they could do more evening activities.

Other Home Inventions

Many inventors worked on inventions that led to the radio in the late 1800s and the television in the early 1900s. These inventions now bring people news from all over the world.

Other inventions have changed people's homes. Many items in kitchens today were once the ideas of inventors. These include stoves, ovens, dishwashers, and refrigerators.

Reading Check **Main Idea and Details**
When was the first practical electric lightbulb invented?

Josephine Cochran (top) invented the first practical dishwasher. Guillermo Gonzalez Camarena (bottom) invented the color television and the remote control.

Summary Inventions have changed the way people live. Many people have worked to invent the things we use every day.

Review

1. **What to Know** What are some inventions that have changed our lives?
2. **Vocabulary** Write about how you use **technology** in your life.
3. **History** Which inventions changed the way people communicate?
4. **Critical Thinking Make It Relevant** What would your life be like if the lightbulb had not been invented?
5. **Make a Chart** Make a chart of inventors and inventions.
6. Focus Skill **Sequence** On a separate sheet of paper, copy and complete the graphic organizer below.

Chart and Graph Skills

Read a Flowchart

Why It Matters People often need to know how to do something or how something works. A chart that shows the steps in order can help them understand.

Learn

A **flowchart** shows how to do something or how something works. It shows the steps in order.

The flowchart below uses words, pictures, and arrows to show the steps to building a car. Cars are put together on assembly lines. On an **assembly line**, each worker adds one kind of part to a product as it passes on a moving belt.

Assembly Line

The car frame is placed on the assembly line.

The top and sides of the car are added to the frame.

Practice

Follow the arrows on the flowchart to answer the questions.

1. What is the next step after the car frame is placed on an assembly line?
2. What happens after the top and sides are added to the frame?
3. When are the engine parts put into the car?

Apply

Make It Relevant Make a list of the things you do every morning to get ready for school. Use your list to make a flowchart that shows the sequence in which you do these things. Draw pictures, label them, and add arrows to show how to read the steps of your chart.

Wheels are attached to the car.

Engine parts are put into the car.

Lesson 4

Communities Long Ago

What to Know
What ideas from ancient communities are used today?

Vocabulary

ancient p. 178
civilization p. 178
modern p. 178
democracy p. 182
republic p. 183
empire p. 184
trade p. 184
port p. 185

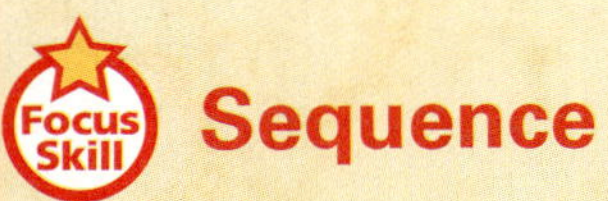

Since **ancient** times, or times very long ago, people have lived in communities. In even the earliest groups, people often shared a government and a culture.

Some of those communities grew to become great civilizations. A **civilization** is a large group of people living in a well-organized way. Ideas from some of those ancient civilizations are still used in modern times. **Modern** is how we describe the time we live in today.

Ruins of ancient Mesopotamia still stand in what is now Iraq.

This Mesopotamian artwork called *Standard of Ur* shows a wheeled cart.

This piece of clay shows Sumerian writing.

Ancient Mesopotamia

One of the world's earliest civilizations was in southwestern Asia. It was in a place called Mesopotamia (meh•suh•puh•TAY•mee•uh). It had some of the world's earliest cities. People built them in a part of Mesopotamia called Sumer (SOO•mer).

The Sumerians developed many new ideas and inventions. They built carts with wheels. Wheels made it easier for people to move things from place to place.

Writing was another important idea developed by the Sumerians. Before people learned to write, they had to keep track of things by remembering them. Writing gave the Sumerians a way to record important information and their history.

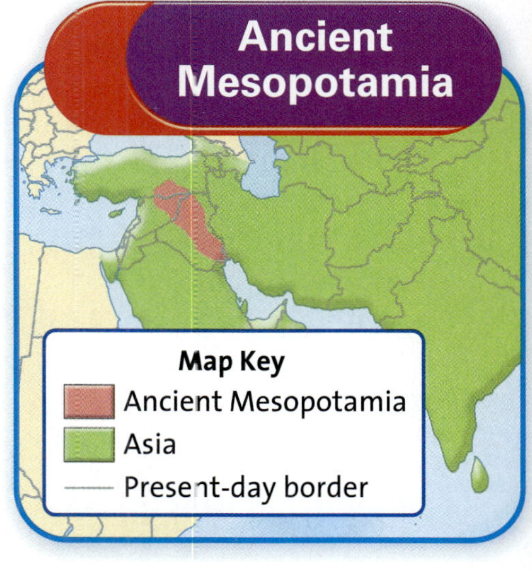

Reading Check **Sequence**

Was writing developed during or after the time of the Sumerians?

Ancient Egypt

The ancient civilization of Egypt, in Africa, is known for its pyramids. An Egyptian pyramid is a tomb, or burial place, for a dead king or queen.

The Great Pyramid is the largest of the pyramids that are still standing today. It is more than 450 feet high. It was built about 4,500 years ago for an Egyptian pharaoh (FAIR•oh), or king, named Khufu (KOO•foo).

The pyramids were made by stacking huge stone blocks in layers. Some of the blocks in the Great Pyramid weigh 5,000 pounds. The ancient Egyptians did not have wheels and pulleys for moving things. They put the giant blocks in place by pushing them up ramps on rollers made of logs.

Reading Check **Summarize**
How was the Great Pyramid of Egypt built?

Hatshepsut (hat•SHEP•soot) was one of Egypt's leaders.

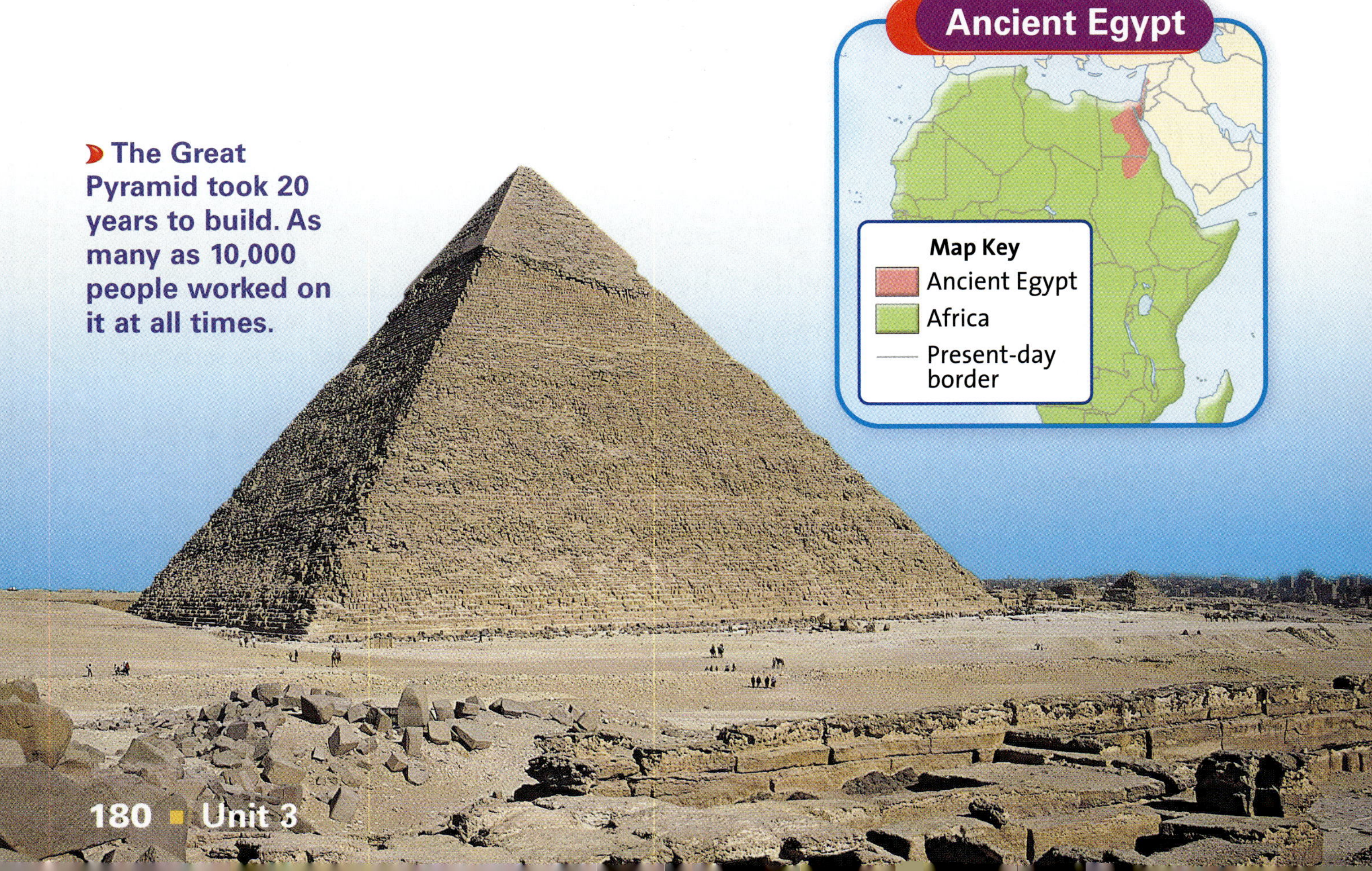

The Great Pyramid took 20 years to build. As many as 10,000 people worked on it at all times.

Chinese Paper Making

Illustration The ancient Chinese made paper by
1. cutting reeds and soaking them to make pulp,
2. mashing the pulp,
3. heating the pulp,
4. pounding the pulp,
5. stretching the paper, and
6. drying the paper.

What happened to the pulp after it was heated?

Ancient China

Every Fourth of July, fireworks light up the night sky all across the United States. But fireworks are not an American invention. They were invented thousands of years ago in China.

The ancient Chinese also invented paper and printing. First, they wrote on paper with brushes and ink. Later, they invented a way to print copies of pages. They carved the writing for a page on a wooden block. Then they put ink on the block and pressed it against paper to make a print. This let them make many copies of a page much faster than they could write them by hand.

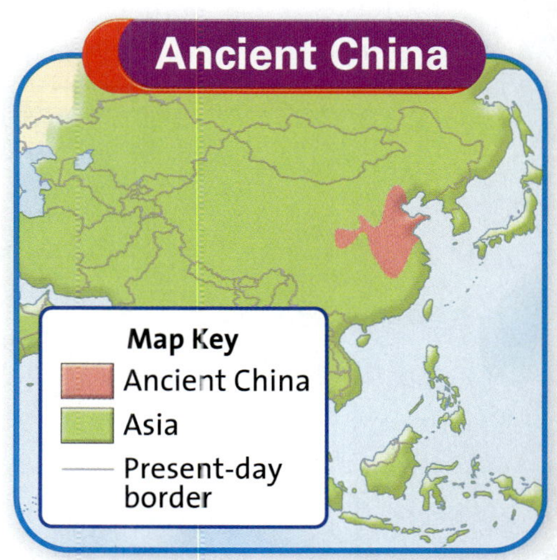

Reading Check **Summarize**
What inventions from ancient China are still used?

Greek Alphabet

Greek Letter	English Sound
Α	a
Β	b
Γ	g
Δ	d
Ε	e

Table In what ways is the Greek alphabet like the alphabet we use today?

Ancient Greece

The Greek civilization began in what is now the country of Greece, in Europe. Athens was one of its most important communities.

The government of Athens was the world's first democracy. In a **democracy**, citizens make the decisions. All free men over the age of 18 could take part in the government of Athens.

In ancient Greece, the male citizens met in a large group, or assembly. Each man had the right to speak. They talked about ideas for new laws and voted on them.

The people of Athens loved the arts and learning. Ancient Greece is still known for its sculptors, potters, painters, builders, and writers.

Reading Check **Main Idea and Details**
What kind of government did Athens have?

The Acropolis (uh•KRAH•puh•luhs) was a religious center in ancient Athens.

The Forum was a public square in the center of Rome. Romans met there to talk about government and business.

Ancient Rome

The Roman civilization began with a number of tiny villages. These were scattered over seven hills above the Tiber (TY•ber) River, in what is today the country of Italy. As the villages grew, they combined to form the city of Rome.

The people of ancient Rome had the world's first republic. In a **republic**, citizens vote to choose government leaders. These leaders make decisions for all the people.

To make the city strong, Rome's leaders built good roads and public buildings. Rome became one of the world's richest cities up to that time.

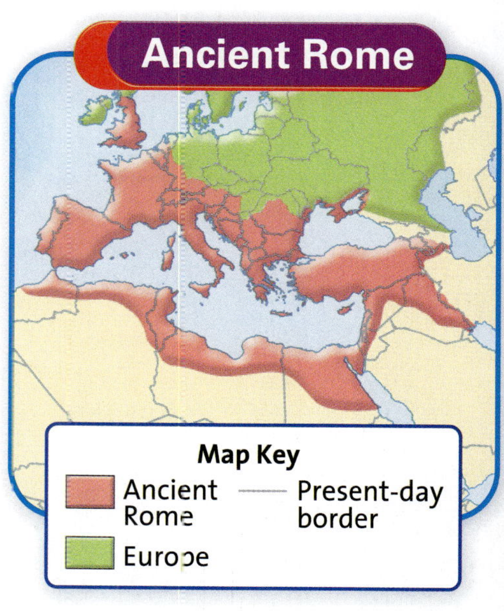

Reading Check **Main Idea and Details**
What form of government did Rome have?

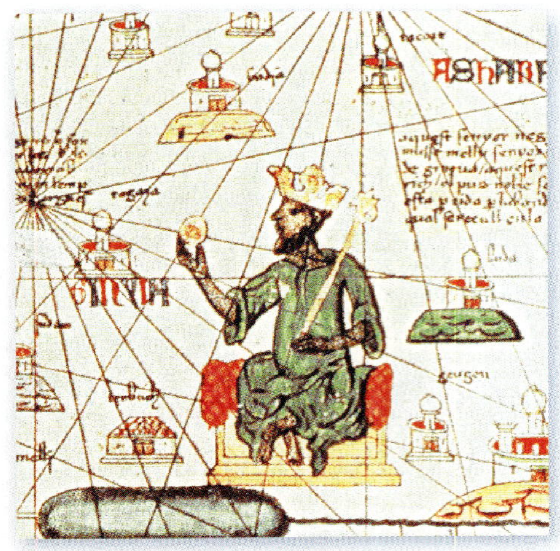

This map shows a leader in ancient Mali named Mansa Musa.

Mali

The empire of Mali, in Africa, was among the richest in the ancient world. An **empire** is all the land and people under the control of a powerful nation.

Between 700 and 1400, Mali was an important trading center. People there traded gold for salt and cloth from the Mediterranean coast. To **trade** is to exchange one good or service for another. The goods that people traded came by camel caravan across the desert. A caravan is a traveling group of traders.

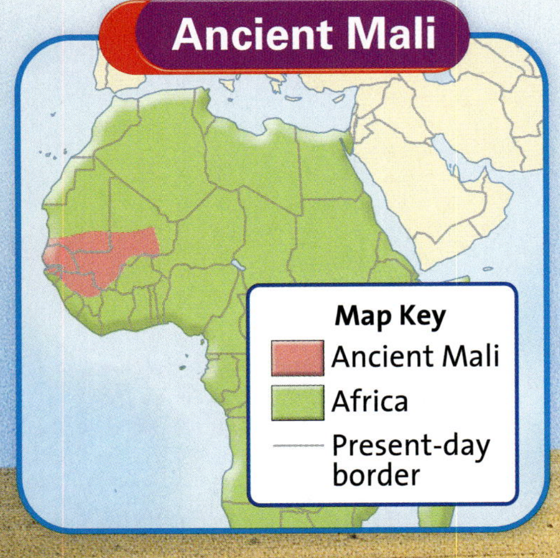

Fast Fact

This camel caravan carries salt across the West African desert. A camel can go for days or even months without water.

Although some ancient buildings still stand, Mali is no longer a powerful trading center. Today, Mali has no lands along the Atlantic coast. It has no port. A **port** is a good place for ships to dock and pick up goods or people. However, many goods, such as cotton and gold, still come from Mali.

Reading Check **Summarize**
What was Mali known as between 700 and 1400?

The Great Mosque (MAHSK) at Timbuktu (tim•buhk•TOO) in Mali

Summary Many communities began in ancient times. Some ideas from ancient times are still important to communities today.

Review

1. **What to Know** What ideas from ancient communities are used today?
2. **Vocabulary** Write a few sentences about one of the **ancient** cultures you read about.
3. **Your Community** Write about a place in your community that shows an idea from one of the ancient civilizations.
4. **Critical Thinking** **Make It Relevant** What invention from an ancient civilization do you use every day?
5. **Create a Radio Interview** With a partner, write an interview with an imaginary person from one of the ancient civilizations. Tape-record your interview, and play it for the class.
6. Focus Skill **Sequence** On a separate sheet of paper, copy and complete the graphic organizer below.

Visual Summary

People change communities with their actions.

Summarize the Chapter

Sequence Complete the graphic organizer to show that you understand changes that have occurred in transportation.

First	Next	Last
People travel by horse and wagon.	**People travel by train.**	

Vocabulary

Identify the term that correctly matches each definition.

1. 100 years

   decade, p. 156

   century, p. 156

2. All of the tools people can use every day

   engineer, p. 164

   technology, p. 170

3. equal treatment for all people

   suffrage, p. 165

   equality, p. 166

4. A large group of people living in a well-organized way

   civilization, p. 178

   modern, p. 178

5. all the land and people under the control of a powerful nation

   republic, p. 183

   empire, p. 184

Inventions have changed the way people live and work.

Ideas from ancient communities are still used today.

Facts and Main Ideas

Answer these questions.

6. How did Chicago change quickly in 1871?
7. How did Dr. Martin Luther King, Jr., work for equality?
8. What are some inventions that changed transportation?

Write the letter of the best choice.

9. Which of the following is an example of continuity in a community?
   A new roads built
   B old roads made wider
   C new buildings built
   D old buildings still used
10. Which civilization was the world's first democracy?
    A the United States
    B ancient China
    C ancient Greece
    D ancient Egypt

Critical Thinking

11. What would life be like without telephones?
12. **Make It Relevant** How have ancient civilizations affected your life?

Skills

Read a Time Line

Use the time line on pages 160 and 161 to answer the question.

13. When did Illinois become a state?

Read a Flowchart

Use the flowchart on pages 176 and 177 to answer the question.

14. What happens before the wheels are added to the car?

writing

Write a Thank-You Note Write a thank-you note to an inventor or another person who caused change.

Write a Diary Entry Imagine that you live in an ancient community. Write a diary entry about your life.

TAKE NOTES

Taking notes can help you remember important ideas in what you read.

- **Write important facts and ideas in your own words.**
- **Organize your notes so that they are easy to understand.**

Our Country's History	
Main Ideas	**Facts**
Lesson 1: • Our First Communities • How the People Lived • ________	• Native Americans formed the first communities in North America. • Native Americans belonged to different tribes. • ________

PREVIEW VOCABULARY

shelter p. 191

patriotism p. 208

pioneer p. 214

CHAPTER 6

Our Country's History

Musicians in Colonial Williamsburg, Virginia

Lesson 1

The First Communities

What to Know
Who formed the first communities in North America?

Vocabulary
language p. 190
oral history p. 190
shelter p. 191

Sequence

The first communities in North America were formed long ago by Native Americans, also called American Indians. Native Americans lived in groups that are now called tribes. The people of a tribe shared the same land and ways of life.

The First People

Each Native American group had its own culture and language. A **language** is a set of words used to communicate. Early Native Americans did not use written languages. They learned about the past from stories told by older family members. These stories made up an **oral history**. *Oral* means "spoken."

This Ute father and son live in Colorado. They are dressed in clothing like the Utes wore long ago for a celebration.

MAP SKILL **Location** What Native American group lived nearest to what is now your community?

Native Americans

Native Americans once lived in every part of what is now the United States. All groups used natural resources to meet their needs for food, clothing, and shelter. A **shelter** is a home or other building that protects people from the weather.

Because Native American groups lived in different places, they had different natural resources. They ate different kinds of foods, wore different clothing, and lived in different shelters.

Native Americans who had forests nearby used wood to build shelters. Many groups built villages along rivers, which they used to travel. Those who lived in drier climates found few trees. They built shelters with grasses or mud bricks dried in the sun.

These moccasins, or shoes, show the skill of a Sioux craftworker.

Reading Check **Sequence**
Who lived in North America first?

Two Different Ways of Life

Native Americans mainly hunted or fished. They also gathered plants, nuts, and wild berries. Other groups added to their food supplies by growing crops and trading.

Hunting Communities

Native Americans who lived on the Great Plains hunted buffalo, or bison. They used every part of an animal. They used the meat for food, the bones for tools, and the skin to make clothes and shelters.

Hunting tribes had to keep moving to follow the buffalo. They needed shelters they could move. Their tepees (TEE•peez) were made from animal skins pulled tight over wooden poles.

Life on the Great Plains

Illustration What are some ways the Plains Indians used the animals they hunted?

Farming Communities

In addition to hunting and gathering, some Native American groups also grew their food. They raised crops, such as corn, beans, and squash. Farmers stored food for the winter.

Unlike hunting groups, Native Americans who farmed stayed in one place. They built stronger homes out of wood. The Iroquois (IR•uh•kwoi) built longhouses, or long, narrow houses made of wood and bark.

Reading Check **Main Idea and Details**
How did Native Americans get their food?

An Iroquois dancer beside a longhouse

Summary Native Americans formed the first communities in North America. They lived in different areas and had different ways of living.

Review

1. **What to Know** Who formed the first communities in North America?
2. **Vocabulary** Use the term **shelter** in a sentence.
3. **Geography** How did Native Americans use natural resources?
4. **Critical Thinking** **Make It Relevant** How might Native Americans have used your community's natural resources?
5. **Make a Map** Make a map to show where Native Americans have lived in your state.
6. Focus Skill **Sequence** On a separate sheet of paper, copy and complete the graphic organizer below.

How Did Change Affect Native Americans?

When Europeans came to North America, life changed for the Native Americans. Here are some thoughts about change from Native Americans in the past and present.

1

Chief Joseph

Chief Joseph was chief of the Nez Perce (nez•PERS), a tribe that lived in what is now Idaho, Oregon, and Washington. When Europeans took land away from Native Americans, Chief Joseph spoke against these actions.

"The Earth is the mother of all people, and all people should have equal rights [the same freedoms as others] upon it. . . ."

2

Satanta

Satanta, or White Bear, was a Kiowa (KY•uh•wah) chief from what is now Kansas and Oklahoma. He fought to keep his tribe's hold on their lands.

"I have heard that you intend [plan] to settle us on a reservation near the mountains. I don't want to settle. I love to roam over the prairies. There I feel free. . . ."

3

Leslie Marmon Silko

Leslie Marmon Silko is a poet and novelist. She grew up on the Laguna Pueblo (PWEH•bloh) reservation in New Mexico. She encourages Native Americans to share their ways of life with others.

"If all of us and all living things on the planet are to continue, we, who still remember how we must live, must join together."

4

Buffalo Tiger

Buffalo Tiger is an elder of the Miccosukee (mik•uh•SOO•kee) tribe in southern Florida. He encourages Native Americans to remember their heritage and further their education.

"Think like Indians, be like Indians, but learn English, learn how to write, be educated. You have two minds and you can work with both. We do not want to lose out on being Indians."

It's Your Turn

Analyze Points of View Summarize the different points of view about change. Answer these questions.

1. How did Chief Joseph and Satanta feel about freedom?
2. Would Silko and Buffalo Tiger agree or disagree on keeping Native American ways of life alive?
3. Who speaks mainly about the importance of learning?

Make It Relevant How do you feel about change in your community?

Lesson 2

Building Communities

What to Know
Why did Europeans build communities in North America?

Vocabulary

explorer p. 196
religion p. 197
claim p. 197
settlement p. 197
settler p. 199
conflict p. 200
slavery p. 201

Sequence

In 1492, an Italian explorer named Christopher Columbus sailed from Spain. An **explorer** is a person who goes to find out about a place. Columbus thought that if he sailed west across the Atlantic Ocean, he would reach the part of Asia that Europeans called the Indies.

Instead, he reached an island off the coast of North America. At that time, people in Europe did not know about the Americas, or the continents of North America and South America.

Christopher Columbus came to the Americas with three sailing ships.

This fort at St. Augustine, completed in 1695, is one of the few remaining Spanish buildings in Florida.

In 1513, Spanish explorer Juan Ponce de León (HWAHN POHN•say day lay•OHN) first claimed the land that is now Florida for Spain.

Exploring North America

Soon, other European explorers came to the Americas. Some hoped to find treasure and to spread their **religion**, or belief system. Others came to claim land. To **claim** something is to say it belongs to you.

Spanish Explorers

In 1565, the king of Spain sent Pedro Menéndez de Avilés (may•NAYN•days day ah•vee•LAYS) to what is now Florida. He built a fort named St. Augustine there. St. Augustine is the oldest lasting settlement in the United States. A **settlement** is a new community.

Spain claimed much of South America and the southern part of North America. Mexico and most countries to its south share a Spanish heritage.

Reading Check **Sequence**
Was St. Augustine built before or after the United States was a country?

Native Americans and settlers leaving after trading fur near what is now Missouri.

A French Settlement

Pierre Laclède founded St. Louis, in what is now Missouri.

French explorers also came to North America. They claimed much of what is today Canada. The French also claimed the middle part of what is now the United States.

In 1763, Pierre Laclède (lah•KLED) traveled up the Mississippi River. He was looking for a good place for a fur-trading post. Laclède chose a spot near a cliff along the river. He knew he could use the river to move furs.

In 1764, he began a settlement there that later became St. Louis. It was named for King Louis XV of France. Laclède said, "This settlement will become one of the finest cities in America."

Building St. Louis

The settlers first built shelters in which to live and work. A **settler** is one of the first people to live in a new community. These buildings included a large house for trading furs, cabins for workers to sleep in, and sheds for storing things. The settlers later built a church and a fort.

Many people traveling west passed through St. Louis. Some stayed and settled there. By 1765, St. Louis had more than 300 settlers. In the 1800s, the city became one of the largest river ports in the nation. Today, St. Louis is a large city.

Sequence

What did the settlers add to St. Louis after building shelters?

St. Louis today

St. Louis was a busy river port in 1874.

An English Settlement

In 1607, three ships sailed from England to North America. They landed in what is now the state of Virginia. Some of the 105 passengers hoped to find riches and a way to the Pacific Ocean. Others wanted to spread their religion. They named their settlement after their king, James I. Jamestown was the first lasting English settlement in North America.

Conflict and Change

An early leader of Jamestown, John Smith, traded with Native Americans to get food for the settlers. Over time, the settlers came into **conflict**, or disagreement, with Native Americans. They fought over food and land.

Today, Jamestown is a National Historic Site.

In 1612, John Rolfe began growing tobacco in Jamestown. To grow tobacco and other crops, the settlers needed more workers. Beginning in the 1600s, people were brought from Africa and forced into slavery. **Slavery** is a system under which people have no choices.

The Africans had been taken from their homes and families. Then traders had brought them to North America, where they worked as enslaved people. An enslaved person is owned by another person and forced to work without pay.

Reading Check **Main Idea and Details**
Why did the English settlers come to North America?

Pocahontas was the daughter of Chief Powhatan. He was the leader of the Powhatan, the Native Americans who lived near Jamestown.

Another English Settlement

Native Americans taught the Pilgrims how to grow corn.

The Wampanoag (wahm•puh•NOH•ag) were the first people to live where Plymouth, Massachusetts, is today. They fished the nearby Atlantic Ocean and grew corn and other crops.

Pilgrims Come to Plymouth

In 1620, a ship called the *Mayflower* carried more people from England to North America. They wanted to live where they could be free to follow their religion. Because they traveled for religious reasons, they became known as Pilgrims.

The Pilgrims looked for a good place to build a settlement. They found a harbor with deep water where ships could come close to shore. John Smith had named the place Plymouth.

Time Line Which of these settlements was built first?

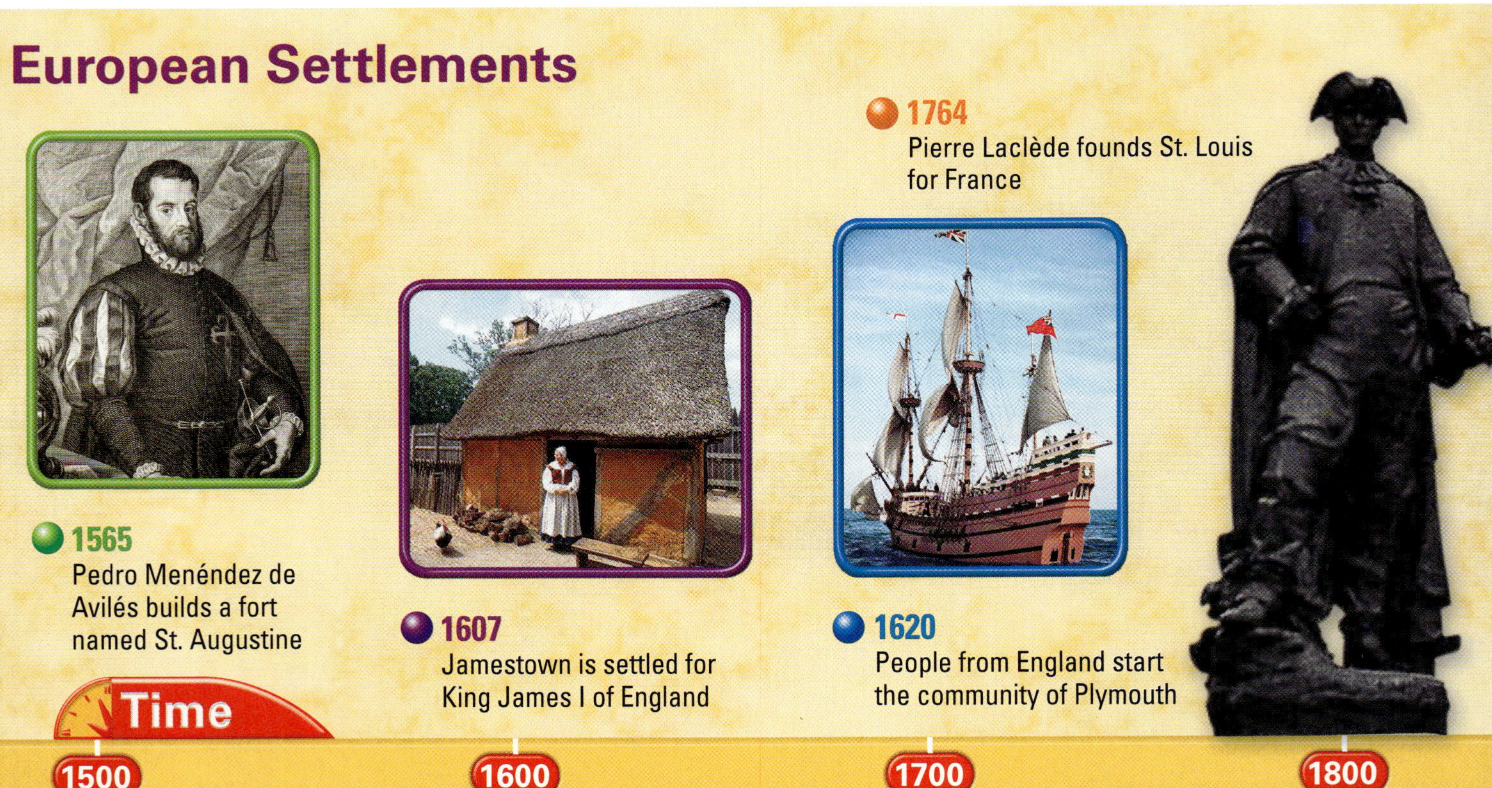

The Mayflower Compact

The Pilgrims wrote a compact, or agreement, that set up a government for their community. In the Mayflower Compact, the Pilgrims agreed to make fair laws for the new community. They also promised to obey these laws. The Pilgrims would govern themselves.

Reading Check **Sequence**
Who were the first people to live in what is now Plymouth, Massachusetts?

In the fall of 1621, the Pilgrims celebrated their first harvest with the Wampanoag. Many people think of this as the first Thanksgiving.

Summary Explorers from Europe claimed many areas of North America. Settlers from different countries built new communities in what is now the United States.

Review

1. **What to Know** Why did Europeans build communities in North America?
2. **Vocabulary** What is the difference between an **explorer** and a **settler**?
3. **Your Community** Find out who started your community.
4. **Critical Thinking** Why do you think there was conflict between the settlers and Native Americans?
5. **Make a Chart** Make a chart showing early settlements. Include their locations, the dates when they were started, and who built them.
6. **Sequence** (Focus Skill) On a separate sheet of paper, copy and complete the graphic organizer below.

Lesson 3

Fighting for Freedom

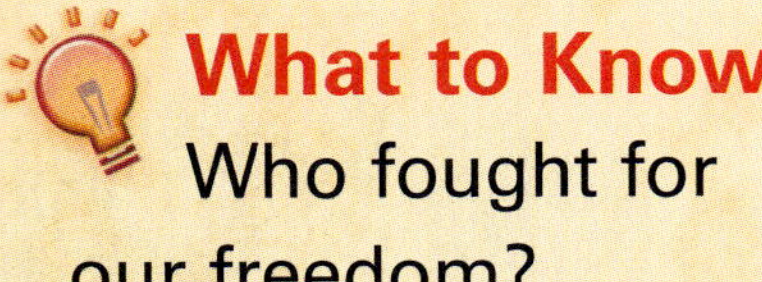

What to Know
Who fought for our freedom?

Vocabulary
freedom p. 204
colony p. 204
tax p. 205
revolution p. 205
independence p. 206
constitution p. 208
patriotism p. 208
President p. 209

Sequence

In the United States, we have many freedoms. **Freedom** is the right to make your own choices. It is one of the ideas on which our country was founded.

Freedom from England

Long ago, most of the settlements along the eastern coast of North America were colonies of England, or Britain. A **colony** is a settlement ruled by a country that is far away. By the 1700s, there were 13 colonies. These colonies were the beginning of the United States.

Fast Fact

The Boston Tea Party was an action taken in 1773 by colonists who were angry about taxes on tea. The colonists dumped 342 crates of tea into Boston Harbor.

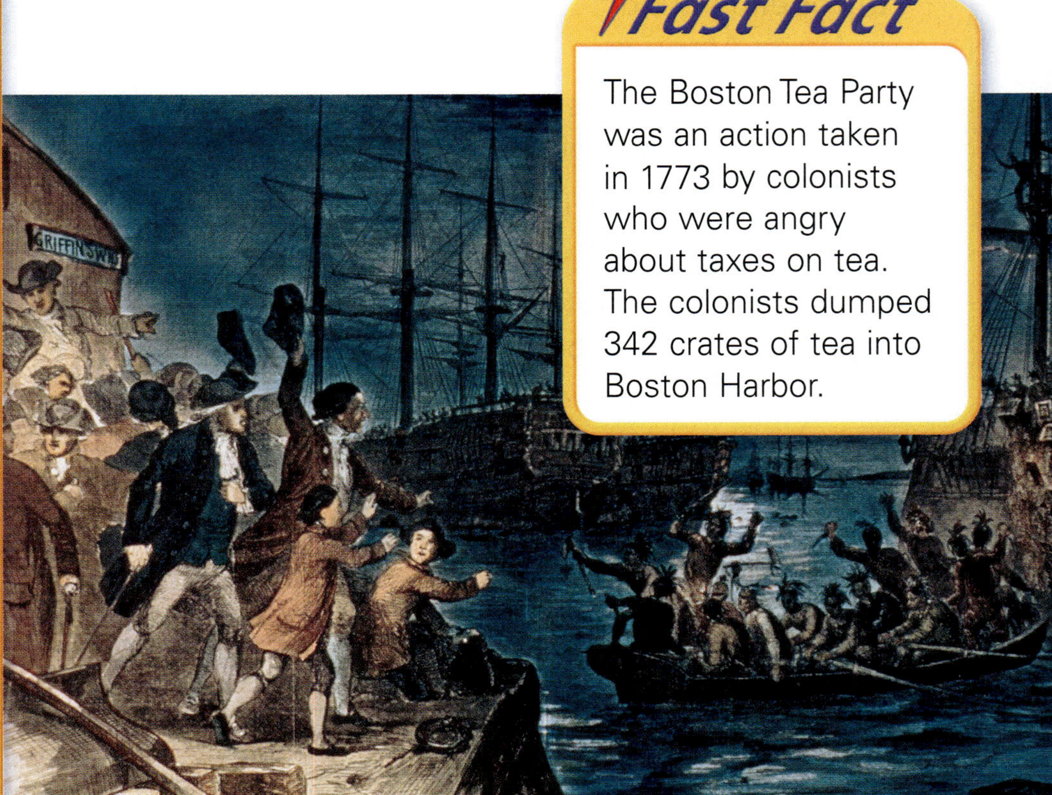

The colonists were people living in the colonies. For a long time they did not mind being ruled by Britain. Then Britain's lawmakers began passing new laws. The colonists felt the laws were unfair. The colonists were also angry that they had no part in making the laws.

Many of the laws included new taxes on goods from Britain, such as sugar and tea. A **tax** is money that people pay to the government.

In 1773, some colonists dumped tea into Boston Harbor. This is known as the Boston Tea Party. The colonists said they would rather throw away tea than pay taxes on it.

Fighting broke out between colonists and soldiers who had been sent from Britain. This fighting was the beginning of the American Revolution, or Revolutionary War. In a **revolution**, people fight for a change in government.

Reading Check **Sequence**
What happened after Britain made the colonists pay new taxes?

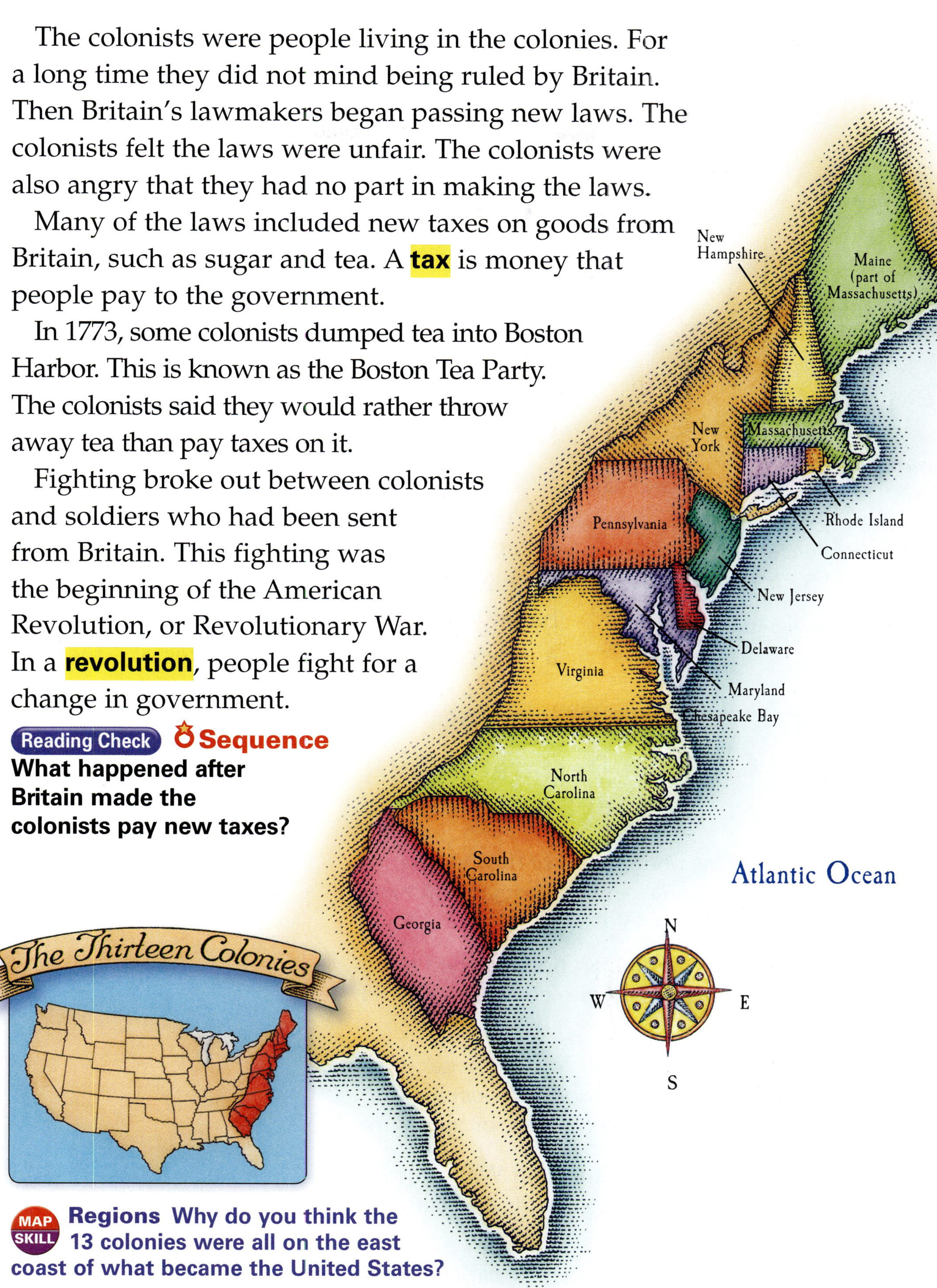

MAP SKILL **Regions** **Why do you think the 13 colonies were all on the east coast of what became the United States?**

▶ The Declaration of Independence was worked on by Benjamin Franklin, John Adams, and Thomas Jefferson.

A Declaration Is Made

In 1776, John Adams, Benjamin Franklin, Thomas Jefferson, and other leaders of the colonies met in Philadelphia, Pennsylvania. They wrote a statement listing reasons the colonists wanted independence. **Independence** is freedom from another country's control.

The statement is called the Declaration of Independence. It says that all people have the right to "Life, Liberty, and the pursuit of Happiness." *Liberty* means "freedom."

On July 4, 1776, the leaders voted to accept the Declaration of Independence. The declaration said that the colonies no longer belonged to Britain. They were now states in a new country, the United States of America.

The Declaration of Independence

Background This photograph of the Declaration of Independence shows what Thomas Jefferson wrote and who signed it.

The first part of the Declaration is called the Preamble. This says why the colonists wanted independence.

One of the colony leaders, John Hancock, wrote his name large. The term *John Hancock* came to mean a person's written name, or signature.

DBQ Document-Based Question What does this photograph tell you about the Declaration of Independence?

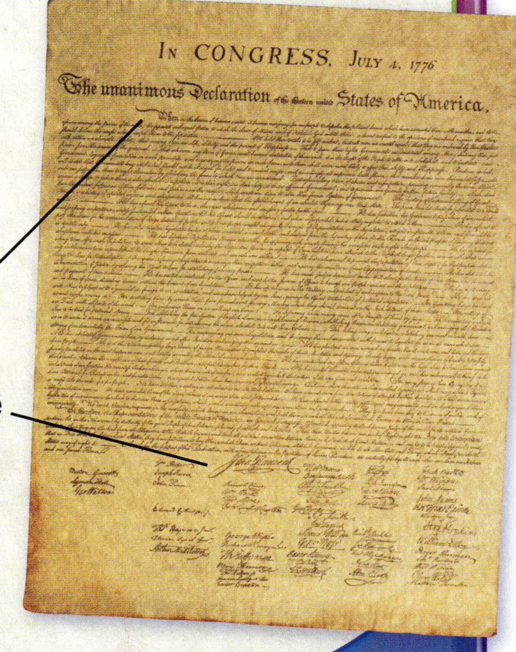
IN CONGRESS, JULY 4, 1776.

The unanimous Declaration of the thirteen united States of America,

This engraving shows George Washington and his army in Morristown, New Jersey.

The War Begins

The Revolutionary War began in 1775, a year before the Declaration of Independence was written. George Washington was chosen to lead the American troops against Britain.

Washington's army was made up of colonists who wanted to help. They were not well trained and sometimes had to get supplies from the towns for which they were fighting. The British soldiers, though, were better trained. Their supplies were sent to them on ships from Britain.

The American soldiers fought many battles. They won some, but they lost others. In 1783, the Americans finally won the war and their independence from Britain. The United States is still an independent country today.

American soldiers wore clothes like these in the Revolutionary War.

Reading Check **Sequence**
Was the Declaration of Independence written before or after the start of the Revolutionary War?

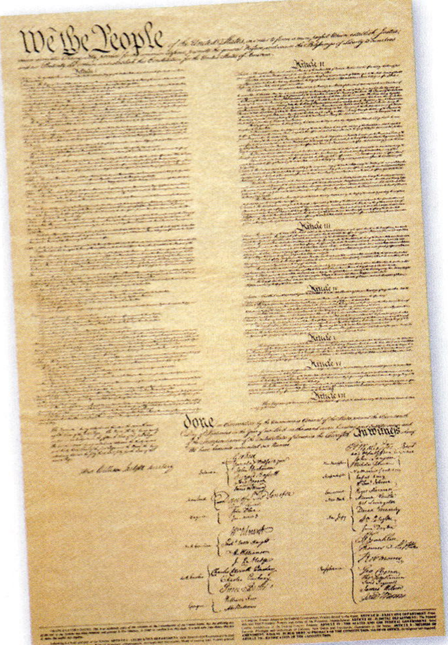
▶ The Constitution of the United States

New Laws Are Made

After the war, people in the United States could make their own laws. They formed a government for the new nation. However, the new government turned out to be weak. By 1787, the country's leaders decided they needed a new constitution. A **constitution** is a set of laws that tells how a government will work.

The leaders wanted to form a government that was strong enough to get things done but would not take away freedoms. They met in Philadelphia to write the Constitution of the United States. In 1789, the Constitution was approved.

The Constitution helped found the republic of the United States. The leaders were proud of the country they had started. A feeling of pride in one's country is called **patriotism**.

▶ This painting shows the signing of the Constitution of the United States.

Our First President

The new Constitution said that the people would choose a **President**, or leader for the country. On April 30, 1789, Americans chose General George Washington to become their first President. He is often called "the father of our country."

Reading Check **Sequence**
What happened after the Constitution was approved?

George Washington arriving in New York City to be sworn in as President

Summary The American colonists fought for freedom from Britain in the Revolutionary War. After the war, their leaders wrote the Constitution of the United States of America.

The quarter coin features George Washington.

Review

1. **What to Know** Who fought for our freedom?
2. **Vocabulary** How are **freedom** and **independence** related?
3. **Civics and Government** What document did the leaders of the United States write to form a new government?
4. **Critical Thinking** **Make It Relevant** How might your life be different if the colonists had not won their independence?
5. **Make a Time Line** Make a time line of important events in the colonists' fight for freedom.
6. Focus Skill **Sequence** On a separate sheet of paper, copy and complete the graphic organizer below.

Biography

Trustworthiness
Respect
Responsibility
Fairness
Caring
Patriotism

Franklin and Jefferson

"We hold these truths to be self-evident, that all men are created equal, that they are endowed by their Creator with certain unalienable Rights, that among these are Life, Liberty, and the pursuit of Happiness."

— The Declaration of Independence

Why Character Counts

How did Franklin and Jefferson show patriotism in their lives?

It was June 1776. The leaders of the 13 colonies had only one thing on their minds—writing a Declaration of Independence. They chose some of the finest minds in the colonies to help. They asked Thomas Jefferson to do the writing, with the help of Benjamin Franklin and John Adams.

Jefferson and Franklin had very different backgrounds. Jefferson was a rich landowner from Virginia. He had a college education. Franklin was from a working-class family. He went to school for only two years and had a job by the age of ten.

Benjamin Franklin

Thomas Jefferson

This painting is called *Congress Voting the Declaration of Independence.*

The first page of Thomas Jefferson's rough draft of the Declaration of Independence

Yet Jefferson and Franklin were alike in many ways. They both were great writers and thinkers. Each loved science and new ideas. They both loved the land of their birth. They believed it could and should be a free and united country. They worked toward a dream of a country that was governed by its people.

On July 4, 1776, the leaders of the 13 colonies approved the Declaration that Jefferson and Franklin had worked so hard to write. With the help of these two patriots, the United States of America began.

For more resources, go to **www.harcourtschool.com/ss1**

1700 — 1830

- **1775** Jefferson and Franklin represent their states in the Continental Congress
- **1776** Jefferson, Franklin, and John Adams draft the Declaration of Independence
- **1787** Franklin signs the Constitution of the United States
- **1801** Jefferson becomes third President of the United States

Lesson 4 Growth and Change

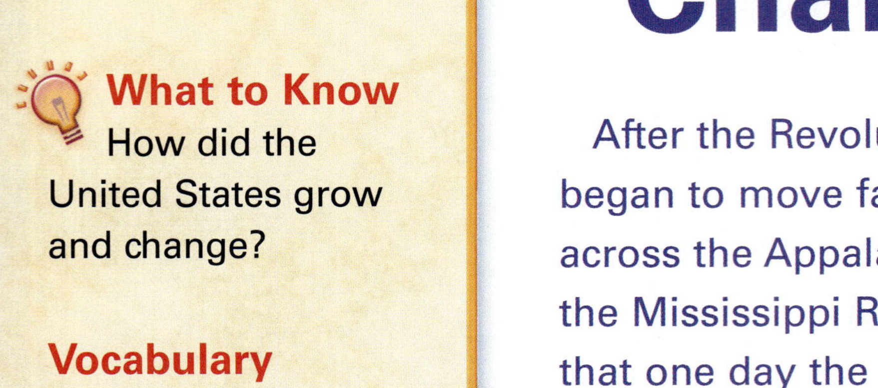

What to Know
How did the United States grow and change?

Vocabulary
pioneer p. 214
civil war p. 216
territory p. 217
amendment p. 217
immigrant p. 218

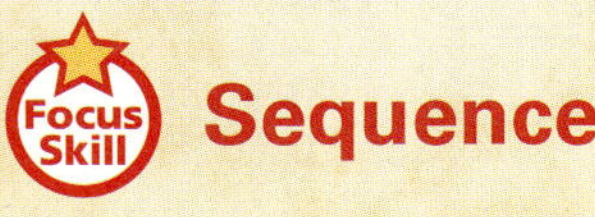

Sequence

After the Revolutionary War, Americans began to move farther west. They moved across the Appalachian Mountains toward the Mississippi River. Many people believed that one day the United States would stretch from ocean to ocean.

The Louisiana Purchase

In 1803, President Thomas Jefferson bought a huge area of land called Louisiana from the French. The Louisiana Purchase made the United States more than twice as large as it had been. Now the nation stretched from the east coast to the Rocky Mountains.

Meriwether Lewis and William Clark (center) explored the West with Sacagawea (right) and York (left).

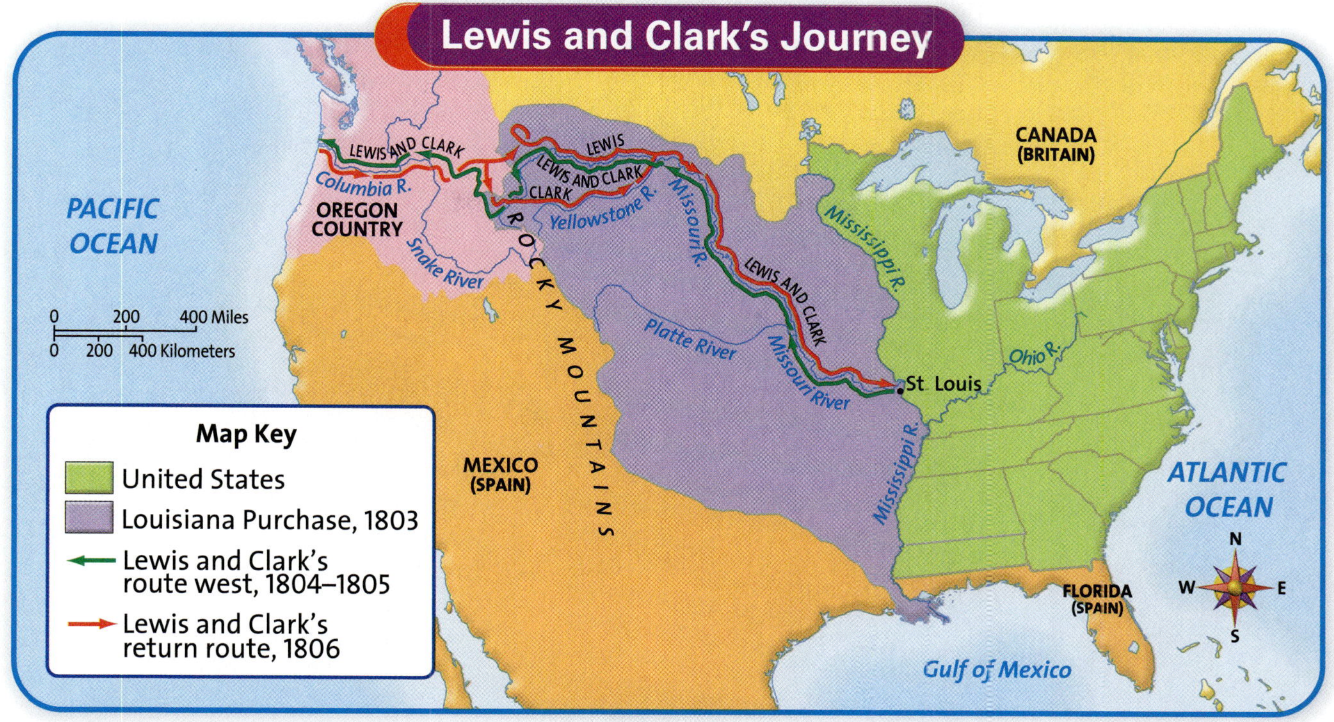

MAP SKILL **Movement** **In which direction did Lewis and Clark travel at the beginning of their trip?**

The Corps of Discovery

President Jefferson asked Meriwether Lewis and William Clark to explore the Louisiana Purchase. He also wanted them to find a way to the Pacific Ocean.

Lewis and Clark traveled with nearly 40 other people, including soldiers and guides. They called themselves the Corps of Discovery. One of the Corps was York, an enslaved African American. York was skilled at hunting and fishing.

A Native American woman of the Shoshone (shuh•SHOH•nee) became a guide for Lewis and Clark. Sacagawea (sa•kuh•juh•WEE•uh) helped them find paths through the mountains.

Reading Check **Sequence**
Was the Corps of Discovery formed before or after the Louisiana Purchase?

The compass that William Clark used

Often children could not ride in the wagon because it was full of goods.

Moving West

On their travels, Lewis and Clark wrote about and drew pictures of plants, animals, and Native Americans. They also drew maps to show rivers and mountain paths. This information helped open the western lands to new settlement. Many people wanted to see this land after they heard or read about it.

Pioneers used churns to make their own butter.

The Pioneers

In the 1800s, many Americans moved west. They traveled in long lines of covered wagons. These **pioneers**, or people who settle lands, included men, women, and children.

Pioneers had many reasons for moving. Some wanted land for farming. Others wanted to find new jobs in the West.

Life in the West

The trip west was very hard. Pioneers faced sickness, accidents, and bad weather along the way. Conflict with Native Americans made some areas unsafe.

Life was not any easier for the pioneers as they settled. First, they had to find water. Many settled near waterways. Others dug wells to reach water under the ground.

Next, they needed shelter. On the plains, some people made homes in the sides of mounds of mud and grass. In forests, people cut trees and used the logs to build cabins. They also planted gardens to grow food.

A pioneer's pitchfork

Reading Check **Sequence**
What did pioneers have to find first as they settled?

Children in History

Pioneer Schools

Children of pioneer families went to school every day of the week except Sunday. In the 1800s, children stayed home during the summer to help their parents plant and gather crops. The schoolhouses had only one room. There were very few books in early classrooms, and often students had to memorize their lessons. The teacher taught all eight grades in the same room. The subjects were math, reading, spelling, and geography. After lunch, students could play outside. They had an entire prairie for their playground!

Make It Relevant **How is your school similar to a pioneer school?**

The Civil War

In 1861, the American Civil War began between the Northern states and the Southern states. In a **civil war**, people of one country fight each other.

People on both sides of the war had different views on many things, including slavery. Many people in the North thought that slavery was wrong. They wanted a law saying that no one in the country could own enslaved people. Many people in the South disagreed. Their way of life was based on enslaved people working for free on their plantations, or large farms.

Harriet Tubman helped enslaved people escape to freedom.

Frederick Douglass wrote and spoke out against slavery.

MAP SKILL **Regions Northern states were called Union states. Border states were part of the Union but still had slavery. Where were the border states located?**

Civil War States

CANADA

Great Lakes

WASHINGTON TERRITORY

DAKOTA TERRITORY

OR

MN

WI

MI

NY

ME

VT

NH

MA

CT

RI

NJ

PA

IA

NEBRASKA TERRITORY

NEVADA TERRITORY

UTAH TERRITORY

COLORADO TERRITORY

IL

IN

OH

MD

DE

WV (1863)

VA

KS

MO

KY

CA

PACIFIC OCEAN

ATLANTIC OCEAN

NC

TN

INDIAN TERRITORY

NEW MEXICO TERRITORY

AR

SC

MS

AL

GA

TX

LA

FL

MEXICO

Gulf of Mexico

N

S

E

W

MAP LEGEND

Union state

Border state

Confederate state

Territory

Abraham Lincoln (center) meets with Northern troops during the Civil War.

Abraham Lincoln

The Southern states started their own country, the Confederate States of America. Abraham Lincoln, President of the United States, felt strongly that the country should stay together.

Lincoln also felt that slavery should not be allowed in new territories. A **territory** is land that belongs to a government but is not a state or a colony. In 1863, Lincoln signed the Emancipation Proclamation. This called for many enslaved people in the Confederate states to be free.

The Civil War ended in 1865. The Thirteenth Amendment to the Constitution was soon passed. An **amendment** is a change to something that is already written. This amendment made slavery against the law.

Reading Check **Cause and Effect**
What was an effect of the Civil War?

Lincoln gave the Gettysburg Address speech to honor soldiers who had died in a famous battle.

Growing into Today's World

After the Civil War ended, the United States continued to grow and change. Communities were affected by changes in transportation, technology, and population.

From Ocean to Ocean

By 1869, railroads starting on the east coast had connected with those from the west coast. All across the country, new routes for travel were built. This opened up more areas to settle.

Ships carried more immigrants to the United States. **Immigrants** come to live in a country from somewhere else in the world. Today, immigrants still move to the United States.

By 1959, Hawaii and Alaska had become states. In less than 200 years, the United States had grown from a small nation of 13 states to a large nation of 50 states.

An airplane flies above San Diego, California.

Space Exploration

In the 1960s, the people of the United States began exploring another new area—space. Astronauts Neil Armstrong and Edwin Aldrin walked on the moon in 1969. Today, nations work together to explore space.

Reading Check **Summarize**
What changes happened after the Civil War?

Summary The settling of the West and the Civil War changed the United States. Changes are still taking place today.

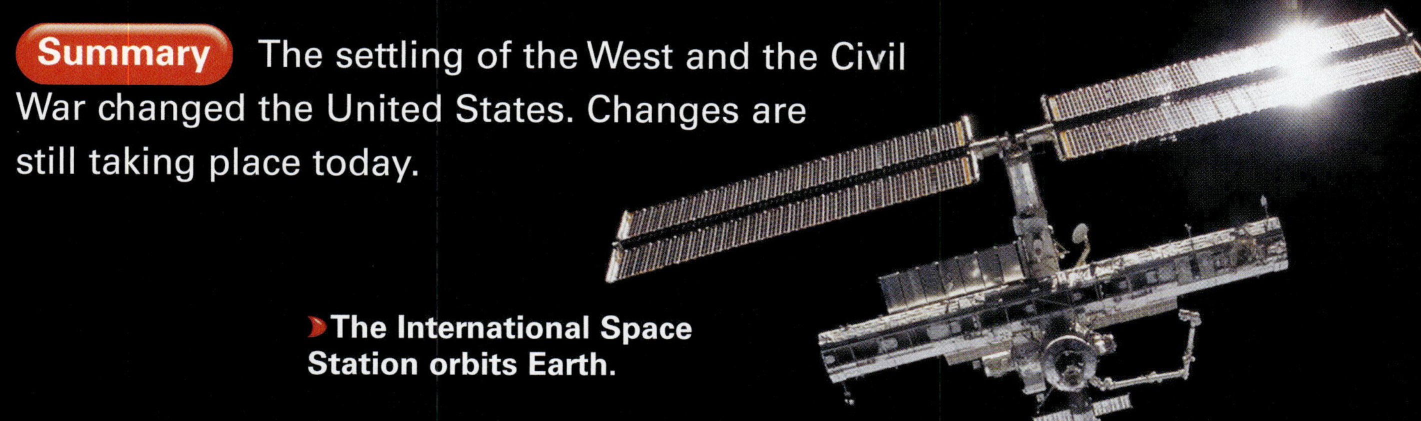

The International Space Station orbits Earth.

Review

1. **What to Know** How did the United States grow and change?
2. **Vocabulary** Use the term **civil war** in a sentence.
3. **Culture** How was pioneer life different from the life of people who did not move west?
4. **Critical Thinking** How might the United States be different if the Lousiana Purchase had not happened?
5. **Write a Journal Entry** Imagine you are a pioneer. Write a journal entry telling about your journey west.
6. Focus Skill **Sequence** On a separate sheet of paper, copy and complete the graphic organizer below.

Compare History Maps

Why It Matters Comparing maps that show the same area at different times helps you see how the area has changed. It also helps you see what has stayed the same.

Learn

A **history map** shows what a place looked like at an earlier time. The maps on page 221 show the United States at two different times. The first shows the United States just before the Louisiana Purchase, in 1803. The other shows the United States in 1903.

Practice

Look at the map keys to see what each color, line, and label shows. Then use the maps to answer these questions.

1. What river marked the western border of the United States before the Louisiana Purchase?
2. How many more states did the United States have in 1903 than it had in 1803?

Apply

Make It Relevant Compare an old map and a new map of your community. What has changed? What has stayed the same?

This telescope was owned by Meriwether Lewis.

For online activities, go to www.harcourtschool.com/ss1

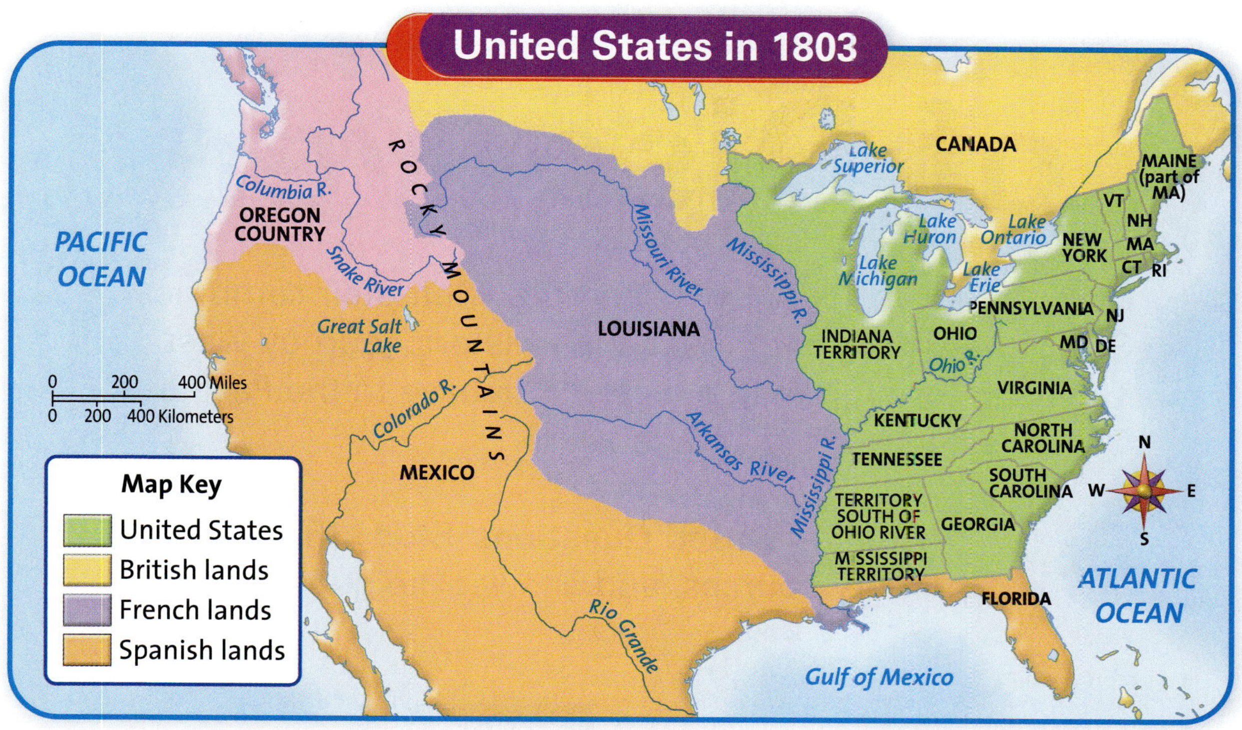

Map and Globe Skills

Primary Sources

The Corps of Discovery

Background In 1804, Lewis and Clark left their camp near St. Louis, Missouri, to make their historic journey west. Their trip through the Louisiana Purchase to the Pacific Ocean lasted more than two years.

DBQ **Document-Based Questions** Study these primary sources, and answer the questions.

Map

Lewis and Clark drew this map during their journey.

DBQ 1 Why do some areas of the map have few details?

Sewing Kit

Lewis and Clark's team used sewing kits to sew tents and sheets and to take care of rips in their clothing.

DBQ 2 Why would a sewing kit be necessary on the journey?

A Nootka Hat

Lewis and Clark collected this wicker hat from Native Americans near the Columbia River.

DBQ ③ Why would the explorers want to take back Native American crafts?

Captain Clark's Journal

Captain Clark recorded daily adventures in his journal.

DBQ ⑤ What might Clark's notes tell about the land he saw?

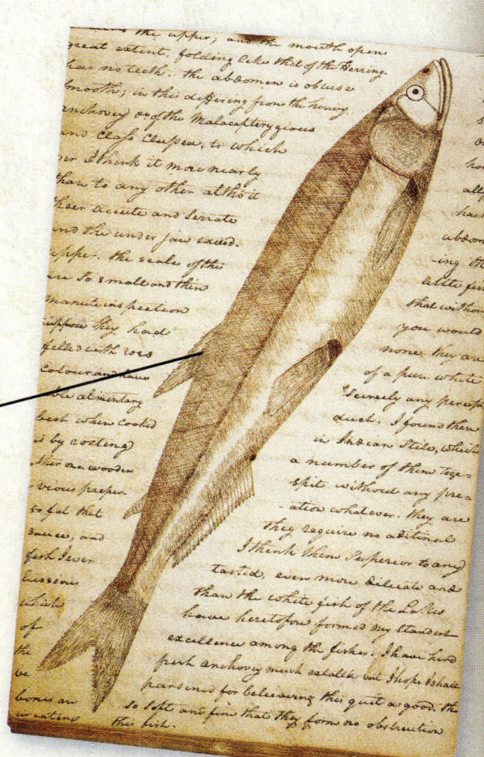

Clark illustrated his journal with drawings.

Peace Medal

Lewis and Clark gave peace medals and other gifts to the Native Americans.

DBQ ④ Why does the peace medal show a picture of Thomas Jefferson?

Thomas Jefferson

WRITE ABOUT IT

What do these primary sources tell you about the journey?

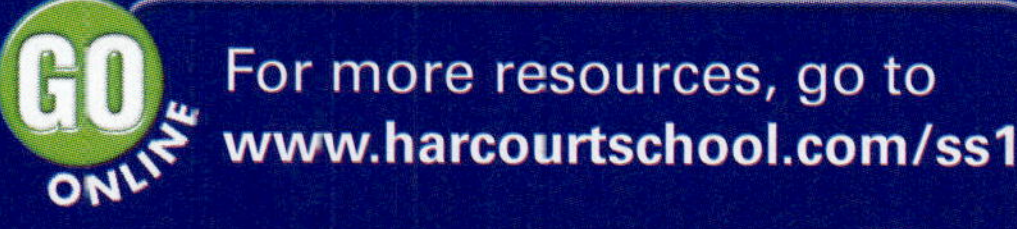

For more resources, go to **www.harcourtschool.com/ss1**

Explore Your Community's History

In this unit, you read about the history of the United States and many of its different communities. You can also explore the past of your own community. These steps explain how to answer the following question.

What was my community like long ago?

STEP 1 Use your community's resources, such as the Internet or newspaper, to find what historic sites are near your town.

STEP 2 Make a list of the historic sites in your community.

STEP 3 Discuss what they have in common.

STEP 4 Choose a historic site that interests you most. Find out more about it, and then share your findings with a partner.

Use Your Community's Resources

Make a Community Time Line

Make a pictorial time line about your community. Start the time line with the date of when your community was founded. Under the date, place a picture of who founded your community. List and illustrate other important events on your time line.

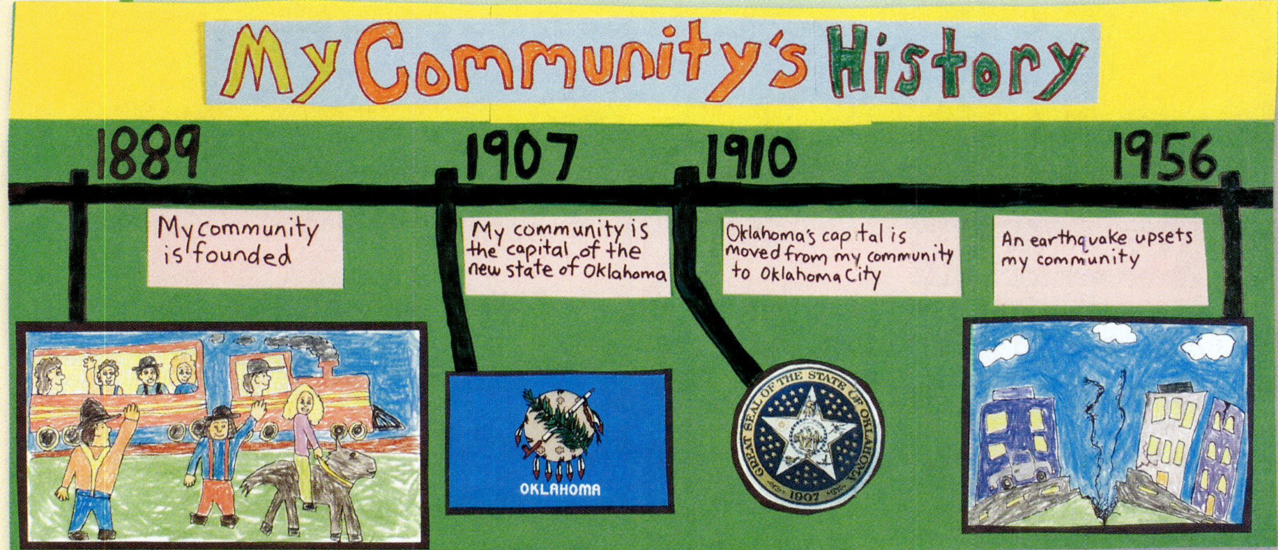

Chapter 6 Review

Visual Summary

Time

1400

1600

1492 Christopher Columbus reaches North America

1620 Pilgrims found Plymouth in Massachusetts

Summarize the Chapter

Sequence Complete the graphic organizer to show you understand the sequence of events in the chapter.

First	Next	Last
Native Americans formed North America's first communities.		The Louisiana Purchase more than doubled the size of the United States.

Vocabulary

Use each term in a sentence that tells the meaning of the term.

1. **oral history**, p. 190
2. **shelter**, p. 191
3. **explorer**, p. 196
4. **settlement**, p. 197
5. **conflict**, p. 200
6. **tax**, p. 205
7. **independence**, p. 206
8. **civil war**, p. 216
9. **territory**, p. 217
10. **immigrant**, p. 218

Facts and Main Ideas

Answer these questions.

5. What inventions for the home have changed the way people live?
6. How did the Native Americans get food?
7. Who was President of the United States during the Civil War?

Write the letter of the best choice.

8. How did George Stephenson change communities?
   - **A** He worked for civil rights.
   - **B** He voted for women's suffrage.
   - **C** He wrote slogans.
   - **D** He developed a train engine.
9. How did John Smith help the settlers in Jamestown?
   - **A** He disagreed with Native Americans.
   - **B** He brought enslaved people to Jamestown.
   - **C** He traded with Native Americans to get food.
   - **D** He agreed with John Rolfe.
10. Which of the following describes an American soldier in the Revolutionary War?
    - **A** well trained
    - **B** received supplies from Britain
    - **C** not well trained
    - **D** did not want to help

Critical Thinking

11. What might have happened if Sacagawea had not helped Lewis and Clark?
12. **Make It Relevant** How might your community change?

Skills

Compare Historical Maps

Use the maps below to answer the following question.

13. What do these maps show about how Frankfort has changed?

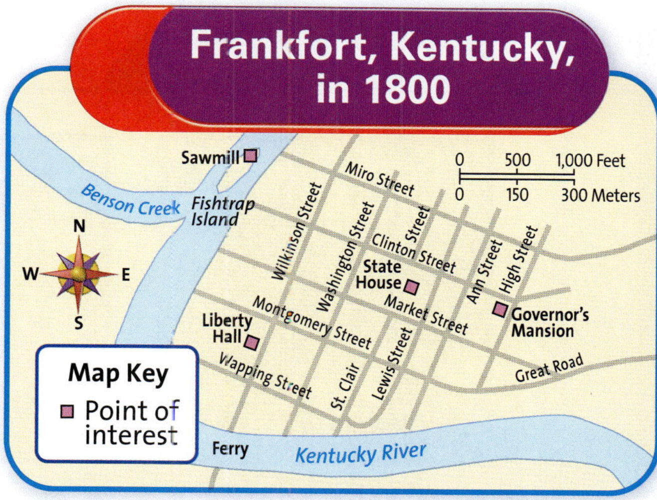

Unit 3

Activities

Show What You Know

Unit Writing Activity

Write a Journal Entry Imagine visiting your community in 100 years. Write a journal entry to describe your experience.

- Explain what has changed.
- Tell which features of your community have stayed the same and why.

Unit Project

Community History Scrapbook Make a scrapbook of your community's history.

- Research your community.
- Write short reports about events in your town's past.
- Add the reports and visuals to a scrapbook.

Read More

- ***Sarah Morton's Day: A Day in the Life of a Pilgrim Girl*** **by Kate Waters. Scholastic Paperbacks.**

- ***My Brother Martin*** **by Christine King Farris. Simon & Schuster Children's Publishing.**

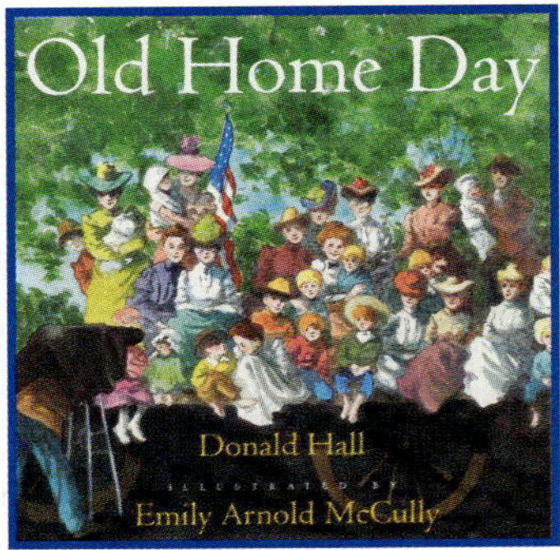

- ***Old Home Day*** **by Donald Hall. Browndeer Press.**

GO ONLINE For more resources, go to **www.harcourtschool.com/ss1**

Citizens and Government

Start with the Standards

Oklahoma Priority Academic Student Skills

1.1 Identify, locate, and compare and contrast information found in resources such as encyclopedias, visual images, atlases, maps, globes, and computer-based technologies.

3.3 Examine the purposes of government and identify representative leaders and their roles in the community.

3.4 Examine the rights and responsibilities of individuals in and to their communities, and identify actions people take to cooperate peacefully and achieve common goals.

The Big Idea

Government

Communities depend on citizens to participate in their government.

What to Know

- ✓ What are our rights?
- ✓ What are our responsibilities?
- ✓ What are the three branches and levels of our government?
- ✓ How do other world communities govern their people?

Unit 4
People
Talk About
People and Government
Francis Scott Key
1779–1843
American lawyer who wrote "The Star-Spangled Banner"

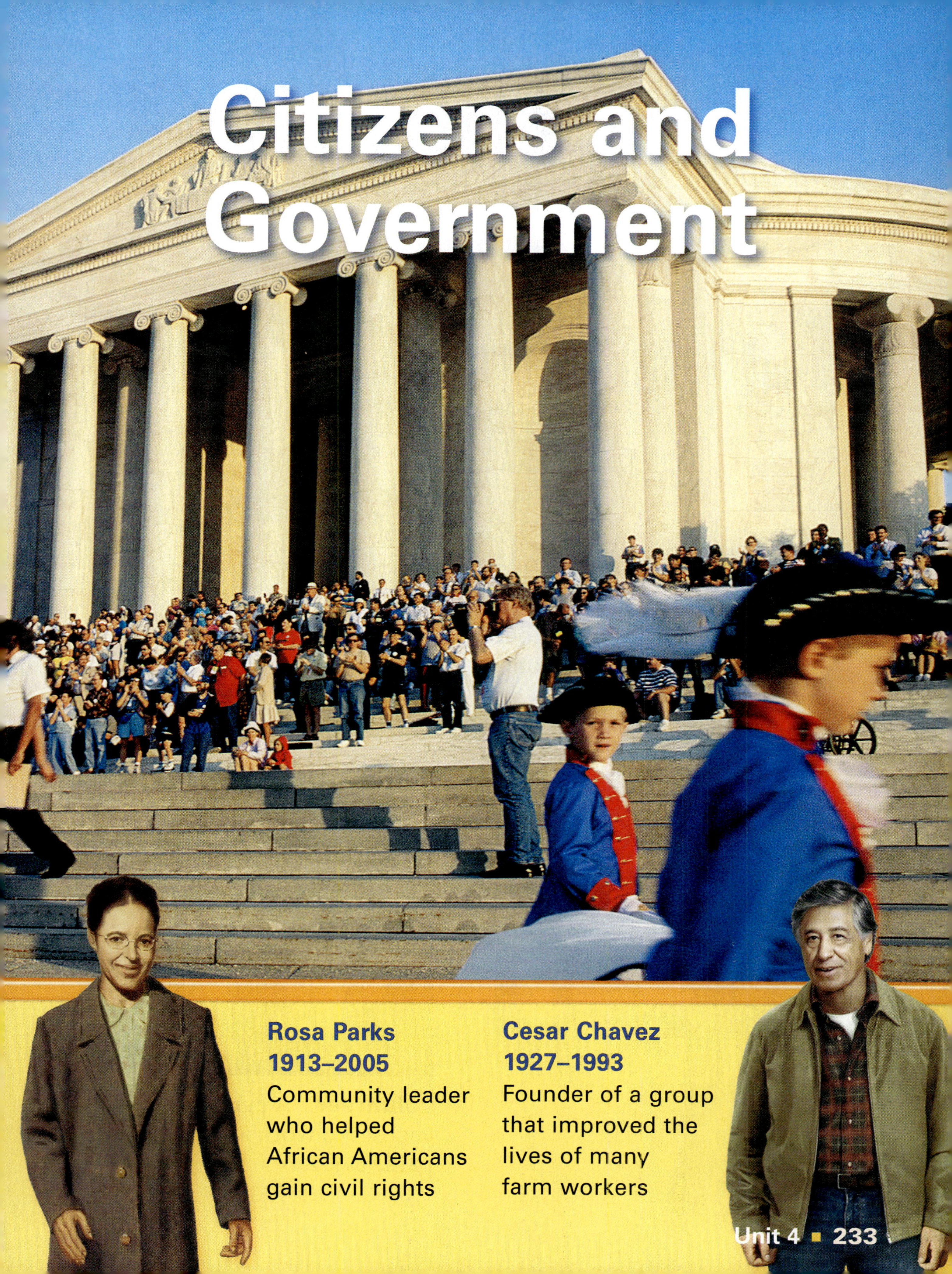

Citizens and Government

Rosa Parks
1913–2005
Community leader who helped African Americans gain civil rights

Cesar Chavez
1927–1993
Founder of a group that improved the lives of many farm workers

Preview

Vocabulary

election A time set aside for voting. (page 246)

volunteer A person who chooses to work without getting paid. (page 251)

government service Work that is done by the government for everyone in a city or town, state, or country. (page 267)

patriotic symbol Something that stands for the ideas in which people believe. (page 290)

monument Something built to honor a person or event. (page 292)

For more resources, go to www.harcourtschool.com/ss1

Reading Social Studies

Summarize

Focus Skill

Why It Matters Summarizing helps you say in a few sentences what is most important in a selection.

Learn

When you **summarize**, you retell the main ideas and details of a passage in your own words.

Key Facts		Summary
Important idea from the reading	→	Important information you read, shortened and written in your own words
Important idea from the reading	→	

- A summary includes only the main ideas and the most important details.
- You can often summarize a paragraph or even a whole selection in just one sentence.

Practice

Read the paragraph. Then summarize it in one sentence.

Key Fact — Indianapolis is the capital city of Indiana. Like all state capitals, it is home to the state's government. Key Fact — Many of Indiana's leaders live in the capital city. They work in the government buildings located there to serve all of Indiana.

Read the paragraphs, and answer the questions.

Indianapolis–At the Heart of Indiana

In 1820, state leaders in Indiana wanted a new city for the state's capital. The capital at the time was Corydon. It was in the southern part of the state.

Indiana leaders wanted a more central capital city. They decided to build Indianapolis in the heart of Indiana. In 1821, they passed a law making Indianapolis the new capital.

The law named Alexander Ralston to help plan the city. Ralston had helped plan Washington, D.C. Like the nation's capital, Indianapolis has many streets named after the 50 states.

Ralston designed the center of the city to have a large circle for government buildings. A home was also built there for the state's leader. However, no leader ever lived in it. No one wanted to live in the town's busy center!

Today, Indianapolis has grown. The circle is still the city's center. Government buildings around the circle include the Statehouse, where lawmakers meet. Indianapolis is still the government's proud home.

Focus Skill Summarize

1. How could you summarize the selection?
2. What key facts helped you summarize the selection?
3. What are some details that are not key facts?

Becoming a Citizen—Just Like Me

As told to Diane Hoyt-Goldsmith
by Shaddai Aguas Suarez
photographs by Lawrence Migdale

Shaddai was born in the United States. That makes her a citizen of this country. This is the story of how Shaddai's father earns his citizenship.

Usually it's the grown-ups who do things first. Even though I'm just a kid, I became a citizen of the United States long before my parents did. My parents were born in Jalisco, Mexico. They both immigrated to the United States when they were just teenagers.

My dad was a student and wanted to become a lawyer. At that time, however, there was no opportunity for him in Mexico. He couldn't afford to pay for college or buy books. My father decided to move to the United States, where he could follow his dreams.

Shaddai and her brother help their mother prepare dinner.

Shaddai's father still likes to fish, just as he did as a boy in Mexico. He likes to take Shaddai with him.

Shaddai's father has his own gardening business. He helps people plant flowers and take care of their lawns.

My mother is the eldest of eleven children. Her mother was struggling to raise the family on her own. So my mother came to the United States to find a good job. That way she could send money back to her family in Mexico.

My father tells me that it was very hard to leave his family and move to a new country. He went to Santa Barbara, California, where he found work. On the job, my father learned how to grow and care for roses. Even though he often felt sad and homesick, my father worked very hard.

My father could speak only Spanish when he came to the United States. He knew he had to learn English in order to succeed. Each night after work, my father went to an ESL class. ESL means "English as a second language." For eight months he studied. Finally he learned enough to begin speaking English.

My parents met in Santa Barbara and soon they were married. My brother came along first, and I was born a few years later. It wasn't until I started going to school that my father decided to become a citizen.

For him, becoming a citizen was hard work. My father had to study the history of the United States. He had to learn about the Constitution and the Bill of Rights. He also had to learn to say the Pledge of Allegiance. After he had learned it, he was so proud.

Soon it was time for my father to take the Citizenship Test. No one was surprised when my father passed.

Then came a special ceremony. On that happy day, in the company of more than a thousand other immigrants, my father was sworn in as a citizen of the United States. Everyone received a special Citizenship certificate.

A friend helped Shaddai's father study for the Citizenship Test.

After studying for many months, Shaddai's father was ready to take the Citizenship Test.

Shaddai's father likes to play soccer on the weekends—and the whole family likes to watch.

Each year on September 17, my family celebrates Citizenship Day. My father knows that on this date in 1787, the Constitution was signed.

He reminds us that we have reasons to be thankful. My father says, "This country has given us everything we have—our home, our jobs, and the chance to build a good life. This country is a place where anyone has the chance to succeed—no matter what his or her race or religion or background might be."

Response Corner

1. Focus Skill **Summarize** How did Shaddai's father become a citizen of the United States?
2. **Make It Relevant** Describe some ways people at your school help new students from other countries. How have you helped your new friends?

USE A K-W-L CHART

A K-W-L chart helps you identify what you know and what you want to learn.

- **Use the *K* column to list what you know about a topic.**
- **Use the *W* column to list what you want to know.**
- **Use the *L* column to list what you learned after reading.**

Citizenship		
What I Know	What I Want to Know	What I Learned
Communities have rules and laws.	How do laws help citizens? Why is it important to follow laws?	______ ______ ______

PREVIEW VOCABULARY

responsibility p. 248

jury p. 248

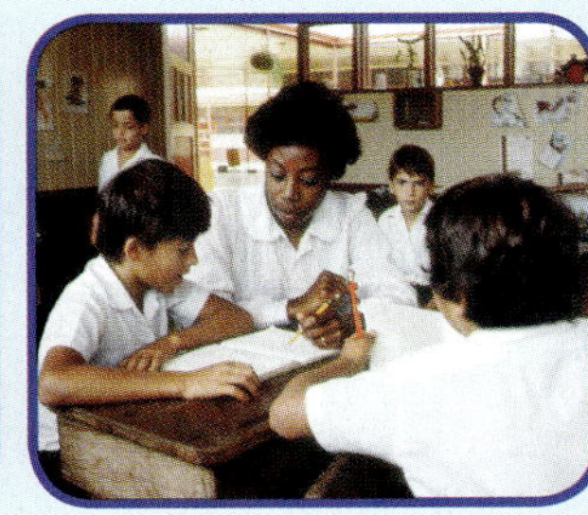

hero p. 257

CHAPTER 7

Citizenship

Students hold a 15-star American flag and learn about the history of Fort McHenry, Maryland.

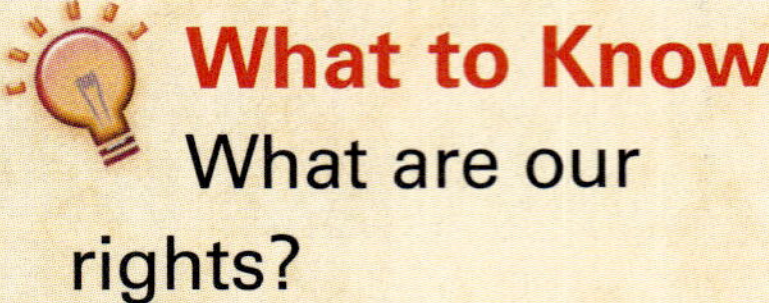

Lesson 1 Rights of Citizens

What to Know
What are our rights?

Vocabulary
elect p. 246
election p. 246
ballot p. 246
majority rule p. 247
minority rights p. 247

Summarize

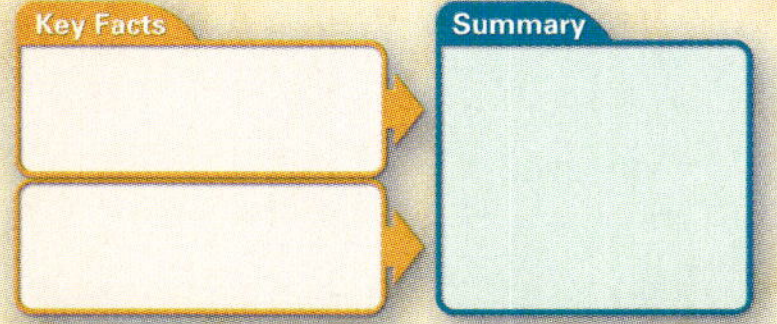

Every citizen of the United States has certain rights, or freedoms. Some of these rights are named in the first ten amendments to the Constitution. Together, these amendments are called the Bill of Rights. The Bill of Rights was added to the Constitution to keep people's rights safe.

The Bill of Rights

The Bill of Rights lists the basic rights that belong to all citizens of the United States. These rights cannot be taken away by the government. Respecting the rights of others is an important part of being a good citizen.

The Constitution is on display in Washington, D.C.

A jury has a responsibility to make careful decisions.

People who break laws face consequences. A **consequence** (KAHN•suh•kwens) is something that happens because of what a person does.

If someone breaks a traffic law, one of the consequences may be an accident. A person who breaks any law may have to pay a fine or go to jail.

Knowing Limits

Citizens need to know the limits to their rights. For example, we have the right to gather in groups, but we must do so peacefully. We have the right to share our opinions, but we should also respect other people's opinions.

Reading Check **Summarize**
What are some responsibilities citizens have?

One consequence of breaking a traffic law is paying a fine.

Serving Your Community

Some responsibilities, such as paying taxes and serving on a jury, are the law. Other responsibilities are not required by law but are still important. One responsibility of being a citizen is to work for the **common good**—the good of everyone in a community.

Wheaton, Illinois

People in communities help one another every day. Helping others is one way to work for the common good.

The community of Wheaton, Illinois, helped one of its citizens. Joel Gomez was hurt while fighting in the war in Iraq. He could no longer move his body and had to use a wheelchair.

Volunteers help build a house for Joel Gomez in Wheaton, Illinois.

A group of volunteers worked together to build Joel Gomez a new house. **Volunteers** are people who choose to work without getting paid. Gomez's new house had technology that would help him live a better life.

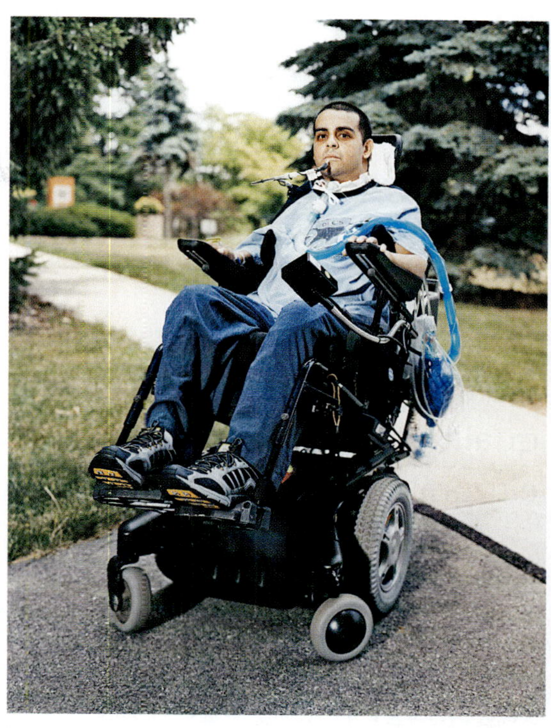

Joel Gomez

Volunteers from more than 50 groups in Wheaton helped in other ways. School groups and firefighters held events to raise money for Gomez. One citizen even bought him a special van.

Reading Check **Summarize**
How can citizens work for the common good?

Summary Citizens have many responsibilities. These include paying taxes, obeying laws, and helping others.

Review

1. **What to Know** What responsibilities do citizens have?
2. **Vocabulary** Use the terms **responsibility** and **jury** in a sentence.
3. **Civics and Government** What responsibilities do voters have?
4. **Critical Thinking Make It Relevant** What responsibilities do you have in your community?
5. **Write a Report** Write a short report that tells how to be a responsible citizen.
6. **Summarize** Focus Skill On a separate sheet of paper, copy and complete the graphic organizer below.

Lesson 3

Being a Good Citizen

What to Know
What are some qualities of a good citizen?

Vocabulary

cooperate p. 252
character trait p. 253
justice p. 253
boycott p. 255
hero p. 257

Summarize

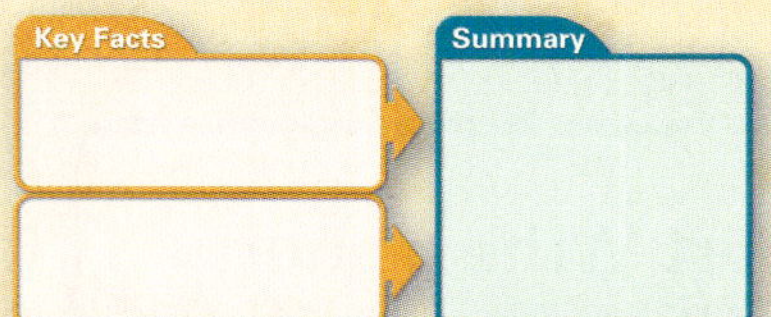

What does it take to be a good citizen? Good citizens take action. They **cooperate** (koh•AH•puh•rayt), or work together, for the good of the community. They try to make the community a better place for everyone.

What Is a Good Citizen?

Good citizens follow the laws of the nation, the state, and the community. They speak out against laws that they think are unfair. They pay taxes and take part in the government by voting. Good citizens also show respect for themselves and for the people around them.

Cooperating with classmates is one way to be a good citizen.

Students in Kentucky made these posters to support Kentucky's Adopt-A-Highway program.

Being Good Citizens

Students are being good citizens when they show respect for their classmates and teachers. They follow rules, do their best work, and take part in class activities.

Good citizens often show helpful character traits. A **character trait** is a quality that a person has, such as responsibility, trustworthiness, respect, fairness, patriotism, and caring. Helpful character traits usually make good citizenship traits, too.

Some citizens become leaders and bring big changes to people's lives. Others work with their neighbors to solve problems. They show a belief in **justice**, or fairness, for everyone.

Reading Check **Summarize**
How would you describe a good citizen?

Jimmy Carter and Rosalynn, his wife, help build homes for Habitat for Humanity.

Jimmy Carter

Jimmy Carter was once President of the United States. Now he works for peace in countries around the world. He helps nations that disagree solve their problems peacefully. In 2002, Carter was awarded the Nobel Peace Prize for his work.

Carter also volunteers for Habitat for Humanity. This is a group that builds homes for people who cannot pay for them. Volunteers like Jimmy Carter give their time and effort for free. They feel a responsibility to help other people.

Jimmy Carter received the Nobel Peace Prize in 2002.

Reading Check **Summarize**

How is Jimmy Carter a good citizen?

Rosa Parks

Rosa Parks wanted to change laws that were unfair to African Americans. In some places in the 1950s, African Americans had to sit in the back of public buses. They could sit in the middle only if the seats were not needed for white people.

In 1955, Parks was sitting in a middle seat of a bus in Montgomery, Alabama. When the bus filled up, Parks refused to give up her seat. The driver called the police, and she was arrested.

Parks and other African Americans in Montgomery had been planning a bus boycott. During a **boycott**, people refuse to buy or use something. After Parks was arrested, many people refused to ride the bus. Their boycott caused the bus company to lose money. After almost a year, the law was changed.

Reading Check **Summarize**
How did Rosa Parks help her community?

Rosa Parks worked for justice.

The bus on which Rosa Parks refused to give up her seat is now in a museum.

➤ Dolores Huerta worked with Cesar Chavez to form the National Farm Workers Association.

Dolores Huerta

As a teacher, Dolores Huerta saw her students come to school hungry and poorly dressed. She decided to help them by helping their parents. The parents were mostly farmworkers from Mexico and other countries. The families traveled all over the United States to find work picking fruits and vegetables.

Because many of the farmworkers were not United States citizens, they did not have many rights. Huerta started classes to teach the workers how to become citizens and how to vote. Later, she helped them earn more money so they could buy the food and clothing they needed.

Reading Check **Summarize**
How did Dolores Huerta help farmworkers?

Everyday Heroes

Many people in a community show that they care by being everyday heroes. A **hero** is a person who does something important and sets an example for others. Some everyday heroes in your community may be parents, firefighters, police officers, teachers, and volunteers.

Reading Check **Summarize**
What is an everyday hero?

Fast Fact

Ryan Hreljac learned at the age of six that some people did not have clean water. That year, Ryan raised $70 to build a well in Africa. He kept working and has now raised more than 1 million dollars. Ryan is shown here with his adopted brother, Jimmy.

Summary Good citizens are responsible, caring, and fair. They work to help people in their community. They may be community leaders or act as everyday heroes.

Review

1. **What to Know** What are some qualities of a good citizen?
2. **Vocabulary** Write a short description of a **character trait**.
3. **Your Community** Who are some of the everyday heroes in your community?
4. **Critical Thinking Make It Relevant** What are some ways you can be a good citizen?
5. **Make a Poster** Make a poster about justice and respect.
6. Focus Skill **Summarize** On a separate sheet of paper, copy and complete the graphic organizer below.

Cesar Chavez

"My motivation comes from my personal life—from watching what my mother and father went through when I was growing up."

— Cesar Chavez, 1984

Why Character Counts

How did Cesar Chavez work for fairness for migrant field workers?

When Cesar Chavez was born in 1927, his family was facing hard times. The family members were migrant, or traveling, workers. They worked mostly with other Mexican Americans, picking grapes, beans, carrots, and lettuce.

Field work is seasonal. Workers are needed only at different times and places. Like other migrant workers, the Chavez family was always traveling around California and Arizona for work.

Cesar Chavez

Cesar Chavez talks to farm workers in Salinas, California.

Buttons and patches like these were worn by Cesar Chavez supporters.

As an adult, Chavez never forgot his family's hardships. In 1958, he became the national director of the Community Service Organization. This group worked to gain civil rights for Hispanic Americans. In 1962, Chavez helped form the National Farm Workers Association. This group worked for higher pay and a better work environment for migrant farmers.

Chavez did not believe in violence. He organized peaceful actions to help the workers. He held public hunger strikes in which he did not eat for many days. These hunger strikes brought attention to the lives of the workers.

Cesar Chavez died in 1993. More than 50,000 people came to his funeral. In 1994, former President Bill Clinton honored him with the Medal of Freedom.

For more resources, go to **www.harcourtschool.com/ss1**

Time

1927 Born

1942 Leaves school to help his family earn money

1958 Becomes director of the Community Service Organization

1962 Forms the National Farm Workers Association

1993 Died

Make a Thoughtful Decision

Why It Matters Thinking about consequences can help you make the best choice.

Learn

A choice is also called a **decision**. Follow these steps to make a thoughtful decision.

Step 1 List the choices.

Step 2 Gather all the information you need.

Step 3 Think about the consequences of each choice.

Step 4 Decide which choice will have the best consequences.

Step 5 Make a choice, and act on it.

Practice

Miguel makes a chart to help him decide what to do with his free time. He wants to volunteer at an animal shelter, but he also wants to play with his friends. He uses the steps in this lesson to make a thoughtful decision.

1. What are Miguel's choices?
2. What information does he need?
3. What consequences will each choice have?
4. Which choice do you think Miguel should make?

Apply

Make It Relevant Think about a decision you have made recently. Make a chart like Miguel's to show the choices and consequences you faced.

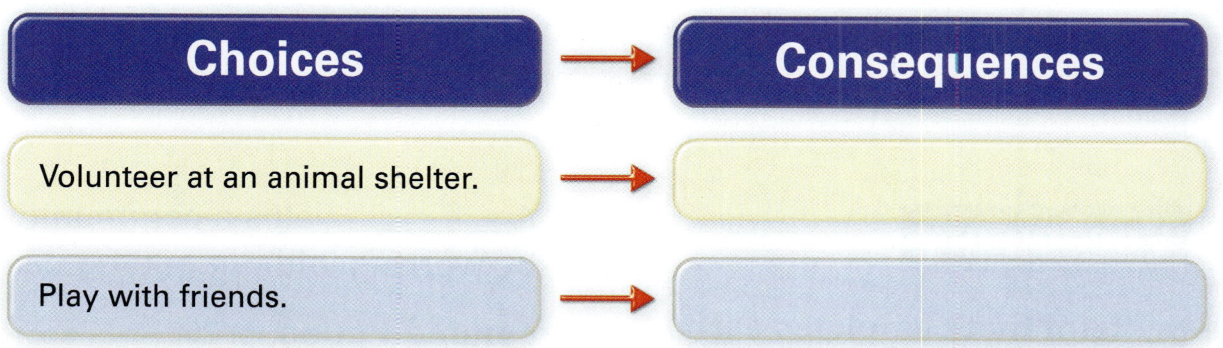

Visual Summary

Citizens of the United States have rights.

Summarize the Chapter

Summarize Complete the graphic organizer to show what you have learned about being a citizen.

Key Facts

Citizens have rights, including freedom of religion and the right to vote.

Responsibilities include voting and obeying laws.

Summary

Write the term that completes each sentence.

1. People vote for a leader in a(n) ________.

   election, p. 246 **ballot**, p. 246

2. There are ________ when someone breaks a law.

   responsibilities, p. 248

   consequences, p. 249

3. A ________ helps a community by working without getting paid.

   common good, p. 250

   volunteer, p. 251

4. Respect is a ________.

   character trait, p. 253

   hero, p. 257

Citizens of the United States have responsibilities.

Good citizens work to improve their community.

Facts and Main Ideas

Answer these questions.

5. What does freedom of speech allow citizens to do?
6. How is voting a responsibility?
7. How can students be good citizens?

Write the letter of the best choice.

8. Which responsibility is required by law?
   - **A** working for the common good
   - **B** voting in elections
   - **C** paying taxes
   - **D** volunteering
9. How did Dolores Huerta work for the common good?
   - **A** She solved conflicts in other nations.
   - **B** She helped farmworkers become citizens.
   - **C** She boycotted buses.
   - **D** She served as United States President.

Critical Thinking

10. **Make It Relevant** How can you show a belief in justice in your daily life?
11. Why is it important to know the limits to your rights?

Skills

Make a Thoughtful Decision
Use the steps on page 260 to answer the question.

12. What do you do after you decide which choice will have the best consequences?

writing

Write an Article Write an article comparing your responsibilities at home, at school, and in your community.

Write a Brochure Create a brochure informing people about their freedoms of the press, assembly, speech, and religion.

SKIM AND SCAN

Skimming and scanning are two ways to learn from what you read.

- **To skim, read lesson and section titles to identify main ideas. Look at the pictures, and read the captions.**
- **To scan, look for key words or facts.**

Skim	Scan
Lesson: Workings of Government	Key Words and Facts • There are three levels of government—local, state, and national. • ______ • ______
Main Idea: Voters elect leaders to all three levels of government.	
Titles/Headings: • The Levels of Government • ______	

PREVIEW VOCABULARY

council p. 273

mayor p. 273

court p. 275

Government

CHAPTER 8

The State capitol building in Oklahoma City, Oklahoma

Lesson 1

Structure of Government

What to Know

What are the three levels and three branches of our government?

Vocabulary

authority p. 266

government service p. 267

legislative p. 268

executive p. 268

judicial p. 268

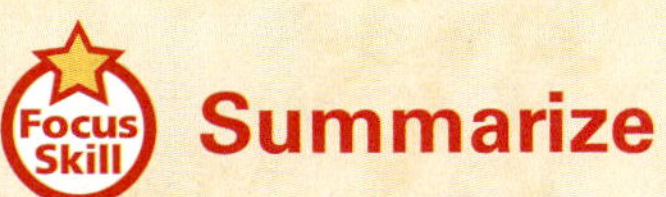

Summarize

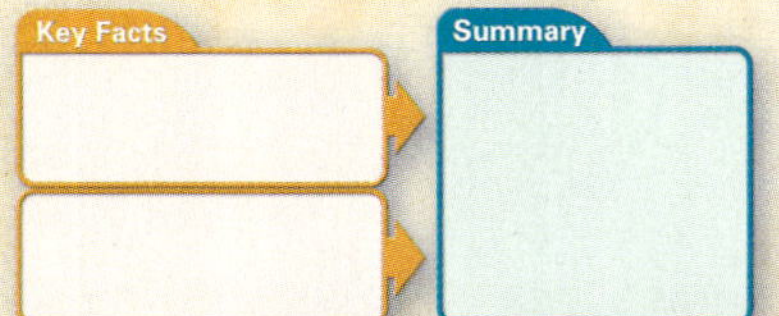

The Constitution is the plan of government for the United States. That plan is based on the idea that government gets its **authority**, or power, from the people. By voting, people give government leaders the authority to make decisions and take action for them.

In the United States, voters elect leaders to run three levels of government—local, state, and national. The three levels handle different kinds of problems for areas that are different sizes.

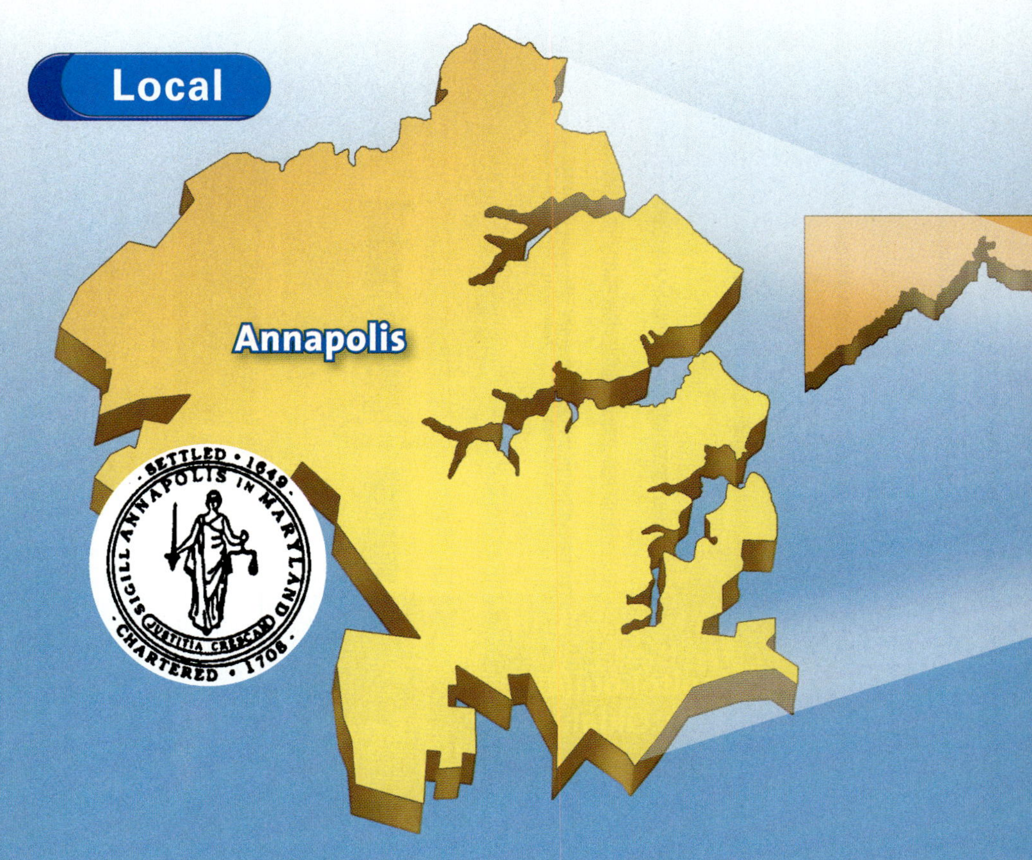

The Levels of Government

A local government governs just one community, such as a city or town. Each of the 50 states is run by a state government. The national government is also called the federal government. It makes laws for the whole nation. Each level of government must obey the Constitution.

Purposes of Government

All three levels of government make laws to keep people safe and to protect their rights and property. However, all three levels of government have their own responsibilities, or jobs to do. Each one provides different government services. A **government service** is work that the government does for the people in its area. People pay for these services with their taxes.

Reading Check **Summarize**
What are the three levels of government?

Levels of Government

Diagram **This diagram shows the levels of government. Which level governs the city of Annapolis?**

Branches of the National Government

Legislative Branch	Executive Branch	Judicial Branch
Makes the laws	Carries out the laws	Makes sure laws are fair
U.S. Capitol Building	White House	Supreme Court Building

Chart Which branch of the United States government makes laws?

The Branches of Government

The President of the United States, George W. Bush, is the leader of the executive branch.

The Constitution divides the national government into three branches, or parts. The three branches are the legislative, executive, and judicial branches. These branches are separate but connected, like the branches of a tree.

Each branch of government has a different job to do. The **legislative** branch makes laws. The **executive** branch sees that the laws are obeyed. The **judicial** branch judges whether the laws are fair and based on the Constitution. The judicial branch also settles conflicts between citizens and businesses.

State governments and most local governments also have three branches. The branches of the state and local levels also make laws, make sure that laws are obeyed, and judge whether laws are fair.

Reading Check **Summarize**
What are the three branches of the United States government?

Members of Kentucky's state government talk about laws.

Summary The three levels of government are local, state, and national. Each level provides services for people in its area. Each level of government also has three branches. Each branch of government does different jobs.

Review

1. **What to Know** What are the three levels and three branches of our government?
2. **Vocabulary** What do you think each word of the vocabulary term **government service** means?
3. **Civics and Government** What document is the plan for our government?
4. **Critical Thinking** What might happen if people did not pay taxes?
5. **Make a Chart** Make a chart that shows the main job of each branch of the national government.
6. **Summarize** On a separate sheet of paper, copy and complete the graphic organizer below.

Citizenship

Constitution Day

"[The Constitution of the United States] was not . . . the offspring [work] of a single brain. It ought to be regarded [thought of] as the work of many heads and many hands."

—James Madison

The Constitution of the United States was signed into law on September 17, 1787. This date is now celebrated as Constitution Day. The idea for the day began with a senior citizen from California, Louise Leigh. After she took a class on the Constitution, Leigh wanted people across the country to celebrate it and learn about it.

James Madison, main author of the Constitution

Students recite the pledge of Allegiance on Constitution Day.

Focus On: Constitutional Principles

President George W. Bush agreed that there should be a day to celebrate constitutional principles. He signed a law to officially declare September 17 as Constitution Day. Each year on this day, people get together to recite, or read aloud, the Preamble. The Preamble is the first part of the Constitution. It outlines the principles of the Constitution, such as freedom and justice.

People across the country recite the Preamble at the same time. Afterward, each state is expected to ring bells. The bells can be heard across the country.

The United States Constitution

Make It Relevant **How will you celebrate Constitution Day this year?**

A Constitution Day concert

Local Governments

What to Know
What are local governments?

Vocabulary

county p. 272
council p. 273
mayor p. 273
county seat p. 274
court p. 275
recreation p. 276
public works p. 277

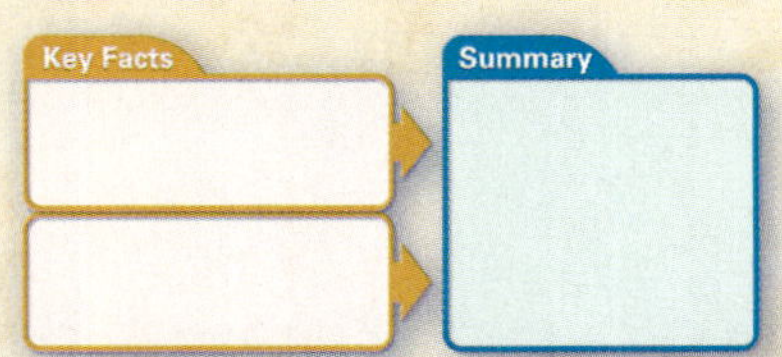

Local governments serve communities, such as cities and towns, as well as counties. A **county** is a part of a state. A county often has several towns or cities within its borders.

City and Town Government

Each city and town in a county has its own local government. In some community governments, all citizens decide things at a town meeting. In others, elected leaders meet to make decisions.

City Hall in Columbus, Ohio, is where members of that city's government meet.

A city council meeting in Columbus, Ohio

Different Local Governments

There are two main types of city government. Both include a **council**, or a group of people who meet to make laws. This is the legislative branch of local government.

In a mayor-council government, voters in a city elect the mayor and the council members. A **mayor** is the leader of a community government. He or she leads the executive branch and makes sure city laws are carried out. The council makes laws and collects taxes.

In a council-manager government, voters also elect council members. Then the council chooses one of its members to be the mayor. It also hires a city manager to help run the city. The city manager hires people to run the fire, police, and other departments.

The mayor of Columbus, Michael Coleman

Reading Check **Summarize**
What are the two main types of city government?

Counties of New Jersey

Map Key
- County seat
- State capital
- County border
- State border

0 20 40 Miles
0 20 40 Kilometers

NEW YORK
CONNECTICUT
PENNSYLVANIA
MARYLAND
DELAWARE
ATLANTIC OCEAN
Delaware Bay

SUSSEX Newton
PASSAIC Paterson
BERGEN Hackensack
WARREN Belvidere
MORRIS Morristown
ESSEX Newark
HUDSON Jersey City
UNION Elizabeth
HUNTERDON Flemington
SOMERSET Somerville
MIDDLESEX New Brunswick
MERCER Trenton
MONMOUTH Freehold
OCEAN Toms River
BURLINGTON Mount Holly
CAMDEN Camden
GLOUCESTER Woodbury
SALEM Salem
CUMBERLAND Bridgeton
ATLANTIC Mays Landing
CAPE MAY Cape May Court House

N S E W

MAP SKILL **Location** What is the county seat of Ocean County in New Jersey?

County Government

County board members meet in Warren County, New Jersey.

Most states are divided into counties. For example, New Jersey has 21 counties. Each county has its own local government.

The County Board

In New Jersey, a group of people is elected by citizens of the county to form a county board. The board members discuss problems in the county and make laws to solve them. These laws affect only the people and area of the county.

The board members meet in the county seat. A **county seat** is the city or town in which the main offices of the county government are located.

County Courts

County governments often have their own courts. A **court** is a place for deciding whether a person has broken a law. County courts are the judicial branch of county government.

Judges are chosen to lead courts. Judges are usually lawyers. Within certain guidelines, a judge may decide what the consequences for breaking a law will be.

Large cities also have their own courts. These courts make decisions about traffic, parking, and other matters important to the community. But most laws are judged in county courts.

Reading Check **Summarize**
What are the parts of a county government?

The county courthouse in Essex County, New Jersey

Many communities have parks and centers where people can meet and have fun.

Community Services

Firefighters protect communities.

A community government provides services for the people in its town or city. The fire department puts out fires and rescues people who are sick or hurt. The police department makes sure traffic laws and other laws are followed.

Education is also a government service. Some communities have groups of citizens who serve on school boards. These citizens make decisions about the community's schools.

Local governments also provide places, such as parks, pools, and sports fields, for recreation (reh•kree•AY•shuhn). **Recreation** is any activity that is done just for fun.

The Public Works Department

The **public works** department provides services to meet the daily needs of citizens. It repairs streets, collects trash, and makes sure that the community has clean water. It also takes care of wastewater. Pipes carry the wastewater to water treatment plants. There, it is cleaned before it is returned to rivers and lakes.

Reading Check **Summarize**
What kinds of services does a local government provide?

This water treatment center in Christmas, Florida, is also a wetlands park.

Summary Local governments include towns, cities, and counties. A city government runs a city or town. A county government runs a county.

Review

1. **What to Know** What are local governments?
2. **Vocabulary** Write a sentence that explains what a **council** is.
3. **Your Community** Do you live in a county? Which city is the county seat for your county?
4. **Critical Thinking** What are some ways citizens in a community can take part in local government?
5. **Make a Diagram** Create a Venn diagram that compares a mayor-council government and a council-manager government.
6. **Summarize** (Focus Skill) On a separate sheet of paper, copy and complete the graphic organizer below.

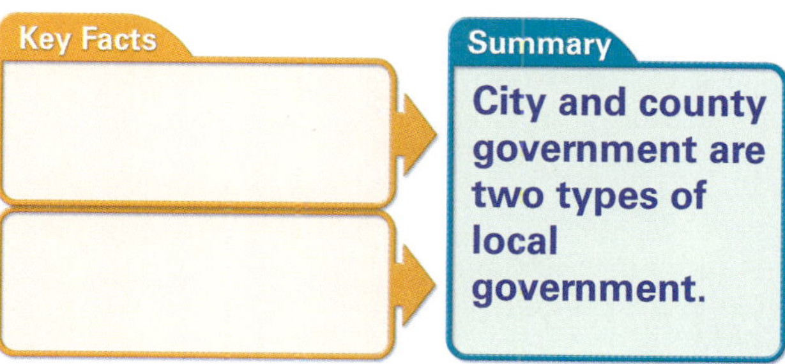

Read a Road Map

Why It Matters A road map can help you locate places and find your way around a community.

Learn

A **road map** shows you the roads and other local features of a community. Follow these steps to read a road map.

Step 1 Find the roads. Roads are shown as solid lines. Thicker lines are used for main roads.

Step 2 Look for points of interest or other local features, such as parks, schools, or railroad tracks. These features will have labels.

Step 3 Trace a road route with your finger. Follow the solid lines from where you are to where you want to go.

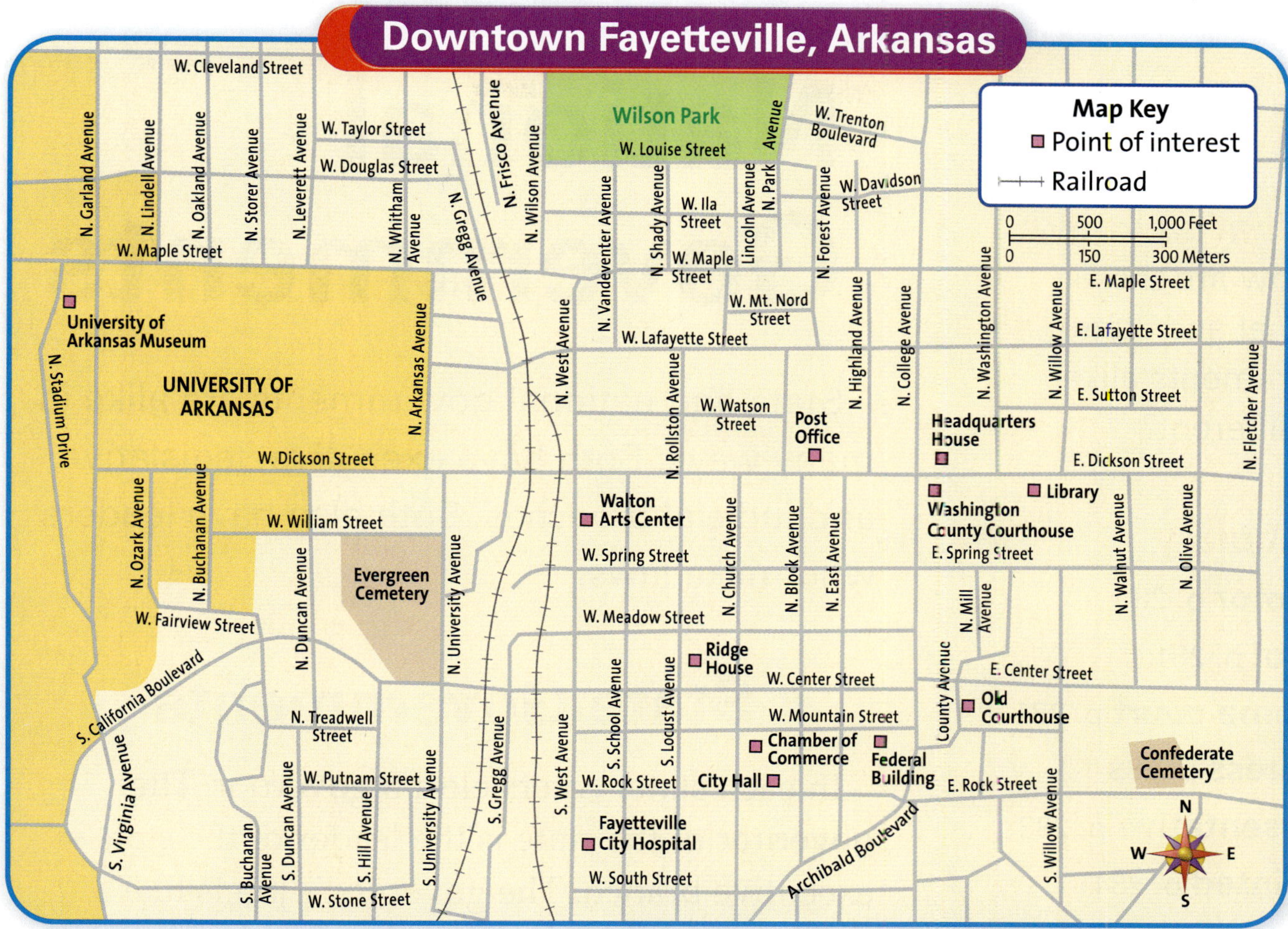

Practice

Use the road map of downtown Fayetteville, Arkansas, to answer these questions.

1. What are some local features shown on this map?
2. Which road would you take to reach Wilson Park—Lincoln Avenue or Maple Street?

Apply

Make It Relevant Find a road map of your community. Trace the route from your home to your school. List the roads you take to get there.

Lesson 3

State and National Governments

What to Know
How are the national and state governments alike and different?

Vocabulary
governor p. 280
capitol p. 281
supreme court p. 281
Congress p. 283
representative p. 283
appointed p. 284

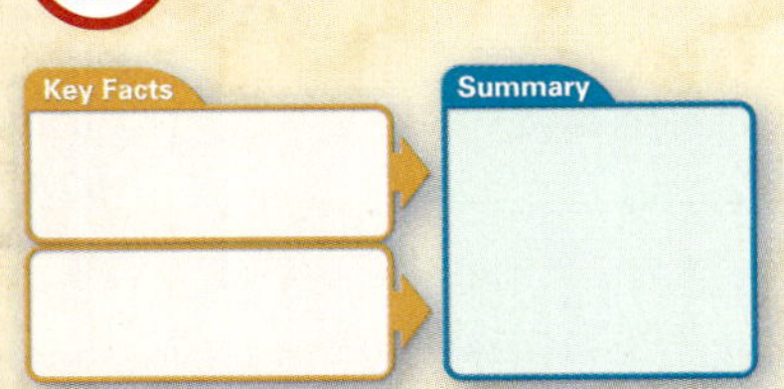

State and national governments are alike in many ways. Both have executive, legislative, and judicial branches. Both also have leaders who make laws.

State Governments

In each state, voters elect a governor. The **governor** of the state is the leader of the state's executive branch. The governor's job is like a mayor's job in many ways. A governor suggests laws for the state and sees that the laws are carried out.

Jennifer Granholm is the governor of Michigan.

Statuary Hall

The *Freedom* Statue on top of the Capitol dome

The iron dome of the Rotunda

The Senate meeting hall

Members of the House of Representatives meet.

A VIRTUAL TOUR

GO ONLINE For more resources, go to www.harcourtschool.com/ss1

Resolve Conflicts

Why It Matters People can have different ideas about things. This can lead to a conflict. Knowing how to resolve, or settle, a conflict is important.

Learn

Follow these steps when you need to resolve a conflict with someone.

Step 1 *Walk Away* Wait until both people can talk calmly about the conflict.

Step 2 *Smile About It* It is easier to resolve a conflict if both people are friendly about it.

Step 3 *Compromise* Two people **compromise** (KAHM•pruh•myz) when each person gives up some of what he or she wants.

Step 4 *Ask for Help* A **mediator** (MEE•dee•ay•ter) is a person who helps other people settle a conflict.

Conflict

Practice

With a partner, roleplay solving a conflict. Tell what happens as you try each of the steps.

1. What happens when one person smiles?
2. What happens when one person is willing to compromise?
3. What happens when one person asks a mediator for help?

Apply

Make It Relevant Think about a conflict you have seen at school. How was the conflict resolved? Write a paragraph that compares the way the people resolved their conflict with the steps in this lesson.

Lesson 4

Symbols of Our Nation

What to Know
What are some of the symbols of our country?

Vocabulary
patriotic symbol p. 290
monument p. 292
memorial p. 292
anthem p. 294

Summarize

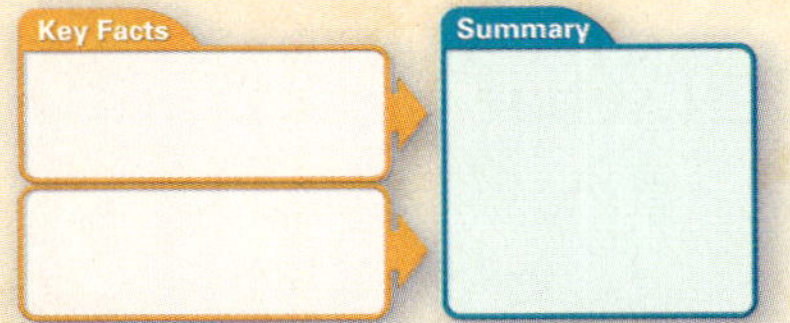

People everywhere feel patriotism for their country. One way they show this feeling is through their patriotic symbols. A **patriotic symbol**, such as a flag, stands for the ideas in which people believe.

Our Nation's Symbols

The United States flag is a symbol of our country's history and beliefs. There are 13 stripes and 50 stars on the flag. The stripes stand for the original 13 colonies. Each star represents one of the 50 states.

A Boy Scout troop carries the United States flag during a parade. The United States flag is a symbol of our country's unity.

Flag Manners

Saluting the Flag

- Stand and look at the flag. Place your right hand over your heart.
- If you have a hat on, remove it and hold it with the hand that is over your heart.

Displaying the Flag

- Fly the flag of the United States above any other flag on the same pole. Raise the United States flag first, and lower it last.
- Flying the flag at half-mast is a sign of mourning, or sorrow for a death. Raise the flag to the top of the pole, and then lower it halfway. At night, raise it to the top before lowering it.

The Bald Eagle

The American bald eagle is the national bird of the United States. It lives only in North America. President John F. Kennedy said, "The fierce beauty and proud independence of this great bird aptly [very well] symbolizes the strength and freedom of America."

The bald eagle is a symbol of the strength and freedom of the United States.

The Liberty Bell

The Liberty Bell, in the city of Philadelphia, Pennsylvania, is another patriotic symbol. It was rung after the first public reading of the Declaration of Independence. People often think of the Liberty Bell when they hear the words *Let freedom ring.*

Reading Check **Summarize**
What do our flag's stars and stripes represent?

The Liberty Bell is a symbol of freedom.

The National Mall in Washington, D.C., has many monuments.

A City of Monuments

Many patriotic symbols are located in Washington, D.C. Some are monuments. A **monument** is built to honor a person or an event in history. It can be a sculpture, a fountain, a building, or any lasting marker. The Washington Monument is a huge stone column in honor of our country's first President.

Some monuments are built as memorials. A **memorial** helps keep the memory of a person or an event alive. The Lincoln Memorial helps people remember President Abraham Lincoln.

The Korean War Veterans Memorial

The Franklin Delano Roosevelt Memorial

War Memorials

Some memorials remember people who died in wars. The Vietnam Veterans Memorial and the Korean War Memorial honor citizens who fought in Vietnam and Korea.

The National World War II Memorial honors soldiers who fought in World War II in the 1940s. It was built in 2004. It is located between the Washington Monument and the Lincoln Memorial.

The National World War II Memorial

Reading Check **Summarize**
What is the purpose of monuments and memorials?

Francis Scott Key

Words of Patriotism

People often use words to express patriotism. Francis Scott Key wrote about his feelings in a poem called "The Star-Spangled Banner." His poem later became the national **anthem**, or song of patriotism.

The Story Behind the Song

Key wrote his poem during the War of 1812. He had watched from a ship as the British attacked a fort in Baltimore, Maryland. The battle went on into the night. When the fighting stopped, it was too dark for Key to tell which side had won.

The next morning, Key could see the American flag flying above the fort. He knew then that the United States had won the battle.

Children in History

The Living American Flag

Each year in May, schoolchildren in Baltimore, Maryland, gather for Flag Day. Wearing red, white, and blue, they create a large "living flag." This tradition began in 1914 to celebrate the 100th anniversary of the battle that defended Baltimore.

The children also wanted people to remember the writing of "The Star-Spangled Banner." To make the first "human flag," 6,500 Baltimore schoolchildren wore colored coats and waved matching handkerchiefs. They made the flag look as if it were waving in the wind!

Make It Relevant **How do you take part in patriotic events?**

The Pledge of Allegiance

The Pledge of Allegiance is a promise that people make to be loyal, or true, to the United States. They stand at attention as they say the words. They place their right hand over their hearts to show respect.

Reading Check **Summarize**
Why do people say the Pledge of Allegiance?

Summary People show their patriotism through symbols. Monuments and memorials are symbols that honor and remember a person or an event. Patriotic words tell the way people feel about their country.

Students say the Pledge of Allegiance in their Maryland school.

Review

1. **What to Know** What are some of the symbols of our country?
2. **Vocabulary** How is "The Star-Spangled Banner" an **anthem**?
3. **History** Why is the Liberty Bell a symbol of freedom?
4. **Critical Thinking** **Make It Relevant** Are there any monuments in your community? How does a monument honor a person or an event?
5. **Draw a Symbol** Draw a picture of a patriotic symbol. Write a sentence to tell what the symbol means.
6. **Summarize** (Focus Skill) On a separate sheet of paper, copy and complete the graphic organizer below.

Use a Line Graph

Why It Matters Sometimes people need to see how things change over time. Graphs can help them.

Learn

A **line graph** uses a line to show changes over time. Look at the graph on page 297. It shows how the number of pairs of bald eagles has grown. The number of bald eagles was once so few that the government made a plan to protect them. You can follow these steps to read the graph.

Step 1 Read the title to learn what the graph shows.

Step 2 Read the labels along the bottom and side of the graph. They tell what the numbers represent.

Step 3 Use the dots on the graph and the numbers along the bottom and side to find the number shown.

Step 4 Follow the line on the graph to see how the number changes over time.

A pair of bald eagles is two eagles that nest together.

Practice

Use the line graph to answer these questions.

1. What information is shown along the bottom? Along the side?
2. Between which years did the biggest change in bald eagle population take place?

Apply

Make It Relevant Make a line graph that shows how your town's population has changed over time.

Population of Bald Eagles, 1995–2000

Primary Sources

State Symbols

Background States have symbols that can tell about life in the states or values important to their citizens. A state flag can express feelings of state pride. A state seal on government buildings or papers is a sign of authority.

DBQ **Document-Based Questions** Study these primary sources, and answer the questions.

Kentucky State Flag

This flag shows a pioneer and a government worker.

"United we stand, divided we fall" is Kentucky's state motto.

DBQ 1 What belief do the picture and phrase show?

Missouri State Flag

The Missouri flag shows the Missouri state seal.

DBQ 2 What values are represented on the Missouri state seal?

Missouri state seal

The grizzly bears on the seal represent strength and courage.

Ohio State Seal

The Ohio state seal shows a bundle of wheat and a bundle of arrows.

DBQ **3** Why might the seal show wheat?

Oklahoma State Flag

The Oklahoma state flag was adopted in 1925. The shield is decorated with symbols of peace.

DBQ **5** What does Oklahoma's flag tell you about who might have lived in the state?

New Jersey State Seal

The New Jersey state seal shows two women.

DBQ **4** What values are most important to the state of New Jersey?

Liberty holds the liberty cap on her staff.

Plenty holds a container filled with food.

THE GREAT SEAL OF THE STATE OF NEW JERSEY

LIBERTY AND PROSPERITY

1776

"Liberty and prosperity" is the state's motto.

WRITE ABOUT IT

Write a paragraph about your state's flag and seal.

GO ONLINE For more resources, go to **www.harcoutschool.com/ss1**

Lesson 5

Governments of the World

What to Know
How do other countries govern their people?

Vocabulary
Parliament p. 301
prime minister p. 301
constitutional monarchy p. 302

Focus Skill Summarize

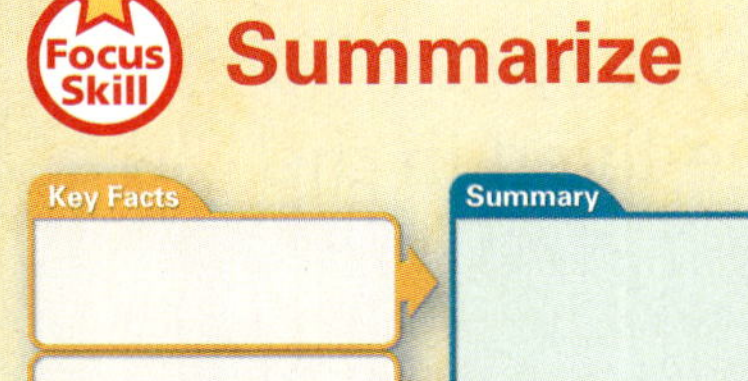

Countries around the world have different governments. Some countries, like the United States, have democracies. Others have governments in which leaders are not chosen by the citizens.

Neighboring Governments

The government of Mexico is somewhat like the government of the United States. Both governments have executive, legislative, and judicial branches. In both countries, the president is the leader of the executive branch.

Government leaders from different countries often meet.

Government members from the United States and Mexico meet to discuss business.

Canada's government is also like that of the United States in certain ways. Canada's legislative branch is **Parliament**. Parliament works with another group called the Cabinet of Ministers. This group is led by the **prime minister**, who heads the executive branch.

Working Together

As neighbors, the United States, Mexico, and Canada have close relationships. Their governments often work together. The three countries also do business together. Mexico, for example, sends most of its goods to the United States.

Reading Check **Summarize**

How are the governments of Mexico and Canada like that of the United States?

Sharing Borders

MAP SKILL **Location** Which country shares the northern border of the United States?

Fast Fact

King Jigme Singye Wangchuck became the king of Bhutan when he was 17 years old.

Bhutan's Government

The government of Bhutan (boo•TAHN) is different from the government of the United States. Bhutan is a country in Asia. Instead of a president, Bhutan has a monarch, or king. King Jigme Singye Wangchuck (JEE•mee SING•ee WANG•choo) is the king of Bhutan. Like other kings, he was born into a royal family. His father and his grandfather were also kings.

A Constitutional Monarchy

Bhutan's government is changing. It is turning into a constitutional monarchy. A **constitutional monarchy** has both a monarch and a government elected by the people. King Wangchuck gave up some of his power to help Bhutan make this change.

Bhutan

CHINA
NEPAL
BHUTAN
Thimphu
BANGLADESH
INDIA
MYANMAR

The Himalayas in Bhutan

Bhutan's legislative branch is the National Assembly. Some of its members are elected. Others are chosen by the king and by religious groups. Wangchuck has given the National Assembly most of his powers.

The executive branch is the Council of Ministers. Its members are chosen by the king but must be approved by the National Assembly.

Reading Check **Summarize**

How is Bhutan's government different from the United States government?

Members of Bhutan's government

Summary Countries around the world have different forms of government. The United States, Mexico, Canada, and Bhutan govern their people in different ways.

Review

1. **What to Know** How do other countries govern their people?
2. **Vocabulary** Write a description of a **constitutional monarchy**.
3. **Civics and Government** How does a person usually become a monarch?
4. **Critical Thinking** How are a president and a monarch alike? How are they different?
5. **Write a Paragraph** Write a paragraph to compare the governments you learned about in this lesson.
6. Focus Skill **Summarize** On a separate sheet of paper, copy and complete the graphic organizer below.

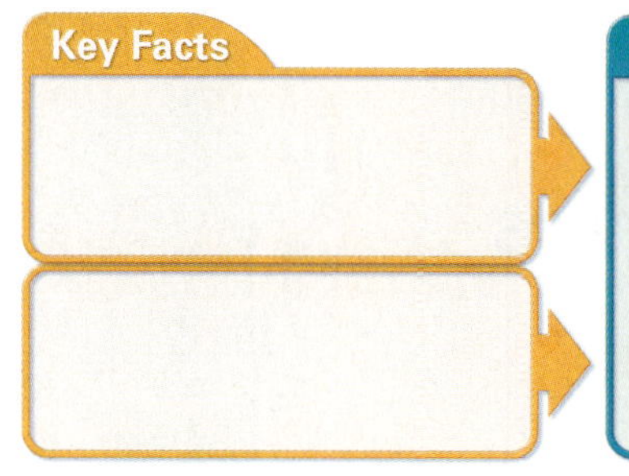

Explore Your Community's Government

In this unit, you read about the different levels and branches of government. You can learn about your own community's government by using the resources below.

Newspapers

Government Offices

Community Websites

Find Out About Your Community

- What type of local government does your community have?
- Who are some leaders in your community?
- Where and when do your community's leaders meet?
- What government services are offered in your community?

Make a Community Website

Make a website for the citizens of your community. Include important information about your community's government, such as your leaders' names, local government offices, and meeting times. Explain what government services your community offers its citizens.

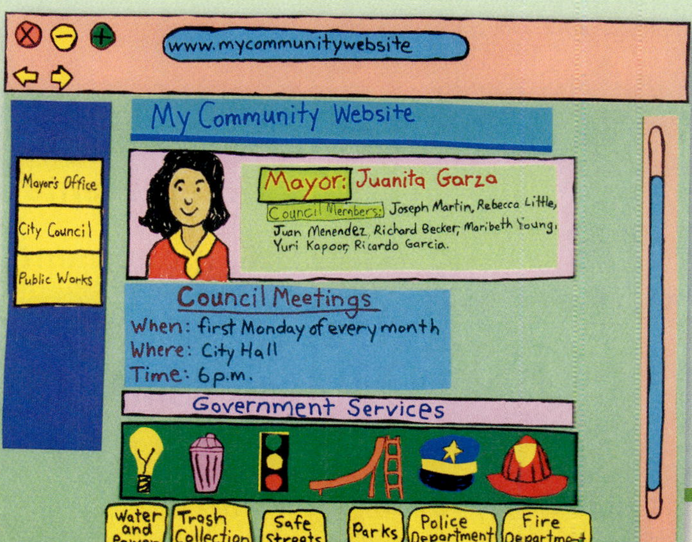

Chapter 8 Review

Visual Summary

The United States has three levels of government.

Summarize the Chapter

Summarize Complete the graphic organizer to show what you have learned about your nation's government.

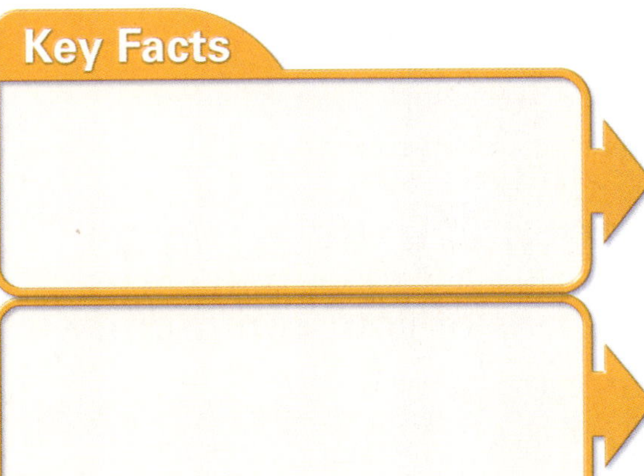

Vocabulary

Write a definition for each term.

1. **government service**, p. 267
2. **judicial**, p. 268
3. **county**, p. 272
4. **public works**, p. 277
5. **governor**, p. 280
6. **Congress**, p. 283
7. **representative**, p. 283
8. **monument**, p. 292
9. **anthem**, p. 294
10. **prime minister**, p. 301

Executive, legislative, and judicial are three branches of government.

Citizens show patriotism for their country through symbols.

Facts and Main Ideas

Answer these questions.

11. Who gives the authority to leaders of our country?
12. What are the three branches of national and state government?
13. What does the Vietnam Veterans Memorial honor?

Write the letter of the best choice.

14. Which best explains a mayor-council government?
    - **A** Voters elect the mayor and council members.
    - **B** Voters hire a judge.
    - **C** The council hires a city manager.
    - **D** The council chooses a mayor.
15. Which of the following governments is a constitutional monarchy?
    - **A** Canada
    - **B** United States
    - **C** Mexico
    - **D** Bhutan

Critical Thinking

16. Why do we need government?
17. **Make It Relevant** What government services does your community provide?

Skills

Read a Road Map

Use the road map on page 279 to answer the question.

18. Which street runs along the southern end of Wilson Park?

Resolve Conflicts

Use the steps on page 288 to answer the question.

19. What happens when one person walks away during a conflict?

writing

Write a Paragraph Write a paragraph about the United States President.

Write a Song Imagine that you saw an important event in history. Write a patriotic song about the event.

This crossword puzzle is complete, but which picture clues match the puzzle words? One is done for you.

1. PATRIOTIC SYMBOL
2. VOLUNTEER
3. BALLOT
4. HERO
5. ANTHEM
6. MONUMENT
7. RECREATION
8. MAYOR

Across

1. 2. 3. 4. 5.

Down

6. 7. 8.

Good Citizens

These four good citizens made a difference. What are their names?

I won the Nobel Peace Prize in 2002. Now I help build houses for people in need.

I did not give up my seat on the bus and went to jail. That helped change unfair laws.

I wrote a poem that was set to music. Now many people sing my words.

I have helped farmworkers and their families.

Online Adventures

GO ONLINE

In this online game, you'll visit City Hall on Election Day. Somebody is trying to stop citizens from voting. To save the election, you'll have to meet all the challenges and catch the person who is responsible. Can you figure out what is happening in time to save the election? Play now at **www.harcourtschool.com/ss1**

Review and Test Prep 

The Big Idea

Government Communities depend on citizens to participate in their government.

Reading Comprehension and Vocabulary

Citizens and Government

As citizens of the United States, we have rights. We also have responsibilities. For example, we have the responsibility to obey laws. To be good citizens, we must cooperate for the good of the community.

Our government has three levels—local, state, and national. Each level provides different government services and has different types of leaders. For example, a mayor leads a community government.

The national, state, and most local governments have three branches that do different jobs. These three branches are the executive, legislative, and judicial branches.

Read the summary above. Then answer the questions that follow.

1. What is one responsibility of citizens?
   A following a religion
   B sharing beliefs
   C obeying laws
   D working

2. What do all three levels of government provide?
   A government services
   B a good community
   C rights
   D responsibilities

3. What does a mayor do?
   A leads state government
   B leads community government
   C leads county government
   D leads national government

4. How many branches do the national, state, and most local governments each have?
   A 2
   B 4
   C 5
   D 3

Facts and Main Ideas

Answer these questions.

5. What right is also a responsibility?
6. What are two kinds of local government?
7. What are the two parts of Congress?

Write the letter of the best choice.

8. What did Jimmy Carter do to be a good citizen?
   - **A** refused to give up a bus seat
   - **B** helped nations solve conflicts peacefully
   - **C** started classes for poor farmworkers
   - **D** helped plan a bus boycott
9. What is the Pledge of Allegiance?
   - **A** our national anthem
   - **B** a promise to be loyal to the United States
   - **C** a war memorial
   - **D** the Constitution
10. How did Bhutan's king become the monarch?
    - **A** He was born into the royal family.
    - **B** He was elected.
    - **C** He was appointed.
    - **D** He was hired by the National Assembly.

Critical Thinking

11. **Make It Relevant** How does the United States Constitution affect you?
12. Why does a state need a government?

Skills

Read a Road Map

Use the map below to answer the following questions.

13. What are some features on the map?
14. Which road would you take to get to Waterworks Park—Forest Avenue or Montgomery Road?

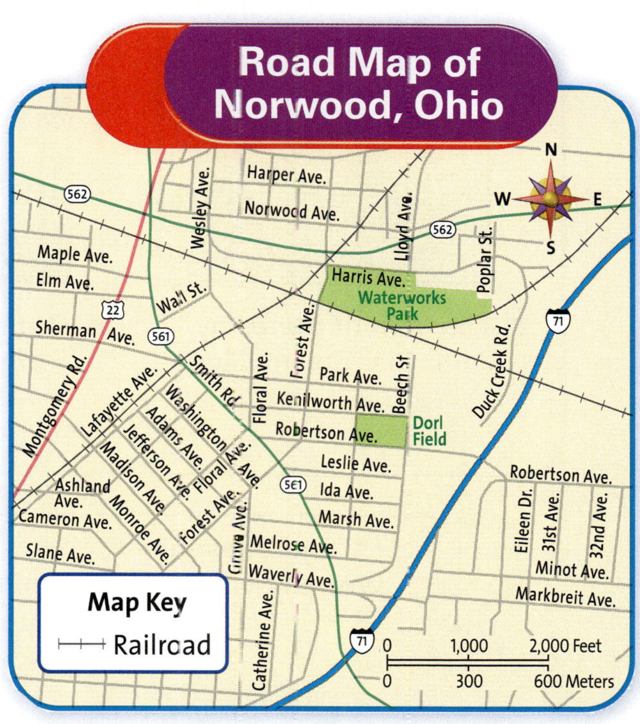

Unit 4

Activities

Show What You Know

Unit Writing Activity

Write a Summary Describe the relationship between citizens and the government.

- List some rights and responsibilities of citizens.
- Explain how the government serves and protects citizens.

Unit Project

Government Handbook Make a handbook that tells about the government.

- Find out about the people and jobs in local, state, and national governments.
- Describe how each level works.

Read More

- *The Train of States* by Peter Sís. Greenwillow.

- *Capital! Washington D.C. From A to Z* by Laura Krauss Melmed. HarperCollins.

- *The Flag Maker* by Susan Campbell Bartoletti. Houghton Mifflin.

For more resources, go to **www.harcourtschool.com/ss1**

People in Communities

Unit 5

Start with the Standards

Oklahoma Priority Academic Student Skills

1.1 Identify, locate, and compare and contrast information found in resources such as encyclopedias, visual images, atlases, maps, globes, and computer-based technologies.

1.2 Examine and use children's literature to compare and contrast his or her own community to other United States and global communities.

3.1 Investigate through children's literature the cultural similarities and differences among people in different regions, and how they have changed over time.

3.2 Compare and contrast the ways people in the United States and other communities in other countries use art, music, and stories to communicate.

The Big Idea

Culture

Cultural differences enrich communities and make them diverse.

What to Know

- ✓ What different cultures can be found in the United States?
- ✓ What makes up our American heritage?
- ✓ How do people express their culture?
- ✓ How are customs different around the world?

Unit 5

People

Talk About

People and Culture

John Chapman
1774–1845
American pioneer known as "Johnny Appleseed"

People in Communities

Emma Lazarus
1849–1887
American poet whose poem "The New Colossus" was placed on the Statue of Liberty

Maya Lin
1959–Present
Artist who designed the Vietnam Veterans Memorial in Washington, D.C.

Unit 5

Preview

Vocabulary

diverse The variety of differences in a group, such as language or beliefs. (page 332)

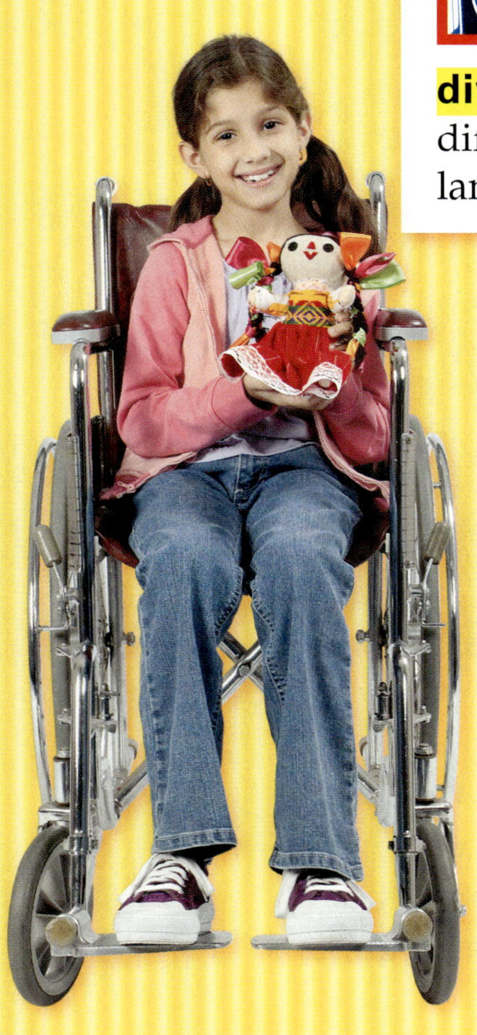

tradition A custom, or way of doing something, that is passed on to others. (page 335)

custom A people's way of doing something. (page 332)

landmark An important human or natural feature that marks a location. (page 338)

festival A joyful gathering for celebration. (page 359)

Unit 5

Reading Social Studies

Cause and Effect

Why It Matters Understanding cause and effect can help you see why events happen.

Learn

A **cause** is something that makes something else happen. An **effect** is the thing that happens as a result of a cause.

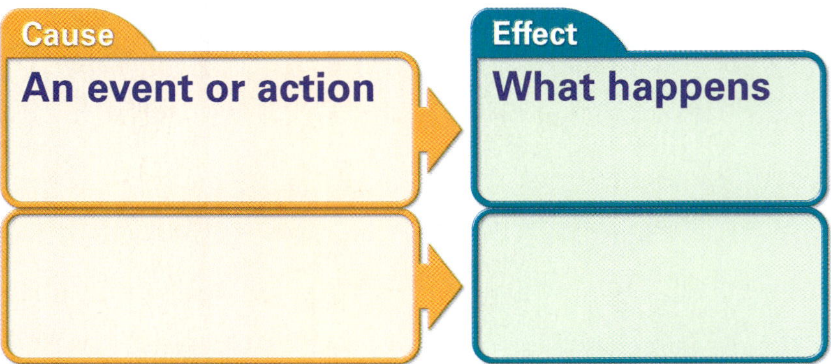

- Words and phrases, such as *because, as a result, since,* and *so,* can help you identify why something happens.
- An effect can also become a cause for another event.

Practice

Read the paragraph. Find a cause and an effect.

Cause

Effect

In the past, people in the Appalachian Mountains did not travel far from home. The steep mountains made it difficult to visit other communities, where they could have learned other ways of life. As a result, the Appalachian region had a different culture from those in the rest of the country.

Apply

Read the paragraphs, and answer the questions.

The Sound of Appalachian Music

The Appalachian region is known for its folk music, or popular music that people learn from each other. The first Europeans in the area came from many cultures. They included English, Scottish, Irish, German, and French settlers. African Americans and Native Americans also settled in the region. As a result, Appalachian folk music blends styles from around the world. Over time, this blend became its own unique, or special, mountain sound.

English settlers brought their love of ballads, or songs that tell stories. German settlers played the dulcimer, a stringed instrument held on the player's lap. A Scottish fiddler started playing the fiddle in a new way, using a short bow. The guitar, banjo, and mandolin were also popular in the region. Each style and instrument helped create the Appalachian sound.

Focus Skill Cause and Effect

1. Why is Appalachian folk music made up of many styles?
2. What effect did Germans have on Appalachian music?
3. Which group brought ballads to Appalachian music?

Dreaming of America

An Ellis Island Story

by Eve Bunting — illustrated by Ben F. Stahl

Annie Moore and her two brothers, Anthony and Philip, left Ireland to come to the United States. Annie's parents had come to this country earlier to work and save money. On January 1, 1892, Annie arrived at Ellis Island, a place where immigrants went before they were allowed to enter the country. This story shows what might have happened when Annie stepped off the ship.

With a squeak and a squeal, the gangplank was lowered.

Mr. Viktor gave Annie a little push. "Be first, Annie. First will be good."

The *Nevada* brought immigrants from Europe to America from 1869–1894.

The original Ellis Island immigration building was completed in 1891.

Annie stepped out, Anthony and Phillip at her heels.

The cheers were like thunder. Small American flags waved. Hats and caps flew in the air. The salty air smelled good. The smell of America.

Two important-looking gentlemen in suits took her hands. "Welcome. You are the first immigrant to enter our country through Ellis Island," one of the gentlemen said.

"First will be good," Mr. Viktor had said. This was what he'd meant. This was why there was a big celebration!

"I am Colonel Weber," the other gentleman said. "What is your name?"

Annie tried not to stammer. "I am Annie Moore of Cork, Ireland. These are my brothers, Anthony and Phillip." She stood, unsure and embarrassed, knowing everyone was watching them. All those hundreds of people pressed behind the barricades. She looked from side to side. Oh, if she could only see her parents!

"We want you to accept this ten-dollar gold piece to commemorate this important day in history," Colonel Weber said.

"And it's Annie's birthday, too," little Phillip piped up.

An important day in history, and she was a part of it! Annie stared down at the gold coin. It seemed to float in her hand, bright as sunshine. Ten dollars? That must be a fortune!

"I'll never part with it. Never," she whispered.

"Now, if you and your brothers will come with us, we will get you registered. . . ."

It was then Annie heard the shouts, so excited they rose above the noise around them.

"It's Annie and little Anthony and little Phillip!"

"Daddy!" Annie called. "Daddy!" She'd know that voice anywhere.

And there was her mother, pushing through to the front of the crowd, her face red with excitement, her hat and hair every which way. "Here we are, darlin's, here we are!" she called.

"How does it feel to be in America?" a man with a notepad asked.

"Grand altogether," Annie said. She looked down at her ring with the red stones that were more precious than rubies. The two hearts. Ireland and America. Was that what her auntie had known when she gave it?

I am Annie Moore of Cork, Ireland, she thought. And I am Annie Moore of America.

This is the real Annie Moore with her first born child, Mary Catherine.

Response Corner

1. **Focus Skill** **Cause and Effect** Why did Colonel Weber give Annie a ten-dollar gold piece?
2. **Make It Relevant** Why do you think people might move to your community from another community?

USE AN ANTICIPATION GUIDE

An anticipation guide helps you anticipate, or predict, what you will read.

- **Look at the lesson and section titles for clues about what you will read.**
- **Preview the Reading Check questions. Use what you know about the subject to predict the answers.**
- **Read to find out whether your predictions were correct.**

Immigration and Migration		
Reading Check	Prediction	Correct?
Why have immigrants come to the United States?	People move to find new opportunities.	✓

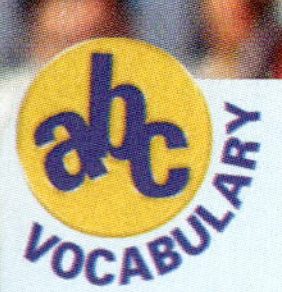

PREVIEW VOCABULARY

opportunity p. 324

multicultural p. 333

holiday p. 340

CHAPTER 9

Our American Culture

A Native American celebration in Los Angeles, California

Lesson 1

Moving to New Places

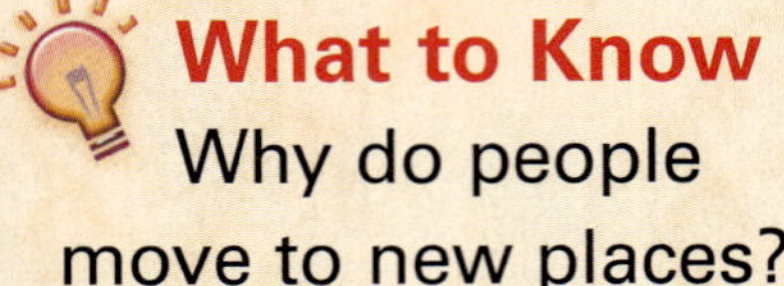

What to Know
Why do people move to new places?

Vocabulary
opportunity p. 324
prejudice p. 325
migrate p. 328

Cause and Effect

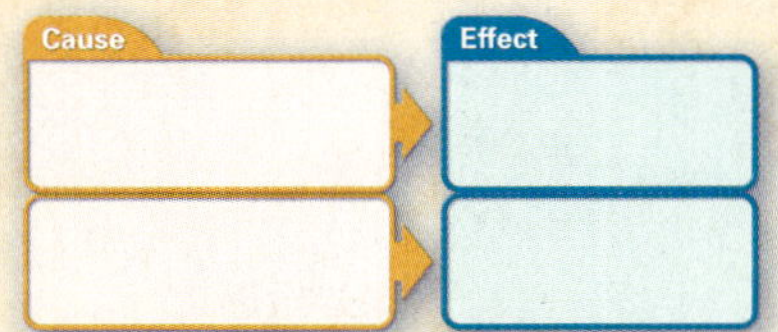

People do not always live in the same place all their lives. Sometimes they move to another community or even another country.

A Nation of Immigrants

Immigrants have been coming to the United States for hundreds of years. Many have come to find new opportunities. An **opportunity** is a chance to have a better way of life. Some came here hoping to find more freedoms. Some came for a better education or job. Others wanted to escape dangers in their own countries.

Immigrant children arriving in the 1930s wave at the Statue of Liberty.

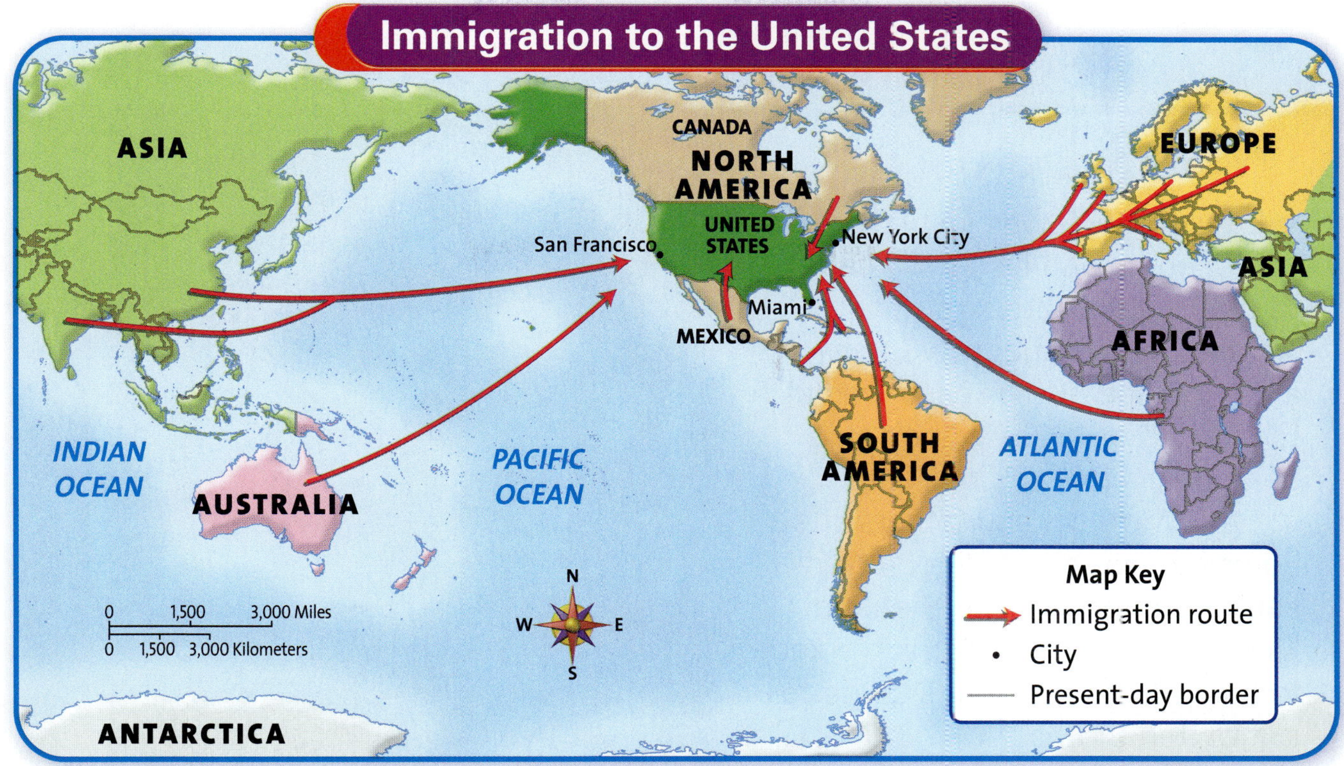

Movement What part of the United States did most immigrants from Europe reach first?

Immigrants Face New Problems

In the past, immigrants to the United States faced many problems. They often had to live in crowded apartments in the older parts of big cities. They had little money for food.

Some immigrants also faced prejudice (PREH•juh•duhs). **Prejudice** is the unfair feeling of hate or dislike for people of a certain group, race, or religion. Immigrants were often paid less money than other workers for the same job. They also had fewer opportunities for good jobs.

A passport of a Russian immigrant

Reading Check **Cause and Effect**
Why have immigrants come to the United States?

Children in History

Edward Corsi

Edward Corsi was just ten years old when he and his family came to the United States from Italy. After a long voyage, the Corsis and 1,600 other Italians arrived at Ellis Island in 1907. As their ship neared Ellis Island, Corsi later wrote, "Mothers and fathers lifted up babies so that they too could see, off to the left, the Statue of Liberty." As an adult, Corsi worked to help other immigrants come to the United States.

These children, like Corsi, were immigrants from Europe.

More than 20 million immigrants passed through Ellis Island.

Beginning New Lives

Between 1880 and 1920, millions of new immigrants arrived in the United States. Most traveled on crowded ships. They wanted the chance to become United States citizens.

After they arrived, immigrants often had to wait in long lines. They had to answer many questions from immigration officers. Then they had to see doctors. They could enter the United States only if they passed all the tests.

Most immigrants from Europe arrived at Ellis Island, in New York Harbor. It was the nation's largest immigration center.

Most immigrants from Asia arrived on the west coast, at Angel Island. Angel Island is located in California's San Francisco Bay.

Building Communities

Many immigrants settled in cities close to Ellis Island or Angel Island. They found jobs and met people from their home countries.

Other immigrants moved to different areas of the country. Some started new communities. They often named these communities for their homelands. Germantown, in Tennessee, was named by the town's early German settlers.

Immigration Today

Today, immigrants arrive from countries all over the world. Most come from countries in Asia and Latin America. The United States government limits the number of immigrants that can enter the country each year.

Reading Check **Generalize**

Why did immigrants settle in cities near Ellis Island or Angel Island?

Immigrants and Their Countries

Country	Number of Immigrants
Mexico	173,664
India	65,472
Philippines	54,632
China	45,942
Vietnam	30,064
Dominican Republic	30,049

Table Many of the immigrants who came to the United States in 2004 were from these countries. How many people came from Vietnam?

Immigrants being sworn in as United States citizens

This African American family migrated from the rural South to Chicago.

Migration in the United States

People also **migrate**, or move, within their own country. Like immigrants, many of them are looking for better opportunities.

The Great Migration

Even after slavery ended, laws limited African Americans' freedoms. During the 1900s, many African Americans left rural areas in the South. They migrated to urban areas in the North and the West. They hoped to find jobs, homes, and equal rights. This movement became known as the Great Migration. African American populations grew in cities such as Detroit, Cleveland, Chicago, and New York City.

A painting from *The Migration* series by Jacob Lawrence

People share customs and make communities diverse.

People in the United States share a common heritage.

Facts and Main Ideas

Answer these questions.

8. What problems did some immigrants to the United States face because of prejudice?
9. How is Adams Morgan in Washington, D.C., a multicultural community?
10. Why do we celebrate Presidents' Day?

Write the letter of the best choice.

11. Where did African Americans move during the Great Migration?
    - **A** to rural areas
    - **B** to urban areas
    - **C** to the South
    - **D** to suburban areas
12. What honors different ethnic groups in Cleveland, Ohio?
    - **A** Friendship Archway
    - **B** Chamblee
    - **C** Cultural Gardens
    - **D** African American Museum

Critical Thinking

13. **Make It Relevant** What symbols of American heritage are in your community?
14. Why do you think immigrants move to the United States today?

Skills

Use a Population Map

Use the population map on page 331 to answer the question.

15. Which color is used for the lowest population density in the map key?

writing

Write an Interview Suppose you are going to interview an immigrant. Write questions you want to ask this person.

Write a Poem Imagine that you are Emma Lazarus. Write another poem for the Statue of Liberty.

WRITE TO LEARN

Write about what you read to better understand and remember information.

- **Keep a learning log to write responses to what you read.**
- **Responses can be personal and creative to make the text more meaningful to you.**

Cultures Around the World	
What I Learned	My Response
People express their culture through storytelling and art.	I can tell a story or make artwork to express my culture.

PREVIEW VOCABULARY

folktale p. 349

folk song p. 350

worship p. 352

CHAPTER 10

Cultures Around the World

People celebrate the Fiesta of San Francisco in Teotihuacán, Mexico

Lesson 1

Expressions of Culture

What to Know
How do people express their culture?

Vocabulary

literature p. 348
myth p. 348
fable p. 348
folktale p. 349
legend p. 349
folk song p. 350
worship p. 352

Cause and Effect

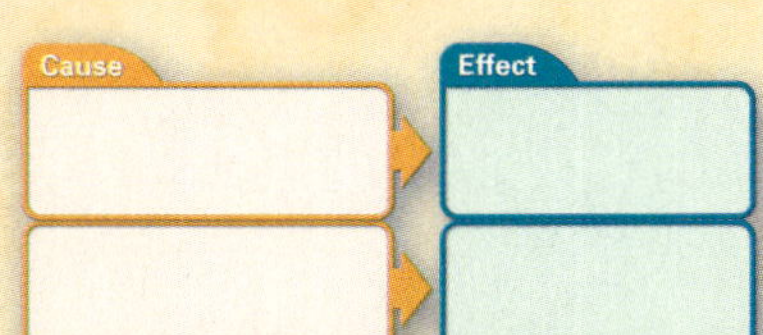

The world has many different cultures. Sometimes different groups express, or share, their cultures in some of the same ways.

Written and Oral Traditions

People can share their culture through literature. **Literature** includes the stories and poems that people use to share their ideas. A **myth** is a story made up to explain the world around us. Children in West Africa hear myths about how Anansi the Spider created the sun, moon, and stars.

A **fable** is a story in which animals speak and act like humans. People enjoy fables that were told by Aesop, a Greek storyteller.

A storyteller tells folktales at a New York public library.

People perform in a play. A play is a story acted out in front of an audience.

Third graders listen to stories at their school in Hawaii.

Folktales and Legends

Folktales help keep the traditions of a culture alive. A **folktale** is a story passed from one generation to the next. A favorite Japanese folktale is about a man named Urashima Taro. While fishing, Taro rescues a turtle. He is rewarded with a visit to the Dragon Palace.

Many people share legends from their culture. A **legend** is a made-up story about a real person or event. One legend is based on John Chapman. He planted apple trees in the United States. He was given the nickname Johnny Appleseed.

Reading Check **Cause and Effect**
Why was John Chapman called Johnny Appleseed?

Detroit Industry, a mural by Diego Rivera

The Arts

Storytelling is just one way people express their culture. Artists, musicians, dancers, and builders also use their talents to express their cultures.

Art and Music

Artists draw, paint, and sculpt artworks. Diego Rivera (ree•VAY•rah) expressed his Mexican culture with colorful murals. A mural is a large painting on a wall.

Musicians use sound to create music, another part of culture. In many African cultures, drums provide the beat for music. The *kalungu*, or "talking drum," comes from Nigeria. Its sounds can be high or low, like a human voice.

Folk songs express the culture of a group of people. In Eastern Europe, people play folk songs with accordions and other instruments.

People dance to folk songs.

Dance

Dancers express culture through traditional clothes, music, and movement. In West Africa, people perform a welcome dance called the Yabara. This dance is named after the beaded rattles that the dancers carry. The rattles are thrown in the air and caught in rhythm.

Women perform an African dance.

Architecture

Architecture is the art of designing buildings. The ancient city of Tikal, in Guatemala, was a center of culture for the Maya. The large step pyramids they built there still stand today. The pyramids show the power and skill of the ancient Maya.

Reading Check **Summarize**
How can people express their culture through the arts?

Fast Fact

Tikal includes the ruins of several step pyramids and a royal palace. There are also courts where the ancient Maya played a ball game.

Church

Mosque

Buddhist Temple

Synagogue

Religions

Religious traditions are also an important part of culture. In the United States, people have the right to choose which religion, if any, they will follow. Some choose to follow the teachings of Christianity or Judaism (JOO•duh•ih•zuhm). Others follow the teachings of Islam (is•LAHM), Hinduism (HIN•doo•ih•zuhm), or Buddhism (BOO•dih•zuhm).

Places of Worship

Communities have special places where people can **worship**, or pray, together. Christians worship in churches. Followers of Islam pray in a mosque (MAHSK), or masjid (MUS•jid). Jewish worshipers meet in a synagogue (SIN•uh•gahg), or temple. Buddhists and Hindus visit temples to meditate.

People gather at places of worship to share religious traditions. There, they meet with other people who share the same beliefs. Some offer programs that help the community. Some places of worship also have schools. These schools teach students about the religion and its beliefs and values. They may also teach regular school subjects.

Reading Check **Summarize**
What are the names of some kinds of places of worship?

Followers of Five Religions in the United States

Religion	Number of Followers
Buddhism	1,082,000
Christianity	159,030,000
Hinduism	766,000
Islam	1,104,000
Judaism	2,831,000

Table This table shows how many people follow the five largest religions in the United States. Which religion has the most followers?

Summary People around the world express their culture. They tell stories and create art. Some people express their culture through religious traditions.

Review

1. **What to Know** How do people express their culture?
2. **Vocabulary** Explain the difference between a **myth** and a **legend**.
3. **Culture** What are some of the different types of literature people use to share their culture?
4. **Critical Thinking** Why do you think people go to places of worship?
5. **Write a Folktake** Write a folktale that takes place in your community.
6. **Cause and Effect** On a separate sheet of paper, copy and complete the graphic organizer below.

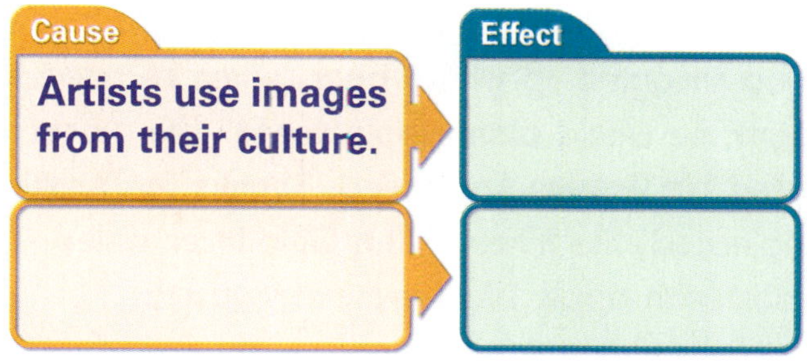

Tell Fact from Fiction

Why It Matters When you read something, it is important to know whether it is fact or fiction.

Learn

Facts are statements that can be proved. They give names, places, and dates that you can check. You can look up these facts in reference works, such as encyclopedias.

Fiction is a story that is made up. The people and events in it may seem real, but they are imaginary. Some works of fiction, such as legends and historical fiction, tell about real people and events. However, many of the details are made up to add interest.

Johnny Appleseed

A long time ago, a man named Johnny decided he would plant apple seeds for settlers in the Ohio River valley. He left his home with only a bag and a cooking pot in which to make his meals. In the bag were so many apple seeds that there was no room for the cooking pot, so he wore it on his head like a hat!

As Johnny traveled, he would sleep outside at night. Once, during a snowstorm, he slept inside a log snuggled up with a bear. When he came to farms, he would plant apple seeds. The pioneers called him Johnny Appleseed. Thanks to Johnny Appleseed, the trees of the Ohio River valley bloom with apple blossoms every spring.

Practice

Read the two selections about Johnny Appleseed. Then answer these questions.

1. Which selection is mainly fiction? Which selection contains the most facts? How do you know?
2. What sources could you use to check the facts?

Apply

Make It Relevant Write a legend about someone you know or have read about. Include both facts and fiction.

John Chapman
(1774–1845)

John Chapman was an American pioneer born in Massachusetts. For more than 40 years, he traveled around Ohio, Indiana, and Illinois. He sold or gave away apple seeds to people he met. He helped hundreds of settlers set up apple orchards. The settlers began to tell stories about him. They gave him the nickname Johnny Appleseed. Chapman became an American legend during his life. He became a symbol of the pioneer spirit in the United States.

National Storytelling Festival

READ ABOUT

Good storytellers make you feel like you are a part of the story. Jimmy Neil Smith has heard many great storytellers spin their tales. These stories led him to create the first National Storytelling Festival in 1973. This festival is held every October in Jonesborough, Tennessee.

Each year, thousands of visitors make their way to Jonesborough. They come to hear stories told about the past. Storytellers take the stage over the festival weekend. Often, their stories share messages about the hopes and dreams of people around the world.

FIND

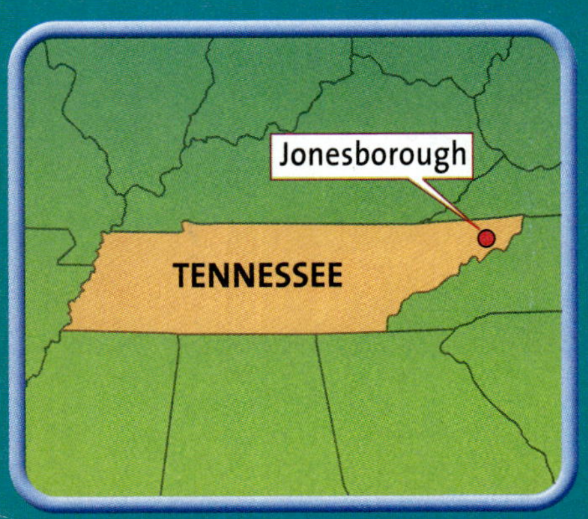

A poster for the National Stoytelling Festival

This Native American shares a story.

A festival performance

Listeners laugh at a story.

A VIRTUAL TOUR

GO ONLINE For more resources, go to www.harcourtschool.com/ss1

Lesson 2

Holidays and Traditions

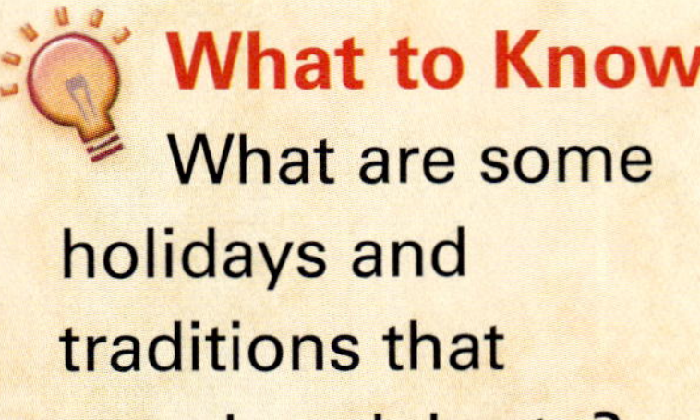

What to Know
What are some holidays and traditions that people celebrate?

Vocabulary

festival p. 359

Cause and Effect

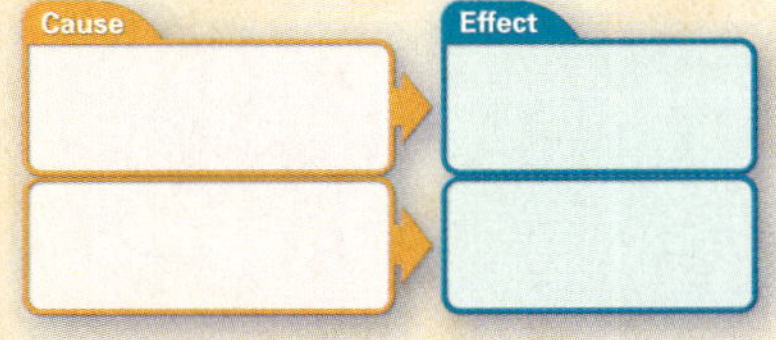

People around the world express their culture with holidays and celebrations. Many of these holidays are also celebrated in the United States.

Cultural Holidays

Some holidays come from different cultures. They are celebrated by many Americans, too.

Saint Patrick's Day

On March 17, the Irish celebrate Saint Patrick's Day. Saint Patrick's Day began as a religious holiday. It has grown to celebrate Irish culture.

Saint Patrick's Day parades are held in many cities in the United States.

➤ Cinco de Mayo is celebrated today with traditional Mexican dances and music.

Cinco de Mayo and Mexican Independence

Cinco de Mayo is celebrated in Mexico. It is also celebrated in many communities in the United States. The name is Spanish for "the Fifth of May." On this day in 1862, a small Mexican army won an important battle against France.

Every September 16, people in Mexico also celebrate their independence from Spain. Many Mexican Americans living in the United States celebrate, too. They decorate their homes with lights. People enjoy food, music, and fireworks.

➤ Each day of Kwanzaa honors a different value, or principle, in the community.

Kwanzaa

Kwanzaa is a week-long holiday in late December. It celebrates the importance of family and community in African American cultures. Many cities have a Kwanzaa **festival**, or a joyful gathering for celebration.

Reading Check **Cause and Effect**

Why do people celebrate Kwanzaa?

New Year's Day

New Year's Day is the beginning of a new calendar year. Countries around the world celebrate the new year in different ways. On New Year's Eve, people in New York City gather in Times Square. They watch as a giant crystal ball is lowered just before the new year begins. Children in Belgium write messages on decorated paper for their parents to read on New Year's Day.

New Year's Eve in Times Square

Chinese New Year

The Chinese New Year falls on a different date each year. This date is between January 21 and February 20. Chinese New Year is celebrated in China and around the world. Chinese families gather for a special meal on New Year's Eve. Children receive red packets with money inside for good luck.

On New Year's Day in China, people gather to watch traditional dragon dances.

Thai New Year

The Thai New Year is called Songkran. *Songkran* is a Thai word that means "to move" or "to change place." It is celebrated in April. April is a hot month in Thailand. People celebrate the new year by throwing cool water on one another. People walk on the streets with bowls of water or even garden hoses. Anyone who passes by is likely to get wet!

Reading Check **Main Idea and Details**
How do people in Thailand celebrate a new year?

Thai children at a Songkran festival

Summary People express their culture by celebrating holidays. People of different cultures celebrate their new year with different traditions.

Review

1. **What to Know** What are some holidays and traditions that people celebrate?
2. **Vocabulary** What does the term **festival** mean?
3. **Geography** Where are some different places that the new year is celebrated?
4. **Critical Thinking** **Make It Relevant** How does your community celebrate New Year's Day?
5. **Write a Description** Write about a holiday that your community celebrates. Describe the traditions for this holiday.
6. **Focus Skill** **Cause and Effect** On a separate sheet of paper, copy and complete the graphic organizer below.

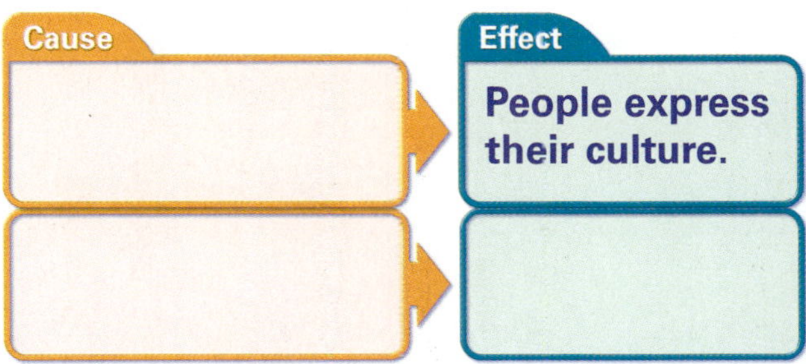

Lesson 3

Cultures of the World

What to Know
How are cultures around the world alike and different?

Vocabulary

cultural identity p. 364

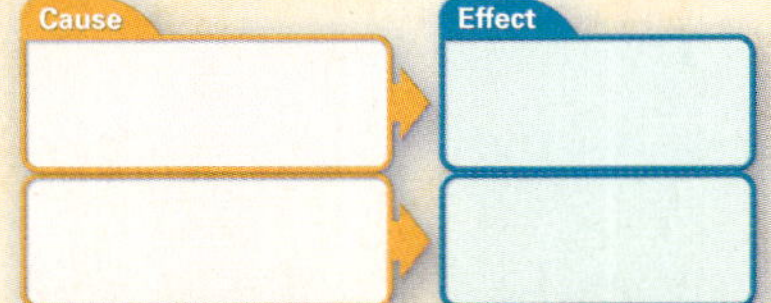

Cause and Effect

Culture groups around the world have similar and different ways of life. These customs affect family, school, language, food, and other parts of life.

Ways of Life

There are many different cultures throughout the world. Africa and Europe are two continents. Each continent has about 700 million people. The people of each continent make up hundreds of culture groups. The people in these groups speak different languages and eat different foods.

Drummers and singers at the Timkat festival in Ethiopia

A market in Spain

Life in Ethiopia

Africa has more than 50 countries. Hundreds of languages, such as Arabic and Somali are spoken. Students in Ethiopia learn different languages in school. At home, families eat vegetables and meat served on *injera* (in•JAIR•uh), a flat, spongy bread.

An Ethiopian woman makes *injera.*

Life in Spain

Europe is made up of more than 40 countries. More than 40 languages are spoken. In Spain, the official language is Spanish. Other languages, such as Basque (BASK) and Catalan, are also spoken. Families in Spain eat their main meal of the day in the afternoon.

Reading Check **Cause and Effect**
Why are several languages spoken on each continent?

People of the World

People everywhere are proud of their own cultures. One way people show their cultural identities is through what they wear. A **cultural identity** is a collection of traits that are seen in a group.

This map shows children from some of the world's cultures. Some are wearing traditional clothing that is worn on special days. Others are in everyday clothes.

Reading Check **Main Idea and Details**
What is one way people show their cultural identity?

People of the World

MAP SKILL **Human-Environment Interactions** The clothes people wear often depend on their environment. What does these children's clothing tell you about how they adapt to their environment?

Expressions of Culture Around the World

People around the world express their culture in different ways. Architecture, music, and dance also help create a group's cultural identity.

A room in a Japanese house

Japanese Architecture

Many historic buildings in Japan share traditional features. They were designed to be close to the natural environment. Most older buildings are made of wood. Some buildings have many openings, so air can move easily through the rooms. In Japan, living close to nature is an important value.

The island of Itsukushima (it•soo•koo•SHEE•mah) in Japan is home to a shrine, or holy place.

Brazilian Music and Dance

Music and dance are important ways to express culture in Brazil. Samba music has a lively rhythm. The samba dance comes from Portuguese, African, and native traditions. Dancers and musicians practice all year for contests held during a festival called Carnaval.

Samba dancers in Rio de Janeiro, Brazil

Reading Check **Cause and Effect**
Why were buildings in Japan built with nature in mind?

Summary People around the world have similar and different customs and ways of life. They express their cultures in many different ways.

Review

1. **What to Know** How are cultures around the world alike and different?
2. **Vocabulary** Explain the meaning of **cultural identity**.
3. **Culture** What cultures are celebrated when Brazilians dance the samba?
4. **Critical Thinking** **Make It Relevant** What cultures from around the world are expressed in your community?
5. **Make a List** List different cultural expressions you learned about in this lesson. Name the countries they came from and find these places on a world map.
6. **Focus Skill** **Cause and Effect** On a separate sheet of paper, copy and complete the graphic organizer below.

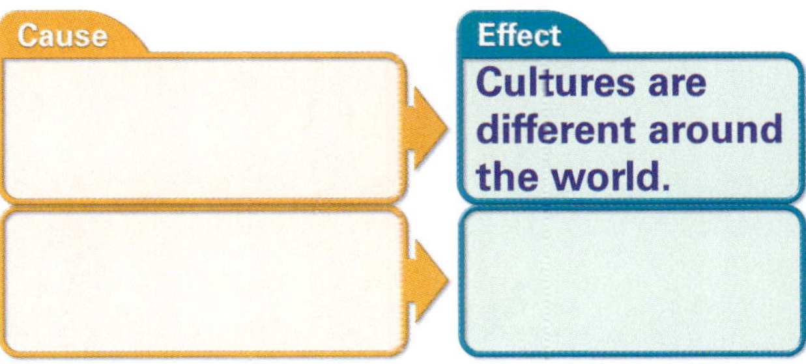

Explore Your Community's Culture

In this unit, you learned about different cultures and the ways people share their culture with others. You can also explore the cultures in your own community.

- What ethnic groups live in your community?
- What are some ways that people in your community express their culture?
- Which cultural holidays or festivals are celebrated in your community?

Use Your Community's Resources

Your Community's Resources

- Historical Societies
- Interviews with Citizens
- Local Newspaper
- Libraries

Design a Culture Guide

Design a guide to the festivals and other cultural events in your community. List the events in order of when they happen in the year. Include a photo or drawing for each event. Describe the customs, food, music, dance, and artwork for each.

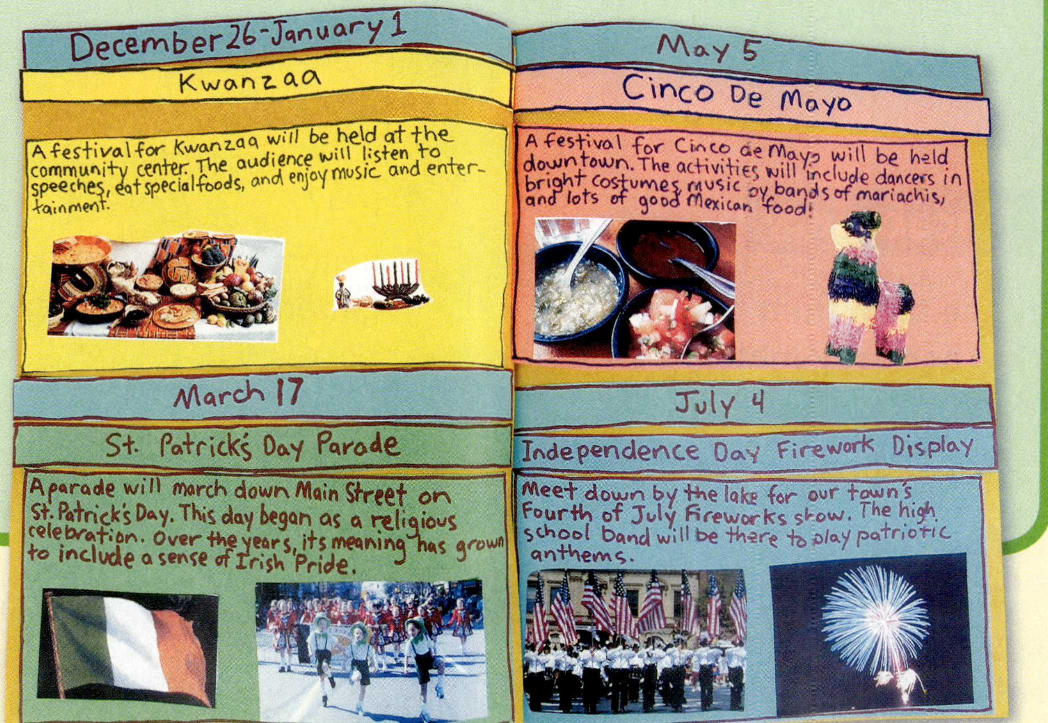

Visual Summary

People express their culture in many ways.

Summarize the Chapter

Cause and Effect Complete the graphic organizer to show that you understand the causes and effects of cultural expression.

Cause	Effect
People want to express their culture and share it with others.	

Identify the term from the word bank that correctly matches each definition.

1. a joyful gathering for celebration
2. a story made up to explain the world around us
3. a collection of traits that are seen in members of the same group
4. pray
5. a story passed from one generation to the next

Word Bank

myth p. 348
folktale p. 349
worship p. 352
festival p. 359
cultural identity p. 364

People celebrate their culture with holidays and traditions.

People all over the world have their own cultures and traditions.

Facts and Main Ideas

Answer these questions.

6. What are some ways people express their culture?
7. How do people celebrate the Chinese New Year?
8. What important value affects Japanese architecture?

Write the letter of the best choice.

9. Which holiday is a celebration of Irish culture?
   A St. Patrick's Day
   B New Year's Day
   C Kwanzaa
   D Cinco de Mayo
10. What is one language spoken in Africa?
   A Spanish
   B Catalan
   C Arabic
   D Basque

Critical Thinking

11. How are churches, mosques, synagogues, and temples alike?
12. **Make It Relevant** How can you learn more about your own cultural heritage?

Skills

Tell Fact from Fiction

Use the selections on pages 354 and 355 to answer the question.

13. What details do you think are made up in the selection that is mostly fiction?

writing

Write a Legend Write a legend about someone in your community. Give your character a name that fits the legend.

Write a Paragraph Make a list of the ways you express your culture. Use this list to write a paragraph.

Button Craze

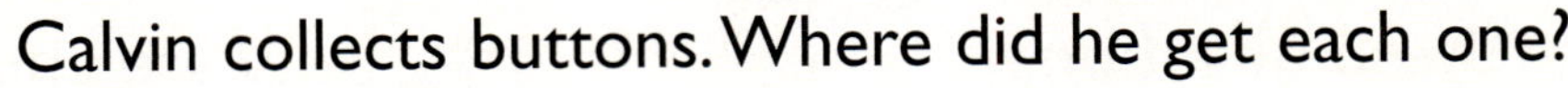

Calvin collects buttons. Where did he get each one?

Put these words into the grid in alphabetical order. Read down the letters in the green squares to answer the riddle.

tradition
folktale
fable
festival
legend
folk song

Riddle:
How can you hear a pin drop?

Online Adventures

GO ONLINE

The cultural fair is in town today! Join Eco to play the online game and visit the fair. You'll get to see games, rides, and prizes. But be ready. To win, you'll need to remember what you learned about culture. Play now at **www.harcourtschool.com/ss1**

Review and Test Prep

The Big Idea

Culture Cultural differences enrich communities and make them diverse.

Reading Comprehension and Vocabulary

People in Communities

Immigrants move to the United States to find more opportunities. By sharing their cultures and customs, these different ethnic groups help make our communities diverse.

People share their cultures through written and oral traditions, such as myths, fables, folktales, and legends. They also express their cultures through art, music, dance, architecture, and religion. In the United States, people of all cultures are united in a common American heritage.

Read the summary above. Then answer the questions that follow.

1. Why do people move to the United States?
   A to find more opportunities
   B to celebrate holidays
   C to honor people
   D to share their art

2. What does diverse mean?
   A better
   B larger
   C different
   D traditional

3. What are some traditions that people share?
   A ethnic groups
   B opportunities
   C landmarks
   D folktales

4. How are all community members in our country united?
   A religious traditions
   B ethnic groups
   C common American heritage
   D art and music

Facts and Main Ideas

Answer these questions.

5. Where did most immigrants arrive in the United States in the past?
6. How is Cleveland, Ohio, multicultural?
7. What are some religions that people follow?

Write the letter of the best choice.

8. Where do most immigrants to the United States come from today?
   A Australia
   B Canada and Mexico
   C Europe
   D Asia and Latin America
9. Which holiday celebrates our common American heritage?
   A Cinco de Mayo
   B Saint Patrick's Day
   C Fourth of July
   D Kwanzaa
10. How do people celebrate the Thai New Year?
    A They gather in Times Square.
    B They write messages on decorated paper.
    C They throw cool water on one another.
    D They watch traditional dragon dances.

Critical Thinking

11. **Make It Relevant** What values and beliefs are taught in your favorite stories?
12. What do you think Emma Lazarus's poem at the base of the Statue of Liberty means?

Skills

Read a Population Map

Use the map below to answer the following questions.

13. Which color is used for the highest population density?
14. What is the population density of Columbia?

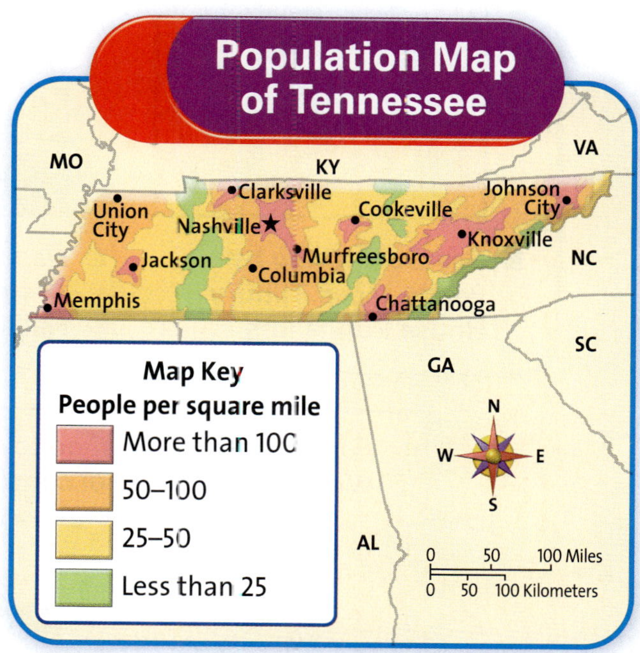

Unit 5

Activities

Show What You Know

Unit Writing Activity

Write a Poem Write a poem about your community's cultures.

- Include details about cultural traditions, such as food, clothing, and art.
- Tell how the cultures make the community a better place to live.

Unit Project

Culture Fair Create a fair exhibit about a culture.

- Research a culture in the United States.
- Make a poster that illustrates the customs of the culture.

Read More

- ***Say Something*** **by Peggy Moss. Tilbury House Publishers.**

- ***Henry and the Kite Dragon*** **by Bruce Edward Hall. Philomel.**

- ***Going North*** **by Janice N. Harrington. Farrar, Straus and Giroux.**

For more resources, go to **www.harcourtschool.com/ss1**

Working in Communities

Unit 6

Start with the Standards

Oklahoma Priority Academic Student Skills

1.1 Identify, locate, and compare and contrast information found in resources such as encyclopedias, visual images, atlases, maps, globes, and computer-based technologies.

4.3 Describe how communities depend upon workers with specialized jobs, giving examples of ways in which they contribute to the exchange of goods and services.

5.1 Describe the difference between goods and services; explaining that, at different times and places, people are both consumers and producers of goods and services.

5.2 Explain that limits on resources require people to make choices about producing and consuming goods and services.

5.3 Compare and contrast the differences among human resources, natural resources and capital resources used to produce goods and services.

5.4 Explain the relationship between saving and spending, and describe the value of setting a financial goal and developing a plan to reach it.

The Big Idea

Economics

People depend on one another to produce, buy, and sell goods and services. Good decision-making helps the economy of a family or a community.

What to Know

- ✓ How do people in a community depend on one another?
- ✓ Why do people and countries trade with each other?
- ✓ How do families earn, spend, and save money?
- ✓ How do businesses around the world make money?

Unit 6

People

Talk About

People and Economics

Madame C. J. Walker
1867–1919

A businesswoman who improved economic opportunities for African Americans

Working in Communities

Katherine Ortega
1934–Present
Former United States treasurer

Ray Tomlinson
1941–Present
Massachusetts engineer who invented e-mail

Unit 6

Preview

Vocabulary

producer Someone who makes a product or provides a service. (page 389)

consumer A person who buys a product or service. (page 390)

barter To trade without using money. (page 418)

supply The goods or services that businesses provide. (page 424)

demand The willingness to buy a good or service. (page 424)

Reading Social Studies

Focus Skill

Generalize

Why It Matters Knowing how to generalize can help you understand and remember what you read.

Learn

To **generalize** is to make a broad statement based on what you know about a group of ideas.

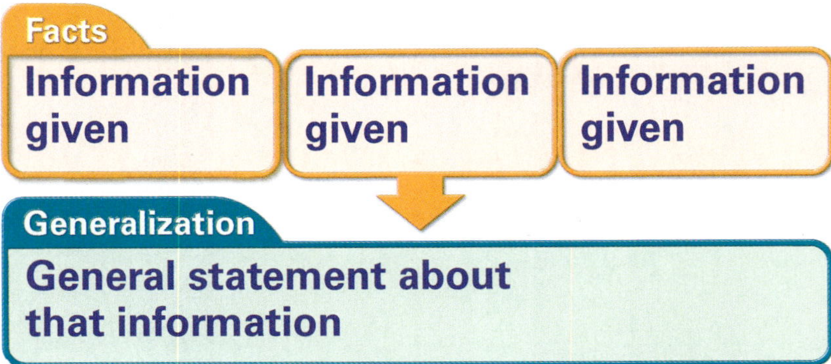

- A generalization should be based on facts.
- To generalize, think about what the facts have in common.

Practice

Read the paragraph. Then make a generalization.

Fact

Fact

Ten years ago, the rural town of Alliance, Nebraska, was in trouble. Its agriculture industry was failing, and the railroad company was getting smaller. Community members feared that their town would become poor. They took action by starting new tourism businesses. Tourism businesses provide goods and services for visitors.

Apply

Read the paragraphs, and answer the questions.

Tourism in Alliance, Nebraska

The people of Alliance, Nebraska, made tourism a major part of the economy. Visitors, or tourists, come to see things such as the huge sculpture Carhenge. The artist, Jim Reinders, modeled it after Stonehenge, an ancient monument in England. His whole family sculpted 38 cars to match the stones in Stonehenge.

Reinders gave the site to the city, and a community group now runs Carhenge. More than 80,000 tourists come each year to see the sculpture. Other tourist sites in town include several museums and a fine arts center.

Tourists bring money to Alliance. They pay to stay in hotels. They buy meals at restaurants and goods in the town's stores. Tourism also helps create jobs in the town. Some townspeople work in the hotels and restaurants. Others help keep the tourist sites clean and safe for visitors.

Focus Skill Generalize

1. What generalization can you make about the selection?
2. How did Jim Reinders help the economy of Alliance?
3. How do tourists help the economy of Alliance?

Alex and the Amazing Lemonade Stand

by Liz and Jay Scott
illustrated by Pam Howard

Alexandra "Alex" Scott was only a baby when her family found out she had cancer. When Alex was eight years old, she decided that she wanted to do something to raise money to fight cancer. She decided to start her own lemonade business. Alex gave the money she made to doctors. She wanted to help find a cure for children's cancers.

Alex was smart. She developed a plan.
She would sell lemonade from a lemonade stand.
Keeping the money was not in her mind.
She would give it to her hospital
for the cure they might find.

When summer came, Alex told her mother
that she would have her stand with the
help of her brothers.
They worked very hard
getting everything ready,
but this work was fun, and their
progress was steady.

The day for the sale came around at last.
There were people outside;
they were lining up fast!
Many people had heard about Alex's stand,
about little Alex and her lemonade plan.

They waited in line, the young & the old,
for a cup of her lemonade,
extra sweet and icy cold.

At the end of the day Alex was happy and amazed
to learn how much money her lemonade had raised.
She also learned
something else that was true.
Other people cared about sick kids too.

Many people learned of Alex's determination.
They found her story an inspiration.
They sent her cards and wrote her letters.
They liked that she helped
sick kids get better.
When next year came along,
Alex stuck with her plan.

On another warm Saturday she set up her stand,
people arrived from near and far.
They had heard about Alex,
the Lemonade Star.

They waited in line, the young & the old,
for a cup of her lemonade,
extra sweet and icy cold.

This year was even better and as her line
grew longer. . .

. . . Alex's determination for a cure
grew stronger.
Again she gave the hospital her money
and a letter.

It said,

Please use
my money to
help ALL kids
get better
-alex

More and more people heard about the good things that were done By the girl named Alex and her Lemonade Fund.

The following year, Alex had a new plan —

"Now I'll sell lemonade
across this great land!
If more kids would help, wouldn't it be great,
we could have lemonade
stands in every state.
Think of the money we could raise to
help kids who are sick.
A cure might be found,
perhaps even quick!"

Other kids listened and held
their own stands,
to help support Alex with her lemonade plans.

Response Corner

1. Focus Skill **Generalize** Why did so many people line up to buy lemonade?
2. **Make It Relevant** Do you think you could start a business to make money and help others? What would the business be? Where would you donate the money?

CONNECT IDEAS

Web organizers can help you connect ideas.

- **Write the chapter title in the top oval.**
- **Add ovals showing main ideas that support the theme.**
- **Add bubbles showing facts and details.**

Working in Our Community

People work.

- to buy goods

People work with each other.

People make and buy things.

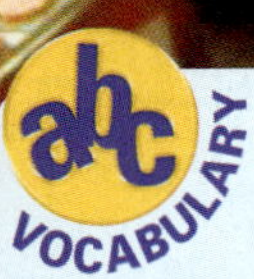

PREVIEW VOCABULARY

wage p. 392

human resource p. 395

capital resource p. 395

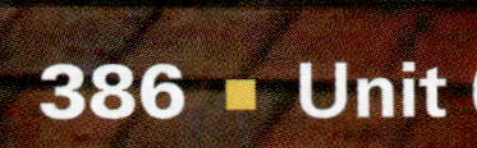

CHAPTER 11

Working in Our Community

This market in Cleveland, Ohio, has many booths that sell foods from different countries.

Lesson 1

Workers and Consumers

What to Know
How do people in a community depend on one another?

Vocabulary
product p. 388
producer p. 389
entrepreneur p. 389
consumer p. 390
interdependence p. 391
wage p. 392
income p. 392

Focus Skill Generalize

In a community, some people grow or make products to sell. A **product** is a good. Other workers provide services, such as haircuts and car washes.

People Work Together

Think about how busy you would be if you had to make all the things you use every day. You would have to grow your own vegetables. If you wanted meat, eggs, and milk, you would have to raise animals.

Early settlers had to make much of what they used. But as towns grew, people were able to share the work with others in their community.

People in a community long ago work together to build a barn.

Oscar Weissenborn's pencil-making business, long ago and today

People Depend on Producers

People in a community depend on producers for goods and services. A **producer** is someone who makes a product or provides a service.

Oscar Weissenborn learned how to use graphite and clay to make pencils. In 1889, he began making pencils in his home in New Jersey. At that time, most pencils were made in other countries.

People began buying Weissenborn's pencils. Weissenborn hired more people. He moved his business into a larger building.

Oscar Weissenborn was an entrepreneur (ahn•truh•pruh•NER). An **entrepreneur** is a person who starts and runs a business. Entrepreneurs provide goods or services and create jobs for workers.

Reading Check **Generalize**
Why are producers important to a community?

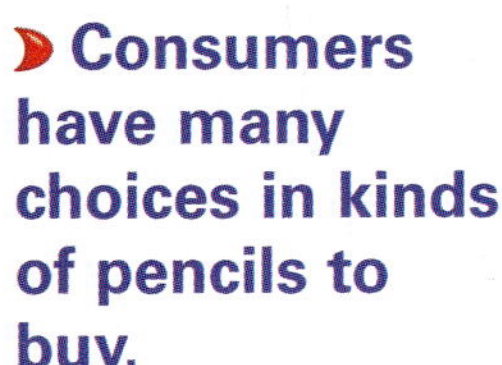

Consumers have many choices in kinds of pencils to buy.

People Buy Things

A person who buys a product or a service is a **consumer**. Consumers buy pencils in all sizes, shapes, and colors. Students buy pencils for school. Some artists buy colored pencils to use for drawing. Other consumers buy pencils to write with at home or at work.

Producers are always trying to make new and better cars, computers, televisions, toys, cereals, and other products. As a result, consumers have more products to choose from all the time.

Reading Check **Generalize**
What is a consumer?

People Help Each Other

Producers and consumers in a community depend on one another. Producers depend on consumers to buy the goods they make. Consumers depend on producers to provide goods and services for them to buy. Depending on one another is called **interdependence**.

Consumers trade, or exchange, things for what they want. They usually trade money for goods or services.

Reading Check **Generalize**
How do producers and consumers depend on one another?

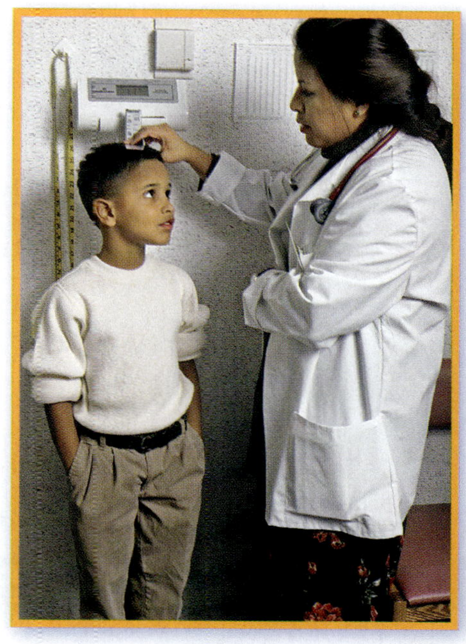

People depend on the services doctors provide to help them stay healthy.

Consumers buy goods at this farmers' market.

Leticia Herrera

People Start Businesses

Leticia Herrera (eh•REH•rah) runs a business that provides cleaning services to other businesses in Chicago. Her workers also fix up old buildings for businesses. Like people everywhere, Herrera's workers depend on their jobs for money.

The money people earn at work is called a **wage**. It is also called **income**. In the United States, people can choose the jobs they will do to make money.

Reading Check **Generalize**
Why do people depend on their jobs?

Summary People depend on one another to provide and buy goods and services. They earn income for the jobs they do. Some start their own businesses.

Review

1. **What to Know** How do people in a community depend on one another?
2. **Vocabulary** Write a description of an **entrepreneur**.
3. **Economics** How do people pay for the goods they need?
4. **Critical Thinking** **Make It Relevant** What are some goods and services that you buy as a consumer?
5. **Write a Help Wanted Ad** Imagine that you are a business owner. Write an ad that describes a job for which you want to hire someone.
6. Focus Skill **Generalize** On a separate sheet of paper, copy and complete the graphic organizer below.

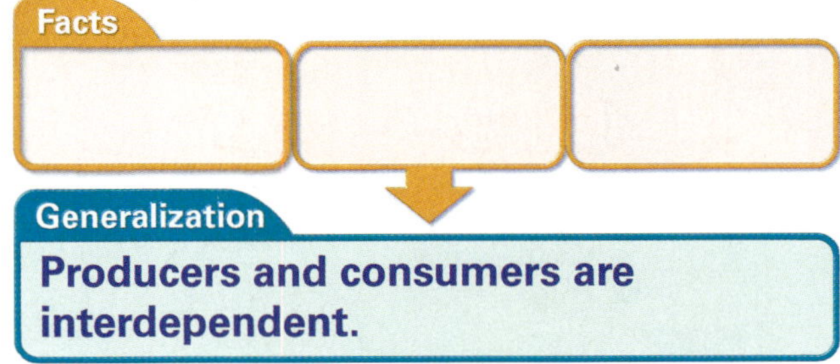

Madame C.J. Walker

"I have built my own factory on my own ground."

— Madame C. J. Walker, 1912

Madame C. J. Walker became one of the first women in the United States to make millions of dollars on her own. She turned her small hair product business, based in Indianapolis, Indiana, into a giant success.

Walker hired and trained many African American women to sell her products. She also donated money to create better opportunities for African Americans. By 1917, she had the largest business owned by an African American in the country. Her generosity and business skills made her a trusted community leader.

Why Character Counts

Why was Madame C. J. Walker trustworthy?

Madame C. J. Walker

Time

1867 Born

1905 Moves to Denver to sell her hair products

1910 Has more than 1,000 employees

1919 Died

Lesson 2

How Business Works

What to Know
What kinds of resources do businesses use?

Vocabulary

capital p. 394
raw material p. 394
human resource p. 395
capital resource p. 395
factory p. 396
manufacture p. 397

Focus Skill **Generalize**

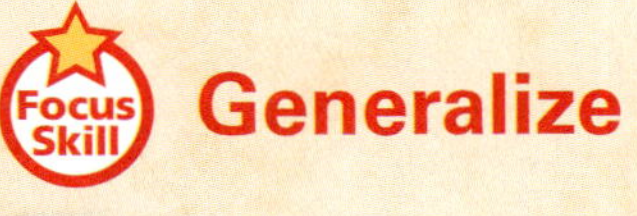

It takes more than just a good idea to start a business. All businesses use **capital**, or money. They also use different resources.

Businesses Start with Resources

Businesses use different resources to make products and provide services. Some businesses begin with a raw material. A **raw material** is a natural resource that can be used to make a product. Some raw materials that businesses use are metals, rock, wood, and water.

Resources Keep a Business Running

One business in Wilmore, Kentucky, uses the natural spring water that bubbles up in parts of central Kentucky. The company bottles the water for people to drink. Then it sells the bottled drinking water to the public.

In addition to natural resources, the business also depends on human resources. **Human resources** are the workers who produce goods and services. Workers at the business collect the water. They clean and bottle it. They also sell and deliver the bottles.

The business uses capital resources, too. **Capital resources** are the tools and buildings a business uses. These include the machines used to make and deliver products.

Reading Check **Generalize**
What three kinds of resources do businesses need?

Natural Resources

Human Resources

Capital Resources

Products, such as bottled water, depend on these three types of resources.

Spring water is found in natural springs all over the United States.

Working with Resources

Many businesses need a factory to make their products. A **factory** is a building in which products are prepared and packaged. A yogurt factory in Minster, Ohio, is the largest yogurt producer in the world.

The yogurt factory depends on many resources to stay in business. It uses milk as a raw material to make the yogurt. It uses human resources to run the factory's machines and other capital resources.

A Yogurt Factory

Illustration The following steps show yogurt making.

1. Fresh milk arrives from farms.
2. The milk is heated.
3. Yogurt cultures are added to the warm milk.
4. Machines put the yogurt into containers.
5. The yogurt is ready to be delivered to grocery stores.

What do the workers do after the milk is delivered?

An Internet cafe provides temporary Internet service for a fee.

The Internet

In the late 1960s, computers at several California universities were connected by wires. This allowed them to "talk" to one another. One of the university students who worked on this project was Vinton Cerf. Along with many others, Cerf helped create what is now known as the Internet.

Ray Tomlinson, a Massachusetts engineer, found a way to use the Internet to send electronic messages. It was his idea to use the *at* symbol (@) in e-mail addresses. He said, "I thought about other symbols, but at [@] didn't appear in any names, so it worked."

E-mail and the Internet have changed the way people work. Both have made it faster and easier to send and receive information.

An early computer

Reading Check **Generalize**
How has technology improved communication?

Electronic Buying and Selling

The Internet is a **communication link**—a kind of technology that lets people share information instantly. Communication links have changed the way people buy and sell products. In the past, people had to meet face to face to buy and sell goods. Now, many businesses sell goods and services online, or on the Internet. Buying and selling in this way is often called **e-commerce**. *Commerce* means "business."

Another communication link that businesses use is the telephone. People place orders over the phone from catalogs. Catalogs are magazines with information about goods and services that can be ordered.

Diagram The flowchart shows how a consumer uses a computer to order a book. Which steps in the process use computers?

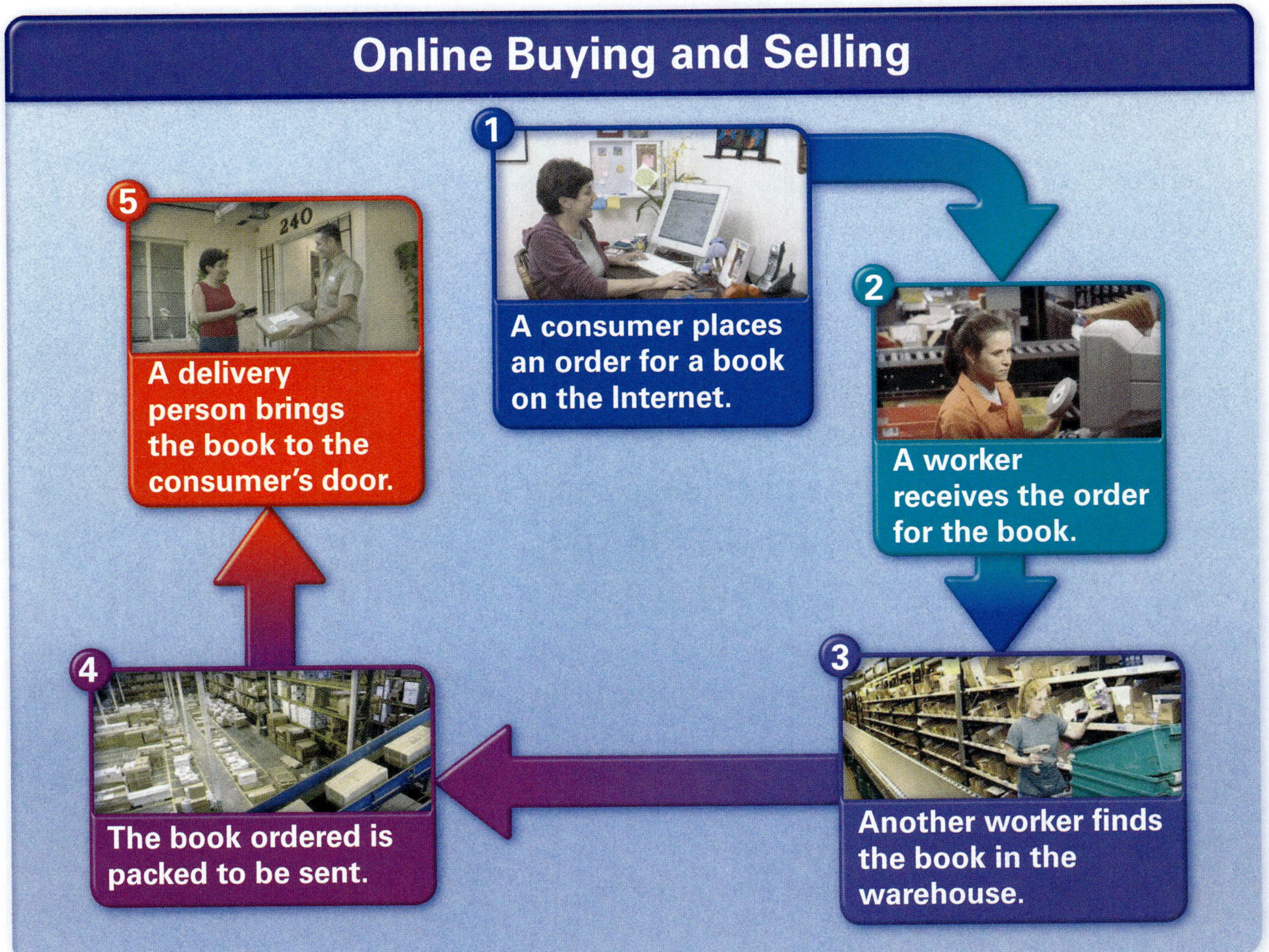

Internet Advertising

Many businesses create Internet websites with advertisements about their goods and services. **Advertisements** are notices made to get people to buy something. Consumers around the world see these ads. They can order what they want from any computer that is connected to the Internet.

A consumer orders products over the Internet.

Reading Check **Generalize**
How have communication links changed businesses?

Summary Technology has changed the way people do business. New inventions provide new ways to communicate. They also give us new ways to buy and sell products.

Review

1. **What to Know** How has new technology changed businesses?
2. **Vocabulary** Use the term **communication link** in a sentence.
3. **Economics** Why might a business decide to sell goods on the Internet?
4. **Critical Thinking** **Make It Relevant** What technology do you use to communicate?
5. **Write an E-mail** Write an e-mail to a local business owner. Ask how changes in technology have affected his or her business.
6. Focus Skill **Generalize** On a separate sheet of paper, copy and complete the graphic organizer below.

Tell Fact from Opinion

Why It Matters To make good decisions, you need to know when a message tells you the facts.

Learn

Many advertisements include both facts and opinions. A fact is a true statement. It can be proved. An **opinion** is a person's belief. Opinions may be supported by facts, but they cannot be proved.

Practice

Study the advertisement on the next page. Read each message, and ask yourself *Can this statement be proved?* Then answer these questions.

1. Which statements are facts?
2. Which statements are opinions?
3. Why might people buy this product?

Apply

Make It Relevant Create an advertisement for a product you enjoy. Share your ad with the class. Invite classmates to point out the facts and opinions.

Example of an Advertisement

Critical Thinking Skills

Primary Sources

Computers, Past and Present

Background In 1974, the first personal computer was invented in California. Computers are machines that store information. People also use computers to solve problems, communicate, and play games. Computer technology has been improved many times.

Document-Based Questions Study these primary sources, and answer the questions.

The First Personal Computer

This computer was the first personal computer made for the public.

DBQ ❶ How was this computer unlike computers used today?

People used a panel of switches to enter commands.

1980s Computer

This computer was a popular home computer in the 1980s. Games helped make this computer a hit.

DBQ ❷ Why do you think more of this computer were sold than the first personal computer?

Computer with Modem

This computer was one of the first personal computers to include a modem, or a part that reads information shared through the Internet.

This computer used icons, or pictures, that could be clicked with a mouse.

DBQ ③ Why do you think the use of a computer mouse became so popular?

Present-Day Computer

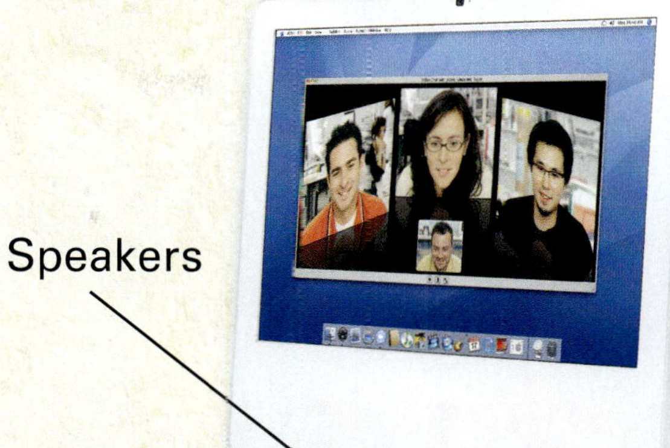

Today's computers can store more information and work faster than computers in the past.

DBQ ④ What features does this computer have that the computers on page 412 do not have?

WRITE ABOUT IT

Write a paragraph about how computers have changed.

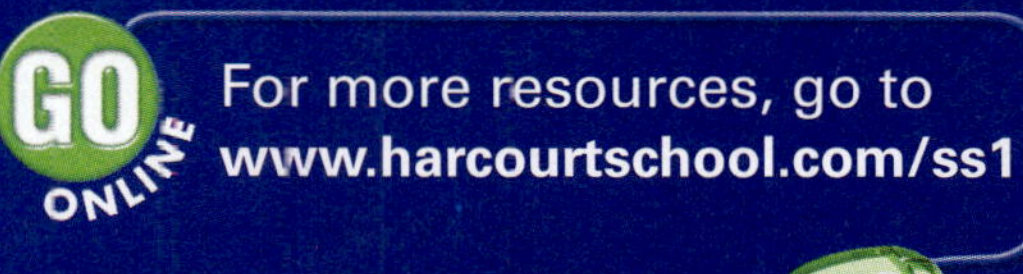

For more resources, go to www.harcourtschool.com/ss1

Chapter 11 Review

Visual Summary

Producers and consumers depend on one another.

Summarize the Chapter

Generalize Complete the graphic organizer to make a generalization about what businesses need.

Facts

People depend on one another.	Businesses use different resources.	People and countries trade with one another.

Generalization

Vocabulary

Identify the term from the word bank that correctly completes each sentence.

1. You are a ________ when you buy a product or a service.
2. The United States ________ products to other countries.
3. An ________ gets people to buy something.
4. A person who starts and runs a business is an ________.
5. All businesses need ________, or money.

Word Bank

entrepreneur p. 389
consumer p. 390
capital p. 394
exports p. 402
advertisement p. 409

People trade goods and services with people in other places.

New technology helps businesses find new customers.

Facts and Main Ideas

Answer these questions.

6. Why do people need an income?
7. How do people transport goods from one place to another?
8. How have e-mail and the Internet changed the way people work?

Write the letter of the best choice.

9. Which is an example of a raw material?
   - **A** capital
   - **B** workers
   - **C** equipment
   - **D** water
10. What was made possible by improvements in transportation?
   - **A** international trade
   - **B** entrepreneurs
   - **C** manufacturing
   - **D** advertisements

Critical Thinking

11. **Make It Relevant** What are some communication links in your house?
12. Why is it better for some businesses to provide only one kind of product or service?

Read a Land Use and Products Map Use the land use and products map on page 399 to answer the question.

13. What are some crops grown in Minnesota?

writing

Write a Business Plan Suppose you are an entrepreneur. Describe what you need to start and run your own business.

Write an E-mail Write an e-mail to a business. Give its owners your opinion about how they can improve their product or service.

ORGANIZE INFORMATION

A graphic organizer can help you make sense of the facts you read.

- **Webs, charts, and tables can show main ideas and details.**
- **Use graphic organizers to classify and categorize information.**

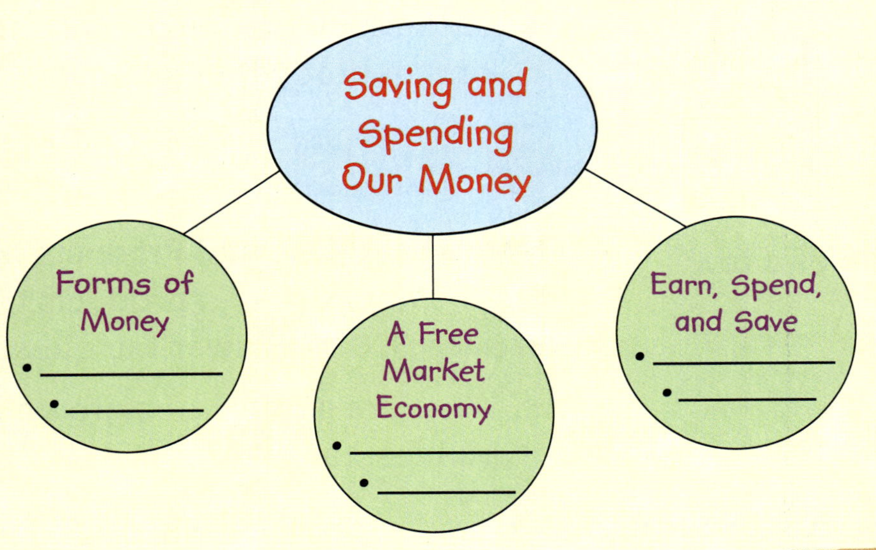

PREVIEW VOCABULARY

savings p. 429

deposit p. 429

budget p. 430

People trade goods and services with people in other places.

New technology helps businesses find new customers.

Facts and Main Ideas

Answer these questions.

6. Why do people need an income?
7. How do people transport goods from one place to another?
8. How have e-mail and the Internet changed the way people work?

Write the letter of the best choice.

9. Which is an example of a raw material?
   A capital
   B workers
   C equipment
   D water
10. What was made possible by improvements in transportation?
   A international trade
   B entrepreneurs
   C manufacturing
   D advertisements

Critical Thinking

11. **Make It Relevant** What are some communication links in your house?
12. Why is it better for some businesses to provide only one kind of product or service?

Skills

Read a Land Use and Products Map
Use the land use and products map on page 399 to answer the question.

13. What are some crops grown in Minnesota?

writing

Write a Business Plan Suppose you are an entrepreneur. Describe what you need to start and run your own business.

Write an E-mail Write an e-mail to a business. Give its owners your opinion about how they can improve their product or service.

ORGANIZE INFORMATION

A graphic organizer can help you make sense of the facts you read.

- **Webs, charts, and tables can show main ideas and details.**
- **Use graphic organizers to classify and categorize information.**

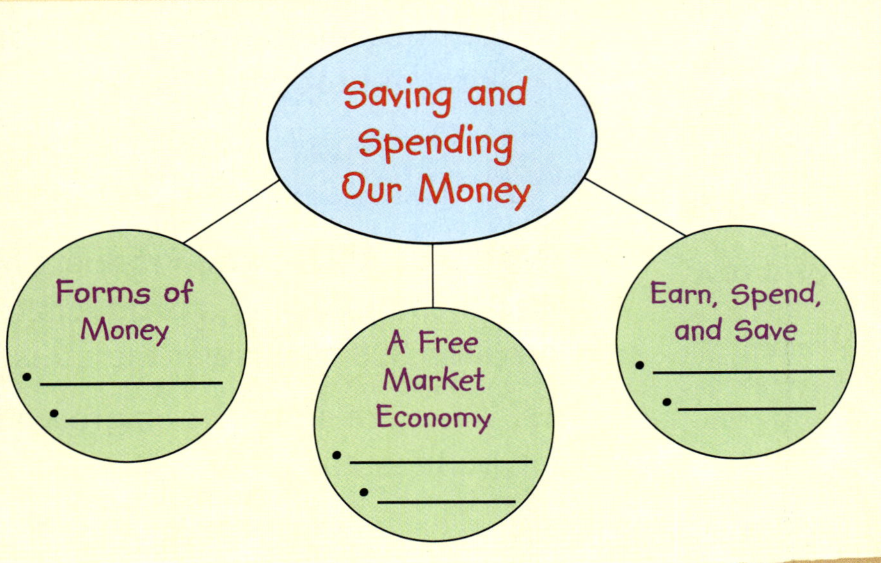

PREVIEW VOCABULARY

savings p. 429

deposit p. 429

budget p. 430

CHAPTER 12

Saving and Spending Our Money

New $100 bills are made at the Bureau of Engraving and Printing in Washington, D.C.

Lesson 1

Forms of Money

What to Know
Why do people use money?

Vocabulary

barter p. 418

mint p. 421

Generalize

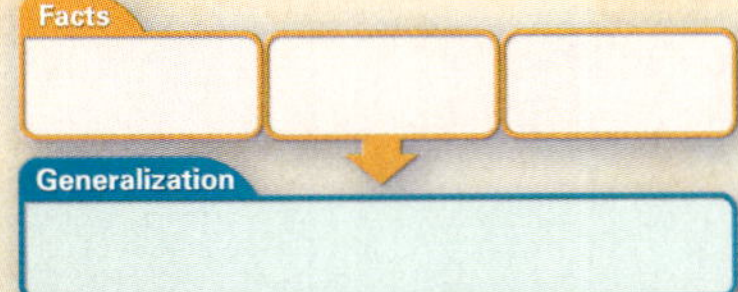

People use money to buy what they want. Different kinds of money are traded for goods and services.

Trading and Bartering

To get goods or services, people need to trade. In the past, people often traded by bartering. To **barter** is to trade without using money. A farmer might have bartered eggs for cloth. Bartering is not always possible. No one may want to trade for your product or service.

Some things are still bartered for, such as trading cards.

Using Money to Trade

Today, people often trade money for goods and services. Money makes trade easier. Coins and bills are small and light. They can be carried easily.

Checks can also be traded for goods and services. The buyer writes on a check the amount to be paid. The bank takes the money from the person's account and gives it to the seller.

Many consumers also use credit cards. Credit cards let people buy goods and services now and pay for them later. Information from their credit card is sent by computers to banks.

Reading Check **Generalize**
How does money make trade easier?

Most goods can be paid for with money.

People usually write checks to make large payments.

This man is buying gas with his credit card.

Primary Sources

Money Through Time

Background People have been using money for thousands of years. But money was not always like the coins and paper bills that most people use today.

Cowrie shells were once used as money in India, Thailand, and countries in Africa.

Wampum belts were used as money by Native Americans.

Today, the euro is the money of countries in the European Union.

Turkish coins were the first coins ever to be used.

DBQ Document-Based Question
How is the euro different from cowrie shells?

United States Money

The United States Mint began making coins in Philadelphia in 1792. A **mint** is a place where coins are made. Metal strips are put into machines that punch out coin shapes. Designs are stamped on both sides of the new coins. The United States Bureau of Engraving and Printing in Washington, D.C., and Fort Worth, Texas, makes our paper money.

Reading Check **Main Idea and Details**
Where are United States coins made?

Katherine Ortega was once United States treasurer. Each dollar has the signature of the treasurer.

Summary People trade money for goods and services. Money has many different forms and has changed over time.

Review

1. **What to Know** Why do people use money?
2. **Vocabulary** Use the term **barter** in a sentence.
3. **History** When were the first coins made in the United States?
4. **Critical Thinking** **Make It Relevant** What goods and services could you use to barter?
5. **Make a Coin Display** Draw a picture of several coins. Label each with its value.
6. Focus Skill **Generalize** On a separate sheet of paper, copy and complete the graphic organizer below.

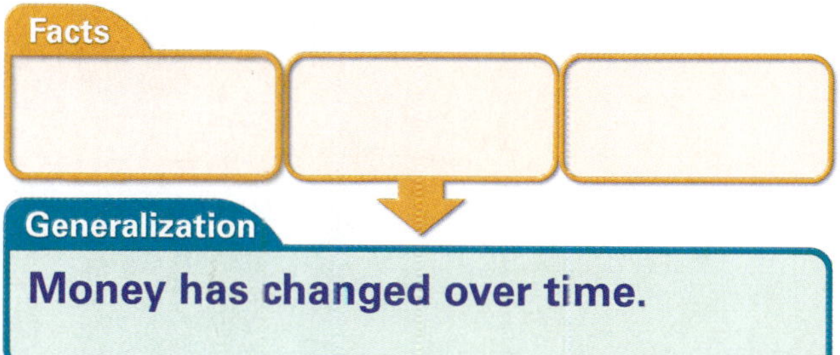

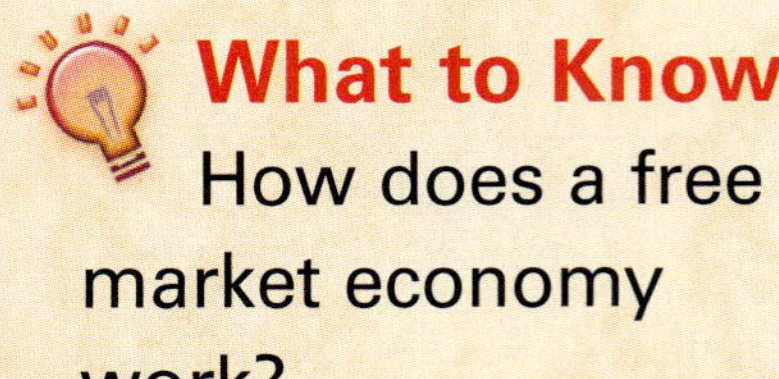

Free Market Economy

What to Know
How does a free market economy work?

Vocabulary
profit p. 422
free market p. 422
competition p. 423
demand p. 424
supply p. 424
scarcity p. 425

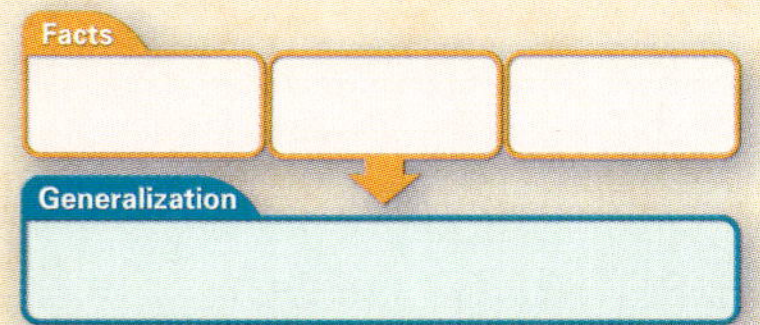

People in the United States have the freedom to start a business. When people start businesses, they hope to make a profit. A **profit** is the money left over after all the costs of running a business have been paid.

A Free Market Economy

The United States has a free market economy. In a **free market** economy, people can make and sell any product or service allowed by law. The government does not tell businesses what goods to make or services to provide.

The Mall of America in Minneapolis, Minnesota

Children in History

Kid Blink, A Famous Newsie

In the 1800s, New York City had many different newspapers. Young people sold the newspapers for a living. These "newsies" bought the papers at a low cost and sold them for more to make a profit.

When the newspaper companies raised their prices, the newsies could not make enough money. One boy, Kid Blink, tried to do something about the problem. He and other newsies refused to sell any newspapers. After two weeks, the newspaper companies agreed to lower their price. The newsies had won!

Make It Relevant **What things do you do to earn money?**

Competition in a Free Market

To make a profit, business owners must offer goods and services that people want to buy. Businesses are often in competition with one another. **Competition** is the contest among businesses to sell the most goods or services. For example, bookstore owners compete with each other. Each one tries to sell the most books.

Competition affects the prices of goods and services. Prices must be low enough to draw consumers from other businesses that sell the same good or service. However, prices must be high enough for the business to make a profit.

Bookstores and other businesses compete with one another to sell the most goods or services.

Reading Check **Generalize**
How does competition affect prices?

Fast Fact

The hula hoop came onto store shelves in 1958. Demand for the new toy was so high, the business that made it sold more than 100 million hoops in two years.

Supply and Demand

What consumers want helps business owners decide what to make or sell. Consumers' wants create a **demand** for, or willingness to buy, goods and services. The products and services that businesses provide are the **supply**.

Sometimes there is a high demand for a product or service. Businesses offer a greater supply of it to meet the demand. For example, if a community has many pets, there will be a demand for pet care products and services. The demand for these goods and services will affect their price.

Table This table shows how supply, demand, and price can change. How does high supply affect prices?

Supply and Demand Affects Prices

Consumers and Producers	Supply and Demand	Usual Prices
Consumers want more	High demand	Higher prices
Consumers want less	Low demand	Lower prices
Businesses produce more	High supply	Lower prices
Businesses produce less	Low supply	Higher prices

The demand for dog-walking services keeps this man busy.

Scarcity of Products

Prices are also affected by the scarcity (SKAIR•suh•tee) of a product. **Scarcity** means that the supply of a product is not enough to meet the demand for it. Suppose that a drought, or a time of dryness, destroys all of the wheat crops. Wheat then becomes scarce, and its price rises.

Reading Check **Generalize**

How do consumers affect the prices of goods and services?

Cotton plants during a drought in North Carolina

Summary The United States has a free market economy. Competition among businesses often helps keep their prices low. Supply and demand affect the prices of goods. Scarcity also affects prices.

Review

1. **What to Know** How does a free market economy work?
2. **Vocabulary** Explain how **scarcity** affects price.
3. **Your Community** How do businesses in your community compete to meet the needs of community members?
4. **Critical Thinking Make It Relevant** What is a product you would like to have that is scarce?
5. **Write a Paragraph** Choose a local business. Write a paragraph that explains how consumers affect what it sells.
6. **Generalize** On a separate sheet of paper, copy and complete the graphic organizer below.

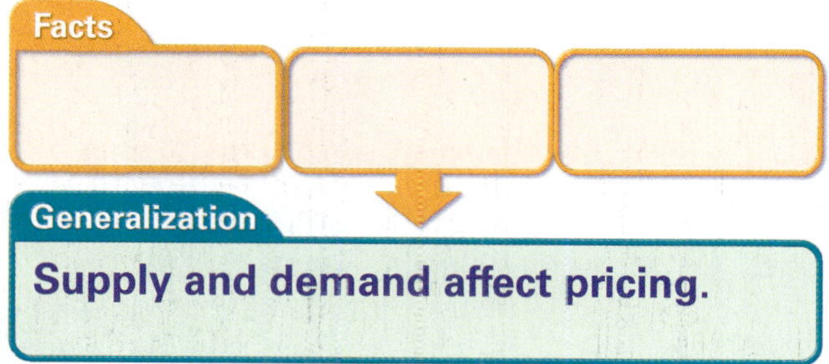

Lesson 3

Earn, Spend, and Save

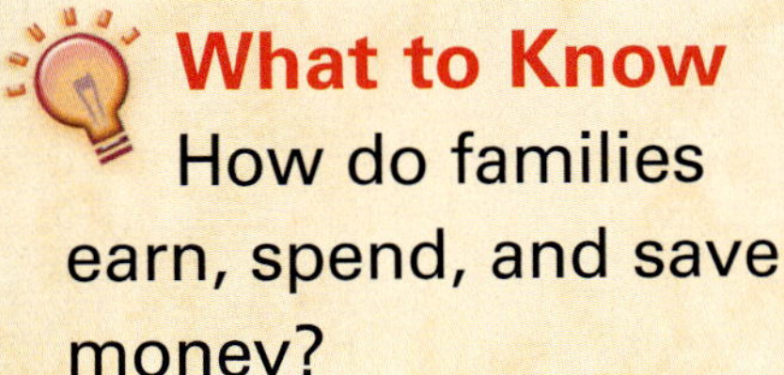

What to Know
How do families earn, spend, and save money?

Vocabulary

savings p. 429
deposit p. 429
interest p. 429
invest p. 429
budget p. 430

Generalize

Facts

Generalization

People must make choices about how they earn, spend, and save money. The choices they make can have big effects. Families make economic decisions every day.

A Family Earns Income

Each member of the Wright family earns an income. The youngest member, James, does yard work. He enjoys earning his own money. He is also glad to help people in his community.

Watering flowers is one of the ways James can earn money.

Bonnie takes photos of children for her photography business.

James's mother, Bonnie, owns a photography business. She takes pictures of people at special events, such as weddings. People pay money for her service. That money is her income.

James's father, Ed, worked at a car parts factory for more than 10 years. He made sure each part was made correctly. When the factory closed, he decided to learn a new skill. He took classes at a local college. He studied how to manage a factory. When he finished, he got a job as a manager in a steel factory. He now earns a higher income.

Ed studies for a test.

Reading Check **Generalize**

How do the members of the Wright family earn income?

The Wrights use part of their income to buy food for their family.

A Family Spends and Saves

The Wrights make decisions about money as a family. They make choices about how to spend and save their income.

Spending Money

Like many families, the Wrights use their income to pay for things they use every day. Much of their income is spent to buy food and to pay for their house. They also buy clothing.

The Wrights buy other things with the money they have left. They spend money on karate lessons for James. James often uses his own money to buy movie tickets and music CDs.

The Wrights do not spend all their money on themselves. They share some with other people. The Wrights give some money to groups that help people in their community and around the world. They also choose to save some of their money.

The Wright family spends money on karate lessons for James.

Saving Money

The money the Wrights save is called their **savings**. They **deposit**, or put, their savings into a bank.

A savings account in a bank earns interest. **Interest** is the money a bank pays people for keeping their money there. It is also the money a person pays to borrow money.

Banks loan to other people some of the money deposited in savings accounts. Those people often borrow that money to start businesses or to buy houses. They pay interest to the bank until all the money is paid back.

The Wrights also invest some of their money. To **invest** is to buy something that will grow in value. One kind of investment involves buying a small part of another person's business. The Wrights hope to make more money when the businesses grow.

Reading Check **Generalize**
How do the Wrights save money?

A bank keeps its customers' money in a vault, a room-sized safe with thick, steel walls.

Bonnie Wright deposits at the bank some of the money she earns.

A Family Makes a Budget

In a note book, the Wright family keeps a budget.

The Wright family keeps a budget. A **budget** is a plan for spending and saving money.

To make a budget, the Wrights first list the ways they earn money. They write down each family member's job. Next to each job, they write the income from it. This part of the budget tells them how much money they have to spend or save.

The Wrights then list the ways they spend money. They organize their list into five groups—shelter, food and clothing, fun, giving, and savings. They add up the amounts of money they spend for different things. Then they write the total for each group.

The Wrights' family budget helps them see how they spend their money. It also helps them make plans to reach economic goals.

The Wright family works on their budget.

Reaching Economic Goals

The Wrights want to take a camping trip. They will need to buy a tent and other supplies before they go. Their budget shows them how much money they can save each week. This lets them see when they will have enough for the camping supplies. If the Wrights follow their budget, they will reach their goal.

Reading Check **Main Idea and Details**
How can a budget help people save money?

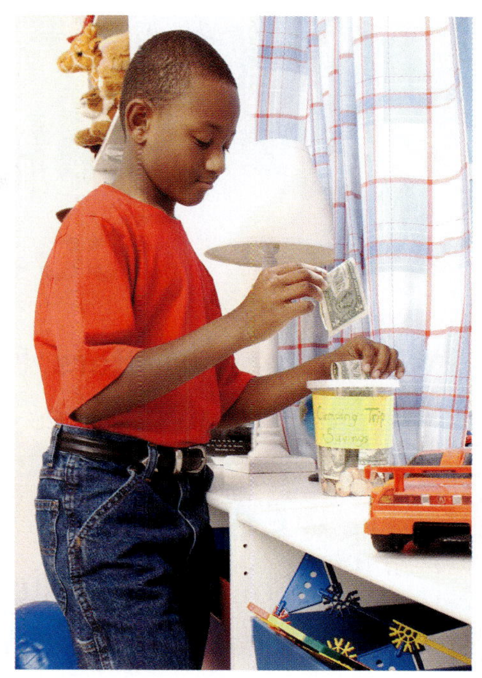

James saves money to buy souvenirs on the family's camping trip.

Summary Families earn, spend, and save money. They use their income to pay for goods and services. Making a budget helps them spend and save wisely.

Review

1. **What to Know** How do families earn, spend, and save money?
2. **Vocabulary** Use the terms **savings** and **interest** in a sentence.
3. **Economics** Why might someone choose to put money in a bank?
4. **Critical Thinking** **Make It Relevant** What is something you want to save money to buy?
5. **Make a Budget** Make a budget that will help you reach an economic goal. Note how long you will need to save to reach your goal.
6. **Generalize** On a separate sheet of paper, copy and complete the graphic organizer below.

Make an Economic Choice

Why It Matters Knowing how to make good economic choices can help you spend money wisely.

Learn

Follow these steps the next time you need to make an economic choice.

Step 1 Consider the **trade-off**. When you choose to buy one product or service, you give up the chance to buy a different one.

Step 2 Consider the **opportunity cost**. This is what you give up to get what you want.

Tent A

Tent B

Practice

The Wrights have $120 in their budget to buy camping supplies. Tent A is $100. It is roomy and has two windows. Tent B is $80. It has less space and only one window.

1. What is the trade-off if the Wrights buy Tent A?
2. What is the trade-off if the Wrights buy Tent B?
3. What is the opportunity cost for each tent?
4. Which tent do you think they should buy? Why?

Apply

Make It Relevant Think about a product or service you bought recently. What was the trade-off? What was the opportunity cost? Do you think you made a good economic decision? Explain.

What Should You Do with Your Money?

Most people agree that it is important to make good decisions about money. Some people think it is best to save money. Others believe it is also important to share money with people who have less.

Lynnette Khalfani

Author Lynnette Khalfani has written several books about budgeting and saving money. She coaches people on how to manage their money.

"... Feel free to spend money on the things you need.... Just live within your means."

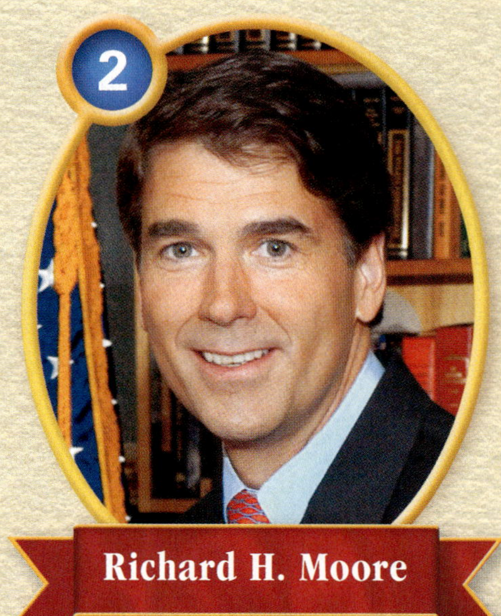

Richard H. Moore

Richard H. Moore is the state treasurer of North Carolina. He believes North Carolina should save money for the future.

"The state should invest in projects that will make our communities stronger like schools and roads."

3

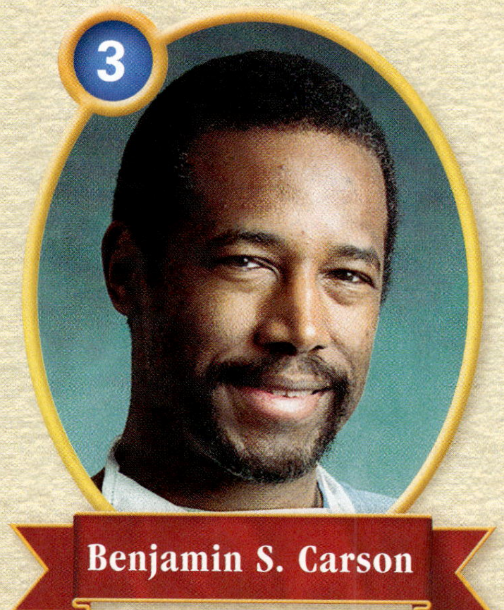

Benjamin S. Carson

Benjamin S. Carson is one of the country's leading brain doctors. Even though his family was poor, Carson was encouraged by his mother to be successful by studying hard. Dr. Carson often takes the time to talk to young people about giving.

"Happiness doesn't result from what we get, but from what we give."

4

Andrew Carnegie

Andrew Carnegie believed people with riches, like himself, should share their money. He gave more than $300 million to help make the world a better place.

"I resolved to stop accumulating [gathering] and begin the infinitely [endlessly] more serious and difficult task of wise distribution [giving]."

It's Your Turn

Compare Points of View Summarize each point of view. Then answer these questions.

1. Who talks about spending money on needs?
2. How does Richard H. Moore feel about saving and investing money?
3. How is Benjamin S. Carson's view like that held by Andrew Carnegie?

Make It Relevant Which ideas about spending, saving, or sharing do you agree with most? Give your reasons.

Lesson 4

World Businesses

What to Know How do businesses around the world make money?

Vocabulary

cooperative p. 438

Focus Skill Generalize

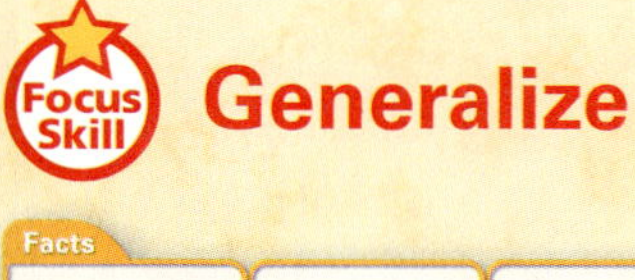

Families around the world depend on businesses. As in the United States, businesses in other countries provide goods, services, and jobs. Some sell goods to other countries. Others sell goods mainly to local markets.

A Business District

In Japan, the city of Tokyo is the main business center. Many Japanese businesses have their main office, or headquarters, in Tokyo. Companies with headquarters in other countries also keep offices in Tokyo.

Businesses Depend on One Another

As in most cities, Tokyo's businesses work together. Workers use technology to communicate with one another by telephone, fax, and e-mail.

Many businesses in Tokyo make goods that they export to other countries. Some high-tech businesses make computers, flat-panel television screens, and cell phones. They depend on other businesses for some of the parts they use. They also depend on transportation companies to ship the finished goods. They depend on stores to sell their products, too.

Reading Check **Generalize**
How do Tokyo's businesses depend on other businesses?

These business people in Tokyo use cell phones to communicate.

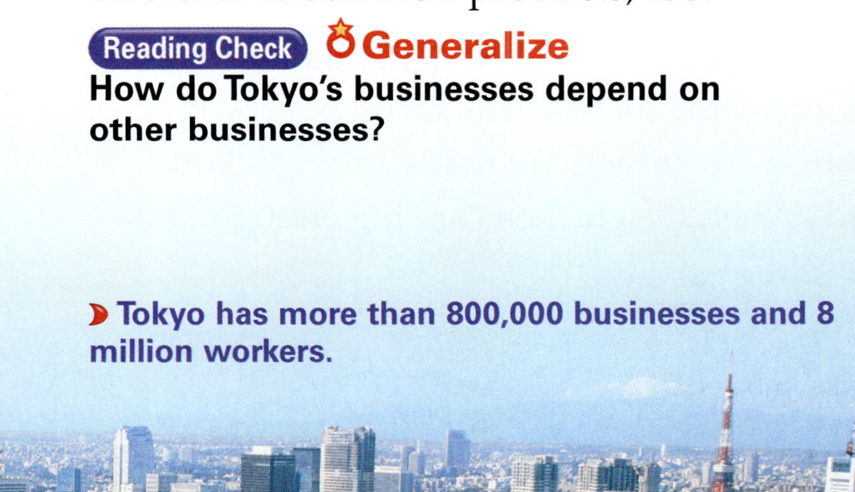

Tokyo has more than 800,000 businesses and 8 million workers.

A Community Cooperative

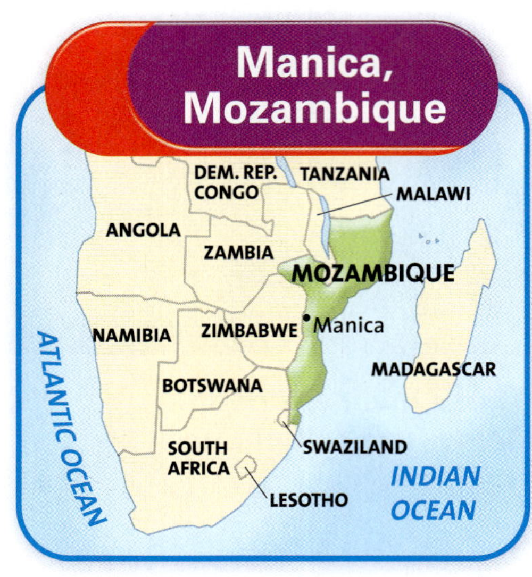

Manica (mah•NEE•kah) is a rural community in eastern Mozambique (moh•zahm•BEEK). The climate there is warm. It is just right for farming and raising animals. Some people in Manica raise chickens.

Some families in Manica are part of a farming cooperative. A **cooperative** is a group of workers who own a business together. Each worker has a vote when the group makes decisions about the business.

A farming cooperative depends on natural resources to survive. The farmers grow sunflowers, which are made into chicken feed. When the chickens are big enough, they are sold.

Farmers raise chickens in Manica.

Cooperatives Help the Community

The money earned from selling the chickens helps the cooperative's economy. Some of the money pays for the cost of the business. The rest of the money pays for things that help the community.

Reading Check **Main Idea and Details**
How do cooperatives help their communities?

These farmers grow sunflowers, corn, and rice and raise chickens.

Summary Businesses around the world make money in different ways. Many companies in Tokyo sell their goods around the world. A cooperative in Mozambique sells its product to local markets.

Review

1. **What to Know** How do businesses around the world make money?
2. **Vocabulary** What clues can you use to remember the meaning of **cooperative**?
3. **Your Community** Are there any businesses in your community like the ones from this lesson? If so, tell how they are the same.
4. **Critical Thinking** In what ways do businesses in Tokyo use technology?
5. **Make a Diagram** Make a Venn diagram to compare and contrast the ways the businesses in this lesson make their money.
6. Focus Skill **Generalize** On a separate sheet of paper, copy and complete the graphic organizer below.

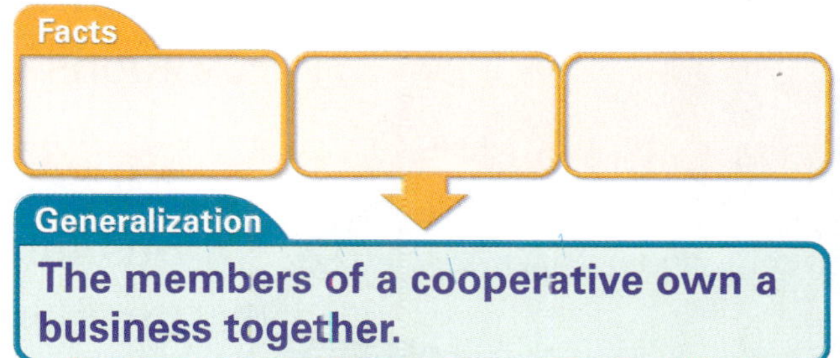

Explore Your Community's Economy

In this unit, you studied the economies of communities around the world. You can also explore your own community's economy. These steps explain how to answer the following question.

What businesses make up my community's economy?

STEP 1 Use your community's resources, such as the newspaper and the Internet, to find what kinds of businesses are in your town.

STEP 2 Make a list of businesses in your community.

STEP 3 Categorize the types of businesses by whether they produce goods or provide services.

STEP 4 Then find out more about a business that interests you. Share it with the class.

Use Your Community's Resources

Make an Advertisement

Make an advertisement about a good or service provided in your community. Your advertisement should name the good or service and include its cost. Illustrate your advertisement, and display it together with your classmates' advertisements.

Visual Summary

People use money to buy goods and services.

Summarize the Chapter

Generalize Complete the graphic organizer to add facts for the generalization about how people spend and save money.

Facts		

Generalization

People spend and save the money they earn.

Write a paragraph about how people make and spend money. Use each of these vocabulary terms in your paragraph. Show that you understand the meaning of each term.

1. **savings**, p. 429
2. **deposit**, p. 429
3. **interest**, p. 429
4. **invest**, p. 429
5. **budget**, p. 430

Competition and supply and demand affect prices in a free market economy.

Families make choices about how to earn, spend, and save money.

Facts and Main Ideas

Answer these questions.

6. Why do people use credit cards?
7. What do businesses do if there is a high demand for a good or service?
8. Why do some people invest in businesses?

Write the letter of the best choice.

9. Which of the following is used by banks to take money from a person's account to pay the seller?
   A bills
   B coins
   C wampum beads
   D checks
10. What do businesses in Tokyo, Japan, depend on stores to do?
   A provide parts
   B ship goods
   C sell their product
   D produce computers

Critical Thinking

11. **Make It Relevant** How might your life be different if you did not live in a free market economy?
12. **Make It Relevant** What might you do if a product you used became scarce?

Skills

Make an Economic Choice
Use the information on pages 432 and 433 to answer the question.

13. How much can the Wrights spend on other camping supplies if they buy Tent B?

writing

Write an Article Interview an adult about his or her economic goals. In an article, tell how to reach those goals.

Write a Paragraph Write a paragraph to explain how competition affects producers and consumers in a free market economy.

Woof Wash

VOCABULARY

Be an entrepreneur, and start a dog-washing business! Play this game with a partner. Be the first to go from START to FINISH!

START

Make a budget. Take an extra turn.

Borrow $20 from Dad for shampoo and brushes. Lose a turn.

There's a demand for your service. Go ahead 2 spaces.

You need more human resources. Hire your little brother to help. Go back 2 spaces.

Your monthly profit is $150! Take an extra turn.

Deposit your profit in a savings account. Go to FINISH.

FINISH

You repay Dad his $20. Go back 1 space.

Barter for your older sister's nail polish. Take an extra turn.

It's slow work to polish a poodle's nails. Lose a turn.

You need an advertisement for your business. Create a website. Go ahead 1 space.

Let customers make reservations on your website. Go ahead 2 spaces.

E-commerce pays off! You get 5 new customers. Take 2 extra turns.

Take a 2-day vacation. Lose a turn.

Demand for your service is up. Go ahead 2 spaces.

Online Adventures

GO ONLINE

Do you think you have learned enough to run a business? In this online game, you and Eco will need to start two successful businesses. In one, you will grow your own vegetable garden on a farm. In the other, you will make and sell fresh-squeezed juice in the city. Play now at **www.harcourtschool.com/ss1**

Review and Test Prep 

The Big Idea

Economics People depend on one another to produce, buy, and sell goods and services. Good decision-making helps the economy of a family or a community.

Reading Comprehension and Vocabulary

Working in Communities

Businesses and consumers are interdependent. People earn wages from their work. Then they spend their money on goods and services. Businesses could not make a profit without consumers. Producers also depend on resources. Competition, supply and demand, and scarcity affect prices set by businesses.

People use their income in many ways. They trade money for goods and services. People also put money into savings. Some invest their money in businesses or give money to help others.

Read the summary above. Then answer the questions that follow.

1. Why are businesses and consumers interdependent?
   A They like to make profits.
   B Both are human resources.
   C They depend on one another.
   D They import products.

2. What do businesses need to make a profit?
   A scarcity of products
   B savings
   C competition
   D consumers

3. Which of the following affects prices in a free market economy?
   A how money is earned
   B amount of profits
   C income
   D competition

4. What does income mean?
   A something bartered
   B money earned
   C plan for spending
   D goods or services

Facts and Main Ideas

Answer these questions.

5. How do businesses depend on natural, human, and capital resources?
6. When is bartering not possible?
7. What can people make and sell in a free market economy?

Write the letter of the best choice.

8. What are producers always trying to do?
   - **A** start their own business
   - **B** make better products
   - **C** buy products
   - **D** help each other
9. For which export is China well known?
   - **A** computers
   - **B** automobiles
   - **C** clothing
   - **D** tea
10. What was used for money in ancient times?
    - **A** trading cards
    - **B** bills
    - **C** beads and shells
    - **D** checks

Critical Thinking

11. **Make It Relevant** Which businesses in your community compete with one another?
12. How might our economy be different if there were no banks?

Read a Land Use and Products Map

Use the map below to answer the following questions.

13. What color shows forest areas in New Jersey?
14. What symbol stands for New Jersey's dairy products?

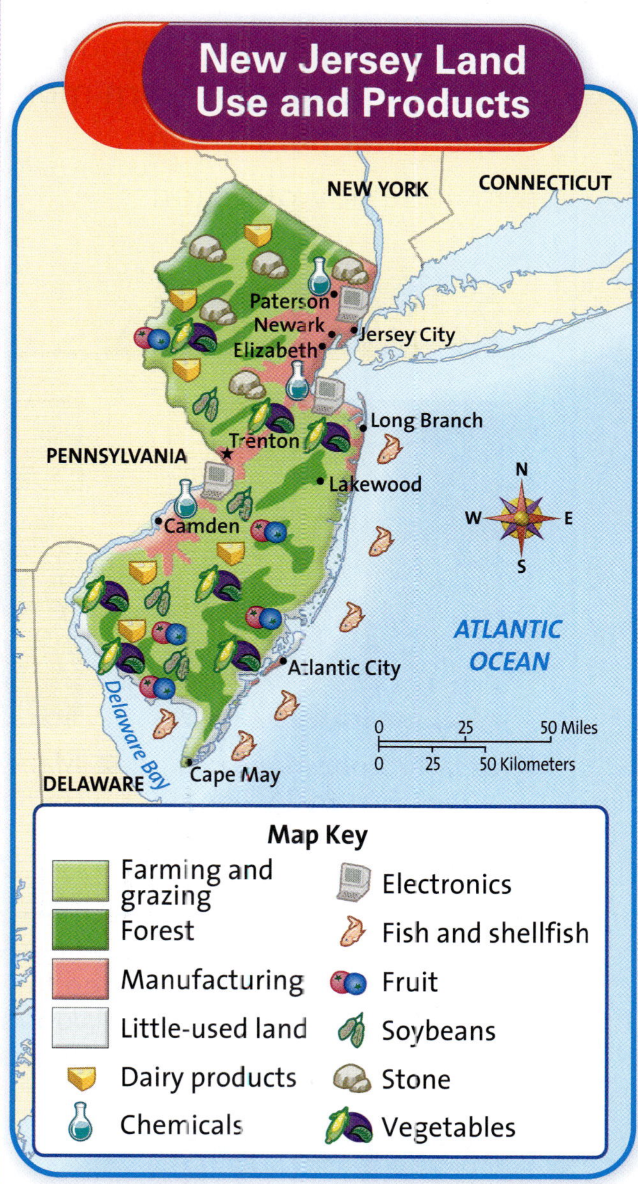

Unit 6

Activities

Show What You Know

Unit Writing Activity

Write a Letter Write a letter to someone who has a job you might like to have someday.

- Introduce yourself. Explain that you are writing to learn more about the person's job.
- Include any questions.

Unit Project

Community Newspaper Make a newspaper for your community.

- Research facts about the local economy to gather topic ideas.
- Write and illustrate the articles.
- Use articles and illustrations to complete the newspaper.

Read More

- *Smart About Money: A Rich History* by Jon Anderson. Grosset & Dunlap.

- *Market!* by Ted Lewin. HarperCollins.

- *Hard Hat Area* by Susan L. Roth. Bloomsbury USA Children's Books.

GO ONLINE For more resources, go to **www.harcourtschool.com/ss1**

For Your Reference

For Your Reference

The World: Political

Abbreviations

DEM. REP. CONGO	DEMOCRATIC REPUBLIC OF THE CONGO
EQU. GUINEA	EQUATORIAL GUINEA
NETH.	NETHERLANDS
N.Z.	NEW ZEALAND
REP. CONGO	REPUBLIC OF THE CONGO
U.A.E.	UNITED ARAB EMIRATES
U.K.	UNITED KINGDOM
U.S.	UNITED STATES

The World: Physical

ARCTIC OCEAN
PACIFIC OCEAN
INDIAN OCEAN
ATLANTIC OCEAN
EUROPE
ASIA
AFRICA
AUSTRALIA
ANTARCTICA
SIBERIA
SAHARA
SAHEL
Greenland
Iceland
Svalbard
Barents Sea
Novaya Zemlya
Severnaya Zemlya
New Siberian Islands
Arctic Circle
Lena River
Yenisey River
Ob River
URAL MTS.
Volga R.
Kamchatka Peninsula
Sea of Okhotsk
Lake Baikal
Amur R.
Kuril Is.
Hokkaido
Honshu
Shikoku
Kyushu
Sea of Japan (East Sea)
East China Sea
Taiwan
North Sea
Baltic Sea
British Isles
North European Plain
Danube R.
ALPS
Mont Blanc 15,771 ft. (4,807 m)
Pyrenees
Iberian Peninsula
Balkan Peninsula
Black Sea
Caucasus Mts.
Mt. Elbrus 18,510 ft. (5,642 m)
Caspian Sea
Aral Sea
Irtysh River
TIAN SHAN
GOBI (DESERT)
HINDU KUSH
K2 (Godwin Austen) 28,250 ft. (8,611 m)
Plateau of Tibet
Huang He
HIMALAYAS
Mt. Everest 29,035 ft. (8,850 m)
Chang Jiang
Asia Minor
Tigris R.
Zagros Mts.
Euphrates R.
Persian Gulf
Mediterranean Sea
Madeira Islands
Canary Islands
Atlas Mts.
Nile R.
Red Sea
Arabian Peninsula
Indus R.
Thar Desert
Ganges R.
Deccan Plateau
Arabian Sea
Bay of Bengal
Hainan
South China Sea
Philippine Islands
Micronesia
Sri Lanka
Maldives
Malay Peninsula
Sumatra
Borneo
Celebes
Java
New Guinea
Melanesia
Fiji
Cape Verde Islands
Lake Chad
Niger River
Ethiopian Highlands
Congo River
CONGO BASIN
Mt. Kenya 17,058 ft. (5,199 m)
Lake Victoria
Mt. Kilimanjaro 19,340 ft. (5,895 m)
Seychelles
Lake Tanganyika
Lake Malawi
Madagascar
Kalahari Desert
Cape of Good Hope
Cape Agulhas
GREAT VICTORIA DESERT
GREAT DIVIDING RANGE
Darling R.
Murray R.
Mt. Kosciusko 7,310 ft. (2,228 m)
Tasmania
North Island
South Island
Ross Sea
0 1,000 2,000 Miles
0 1,000 2,000 Kilometers
Scale accurate at equator
Winkel Projection
N
S
E
W
Southern Polar Region
South Shetland Islands
South Georgia
Bellingshausen Sea
Antarctic Peninsula
Alexander I.
ELLSWORTH LAND
Weddell Sea
SOUTHERN OCEAN (ATLANTIC)
MARIE BYRD LAND
Vinson Massif 16,066 ft. (4,897 m)
Ronne Ice Shelf
Ross Sea
Ross Ice Shelf
TRANSANTARCTIC MOUNTAINS
POLAR PLATEAU
SOUTH POLE
QUEEN MAUD LAND
SOUTHERN OCEAN (PACIFIC)
ANTARCTICA
WILKES LAND
ENDERBY LAND
Antarctic Circle
SOUTH MAGNETIC POLE
0 400 800 Miles
0 400 800 Kilometers
Azimuthal Equidistant Projection

Western Hemisphere: Political

Western Hemisphere: Physical
ARCTIC OCEAN
NORTH MAGNETIC POLE
Queen Elizabeth Islands
Ellesmere Island
Melville Island
Viscount Melville Sound
Devon Island
Banks Island
Victoria Island
Beaufort Sea
Baffin Bay
Greenland
Bering Strait
Point Barrow
Brooks Range
Yukon River
Mt. McKinley 20,320 ft. (6,194 m)
Alaska Range
Yukon Plateau
Mackenzie Mts.
Mackenzie River
Great Bear Lake
Great Slave Lake
CANADIAN SHIELD
Baffin Island
Foxe Basin
Davis Strait
Arctic Circle
Hudson Strait
Liard R.
Mt. Logan 19,550 ft. (5,959 m)
Gulf of Alaska
Bering Sea
Kodiak Island
Alaska Peninsula
Aleutian Islands
Coast Mountains
ROCKY MOUNTAINS
Peace River
Athabasca R.
Lake Athabasca
Hudson Bay
Labrador
Labrador Sea
Cape Farewell
60°N
Queen Charlotte Islands
Saskatchewan River
Lake Winnipeg
James Bay
Vancouver Island
Puget Sound
GREAT PLAINS
NORTH AMERICA
Newfoundland
Gulf of St. Lawrence
St. Lawrence R.
Niagara Falls
Great Lakes
Cascade Range
Coast Ranges
Snake R.
Black Hills
Missouri R.
Mississippi
Nova Scotia
Bay of Fundy
Great Salt Lake
GREAT BASIN
Sierra Nevada
Platte R.
INTERIOR PLAINS
Ohio R.
APPALACHIAN MTS.
Cape Cod
Long Island
Mt. Whitney 14,495 ft. (4,418 m)
Colorado R.
Arkansas
Ozark Plateau
Chesapeake Bay
Death Valley (lowest point in N.A.) -282 ft. (-86 m)
Sonoran Desert
River
COASTAL PLAIN
Cape Hatteras
Rio Grande
ATLANTIC OCEAN
30°N
Baja California
Gulf of California
Sierra Madre Occidental
Sierra Madre Oriental
Gulf of Mexico
Bahamas
Tropic of Cancer
Hawaiian Islands
Yucatán Peninsula
Cuba
Hispaniola
Puerto Rico
Greater Antilles
Pico de Orizaba 18,855 ft. (5,747 m)
Caribbean Sea
Lesser Antilles
PACIFIC OCEAN
Lake Maracaibo
Lake Nicaragua
Isthmus of Panama
Llanos
Orinoco R.
Angel Falls
Guiana Highlands
Chimborazo 20,702 ft. (6,310 m)
Rio Negro
Amazon R.
Equator
Galápagos Islands
AMAZON BASIN
ANDES
Cape São Roque
Line Islands
Marquesas Islands
Tapajós River
Xingu River
Tocantins R.
São Francisco River
Huascarán 22,205 ft. (6,768 m)
Mato Grosso Plateau
Brazilian Highlands
Tuamotu Archipelago
Cook Islands
Society Islands
Lake Titicaca
Altiplano
SOUTH AMERICA
Tropic of Capricorn
Atacama Desert
MOUNTAINS
Gran Chaco
Paraguay R.
Paraná R.
Iguazú Falls
30°S
Uruguay R.
0 1,000 2,000 Miles
0 1,000 2,000 Kilometers
Miller Cylindrical Projection
Mt. Aconcagua 22,834 ft. (6,960 m)
Río de la Plata
Pampa
Mountain peak
Point below sea level
National border
Waterfall
N
W
E
S
Valdés Peninsula (lowest point in S.A.) -131 ft. (-40 m)
Patagonia
Tierra del Fuego
60°W
Falkland Islands
South Georgia
Strait of Magellan
Cape Horn
150°W
120°W
90°W
30°W

United States: Political
CANADA
ARCTIC OCEAN
RUSSIA
ALASKA
Arctic Circle
Yukon River
Fairbanks
CANADA
Yukon River
Bering Sea
Anchorage
Gulf of Alaska
Juneau
PACIFIC OCEAN
0 250 500 Miles
0 250 500 Kilometers
Northeast
Southeast
Midwest
Southwest
West
National capital
State capital
Major city
National border
State border
Seattle
Tacoma
Olympia
Spokane
WASHINGTON
Portland
Columbia River
Salem
Eugene
OREGON
Great Falls
Helena
MONTANA
Billings
Yellowstone R.
IDAHO
Boise
Snake River
Pocatello
WYOMING
Casper
Ogden
Great Salt Lake
Salt Lake City
Provo
Cheyenne
NEVADA
Lake Tahoe
Reno
Carson City
Sacramento
San Francisco
Oakland
San Jose
UTAH
Denver
Colorado Springs
COLORADO
Pueblo
Colorado River
Fresno
CALIFORNIA
Las Vegas
Bakersfield
PACIFIC OCEAN
Flagstaff
ARIZONA
Santa Fe
Albuquerque
NEW MEXICO
Los Angeles
San Bernardino
San Diego
Phoenix
Tucson
Roswell
El Paso
Rio Grande
MEXICO
Gulf of California
N
W
E
S
PACIFIC OCEAN
Honolulu
HAWAII
Hilo
0 100 200 Miles
0 100 200 Kilometers
0 250 500 Miles
0 250 500 Kilometers
Albers Equal-Area Projection

CANADA
ATLANTIC OCEAN
Gulf of Mexico
BAHAMAS
CUBA
Lake Superior
Lake Michigan
Lake Huron
Lake Ontario
Lake Erie
Lake of the Woods
Lake St. Clair
Lake Champlain
St. Lawrence River
Mississippi River
Missouri River
Platte River
Arkansas River
Red River
Lake Texoma
Ohio River
Tennessee River
Rio Grande
Chesapeake Bay
Lake Okeechobee
NORTH DAKOTA
SOUTH DAKOTA
NEBRASKA
KANSAS
OKLAHOMA
TEXAS
MINNESOTA
IOWA
MISSOURI
ARKANSAS
LOUISIANA
WISCONSIN
ILLINOIS
MICHIGAN
INDIANA
OHIO
KENTUCKY
TENNESSEE
MISSISSIPPI
ALABAMA
GEORGIA
FLORIDA
SOUTH CAROLINA
NORTH CAROLINA
VIRGINIA
WEST VIRGINIA
PENNSYLVANIA
NEW YORK
MARYLAND
DELAWARE
NEW JERSEY
CONNECTICUT
RHODE ISLAND
MASSACHUSETTS
VERMONT
NEW HAMPSHIRE
MAINE
Washington, D.C.
Grand Forks
Bismarck
Fargo
Rapid City
Pierre
Sioux Falls
Duluth
St. Paul
Minneapolis
Sioux City
Omaha
Lincoln
Des Moines
Cedar Rapids
Davenport
Topeka
Kansas City
Wichita
Jefferson City
Springfield
St. Louis
Tulsa
Oklahoma City
Amarillo
Lubbock
Odessa
Abilene
Fort Worth
Dallas
Austin
San Antonio
Houston
Beaumont
Laredo
Corpus Christi
Fort Smith
Little Rock
Shreveport
Baton Rouge
New Orleans
Green Bay
Madison
Milwaukee
Rockford
Chicago
Peoria
Decatur
Springfield
Sault Sainte Marie
Grand Rapids
Lansing
Flint
Detroit
Gary
South Bend
Toledo
Cleveland
Akron
Columbus
Dayton
Cincinnati
Indianapolis
Louisville
Evansville
Frankfort
Lexington
Wheeling
Charleston
Memphis
Nashville
Knoxville
Chattanooga
Huntsville
Birmingham
Montgomery
Mobile
Meridian
Jackson
Biloxi
Atlanta
Macon
Columbus
Savannah
Tallahassee
Jacksonville
Orlando
Tampa
St. Petersburg
West Palm Beach
Miami
Charleston
Columbia
Charlotte
Winston-Salem
Greensboro
Raleigh
Roanoke
Richmond
Norfolk
Newport News
Virginia Beach
Pittsburgh
Harrisburg
Philadelphia
Trenton
Newark
New York City
Baltimore
Annapolis
Wilmington
Dover
Buffalo
Rochester
Syracuse
Albany
Burlington
Montpelier
Manchester
Concord
Worcester
Boston
Providence
Hartford
Bridgeport
Augusta
Portland
100°W
90°W
80°W
70°W
50°N
40°N
30°N

United States: Physical

100°W
90°W
80°W
70°W
50°N
40°N
30°N
CANADA
Lake of the Woods
Isle Royale
Lake Superior
Keweenaw Peninsula
Upper Peninsula
Lake Huron
Lake Michigan
Lower Peninsula
Lake St. Clair
Lake Erie
Lake Ontario
Niagara Falls
St. Lawrence River
Moosehead Lake
Mt. Katahdin 5,269 ft. (1,606 m)
Mt. Washington 6,288 ft. (1,917 m)
Lake Champlain
Adirondack Mountains
Green Mts.
White Mts.
Connecticut R.
Hudson R.
Finger Lakes
Cape Ann
Cape Cod
Long Island
ME
VT
NH
MA
NY
CT
RI
NJ
PA
MD
DE
Delaware Bay
Cape Charles
Chesapeake Bay
Albemarle Sound
Cape Hatteras
Cape Fear
ATLANTIC OCEAN
Upper Red Lake
Lower Red Lake
Mesabi Range
Leech Lake
Mille Lacs Lake
Lake Sakakawea
ND
MN
WI
Wisconsin River
Mississippi River
Lake Winnebago
MI
Lake Oahe
SD
Black Hills
Missouri River
G R E A T P L A I N S
Sand Hills
NE
North Platte R.
South Platte R.
Platte River
IA
I N T E R I O R P L A I N S
Illinois River
IL
Wabash River
IN
CENTRAL PLAINS
OH
Ohio River
WV
Allegheny Mts.
Potomac R.
VA
James R.
Roanoke R.
A P P A L A C H I A N M O U N T A I N S
P I E D M O N T
C O A S T A L P L A I N
Smoky Hills
KS
Missouri River
MO
Lake of the Ozarks
Harry S. Truman Reservoir
Ozark Plateau
Red Hills
KY
Cumberland Gap
Lake Barkley
Mt. Mitchell 6,684 ft. (2,037 m)
NC
Cape Fear River
Cumberland R.
TN
Tennessee R.
OK
Canadian River
Arkansas River
Ouachita Mountains
Lake Texoma
Red River
AR
Mississippi River
SC
Savannah River
Clark Hill Lake
Stone Mountain
Oconee R.
Ocmulgee R.
Altamaha R.
Okefenokee Swamp
Llano Estacado
Sabine River
TX
Brazos River
Pecos River
Edwards Plateau
Colorado River
Sam Rayburn Reservoir
Toledo Bend Reservoir
LA
C O A S T A L P L A I N
Lake Maurepas
Lake Pontchartrain
Mississippi Delta
MS
Tombigbee R.
AL
Alabama R.
Chattahoochee R.
GA
Mobile Bay
St. Johns River
Cape Canaveral
FL
Tampa Bay
Lake Okeechobee
Everglades
Cape Sable
Florida Keys
Straits of Florida
BAHAMAS
CUBA
Galveston Bay
Rio Grande
Gulf of Mexico

Research Handbook

To write a report or complete a project, you must gather information about your topic. You can find information in different sources, such as maps, photos, illustrations, and artifacts. You can also find information in your textbook. Other sources of information are technology resources, print resources, and community resources.

Technology Resources

- Internet
- Computer disk
- Television or radio

Print Resources

- Almanac
- Atlas
- Dictionary
- Encyclopedia
- Nonfiction book
- Periodical
- Thesaurus

Community Resources

- Teacher
- Museum curator
- Community leader
- Older citizen

Technology Resources

The main technology resources you can use to find information are the Internet and computer disks. Your school or local library may have CD-ROMs or DVDs that contain information about your topic. Television or radio can also be good sources of information.

Using the Internet

The Internet contains large amounts of information. By using a computer to go online, you can read letters and documents. You can see pictures and artwork. You can listen to music or take a virtual tour.

Keep in mind that some websites have mistakes or incorrect information. To get accurate information, be sure to visit only trusted websites. These include museum and government sites.

Plan Your Search

- Identify the topic.
- Make a list of questions that you want to answer.
- List key words or groups of words that you might want to use to write or talk about your topic.
- Look for good online resources to find answers to your questions.
- Decide if the information is relevant.

Use a Search Engine

A search engine is an online collection of websites. It can be sorted by entering a key word or group of words. Ask a librarian, a teacher, or a parent for suggestions about which search engine to use.

Search by Subject To search by subject, or topic, use a search engine. Choose from the list of key words that you made while planning your search. Enter a key word or group of words in the search engine field on your screen. Then click SEARCH or GO. You will see a list of websites that relate to your topic. Click on the site or sites you think will be most helpful.

Search by Address Each website has its own address, called a Uniform Resource Locator, or URL for short. To get to a website by using a URL, simply type the URL in the LOCATION/GO TO box on your screen, and hit ENTER or click GO.

Use Bookmarks The bookmark feature is an Internet tool for keeping and organizing URLs. If you find a website that seems helpful, you can save the URL. This way you can quickly return to it later. Click BOOKMARKS or FAVORITES at the top of your screen, and choose ADD. Your computer makes a copy of the URL and keeps a record of it.

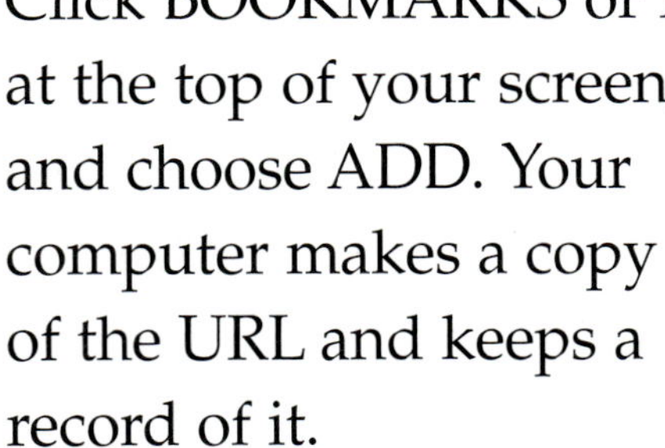

Print Resources

Books in libraries are organized through a system of numbers. Every book has its own title and call number. The call number tells where in the library the book can be found. You can then find information in the book by using its table of contents, title page, and index. You may also need to look at illustrations to learn more about the topic you are researching.

Some reference books, such as encyclopedias, are usually kept in a separate section of a library. Each book there has R or RE—for *reference*—on its spine.

Almanac

An almanac is a book or an electronic resource that has facts about different subjects. The subjects are listed in alphabetical order in an index.

Atlas

An atlas is a book of maps. It gives information about places. Different kinds of atlases show various places at different times. Your teacher or librarian can help you find the kind of atlas you need for your research.

Dictionary

A dictionary gives the correct spelling of words and their definitions, or meanings. It also gives the words' pronunciations, or how to say the words aloud.

Encyclopedia

An encyclopedia is a book or set of books that gives information about many different topics. The topics are arranged alphabetically. An encyclopedia is a good source to use when beginning your research.

Nonfiction Books

A nonfiction book gives facts about real people, places, and things. All nonfiction books in a library are arranged in order and by category according to their call numbers. To find a book's call number, you use a library's card file or computer catalog. You can search for a book in the catalog by subject, by author, or by title.

Periodicals

A periodical is a publication that appears each day, each week, or each month. Periodicals are good resources for current information on topics not yet recorded in books.

Thesaurus

A thesaurus (thih•SAWR•uhs) lists words that mean the same or nearly the same as another word. A thesaurus also lists words that have the opposite meaning. Using a thesaurus can help you find words that better describe your topic and make your writing more interesting.

Community Resources

People in your community can share oral histories or information about your research topic. Before you talk to any of them, always ask a teacher or a parent for permission.

Listening to Find Information

It is important to plan ahead whenever you talk with people as part of your research.

Before

- Find out more about the topic you want to discuss.
- List the people you want to talk to.
- Make a list of questions you want to ask.

During

- Speak clearly and loudly when asking questions.
- Listen carefully. Make sure you are getting the information you need.
- Be polite. Do not talk when the other person is speaking.
- Take notes to help you remember important ideas.
- Write down the person's exact words if you think you will want to use them in your report. If possible, use a tape recorder. Be sure to ask the speaker for permission in advance.

After

- Thank the person you spoke with.
- Later, write a thank-you note.

Writing to Get Information

You can also write to people in your community to get information. You can send them an e-mail or a letter. Keep these ideas in mind as you write:

- Write neatly or use a computer.
- Say who you are and why you are writing. Check your spelling and punctuation.
- If you are writing a letter, always provide a self-addressed, stamped envelope. The person can use it to send you a response.
- Thank the person.

Reporting

Written Reports

Your teacher may ask you to write a report about the information you find. Knowing how to write a report will help you make good use of the information. These tips will help you write your report.

Before Writing

- Choose a main idea or topic.
- Think of questions about your topic.
- Gather information from more than one source.
- Take notes on the information you find.
- Review your notes to be sure you have the information you need. Write down ideas to put in your report.
- Use your notes to make an outline of the information you found.

Citing Sources

An important part of research and writing is citing, or listing, sources. When you cite a source, you write down where you got your information. The list of sources will make up a bibliography. A bibliography is a list of the books and other sources that you used to find the information in your report.

Bibliography Card

Wyatt, Adam. *The History of Arkansas*. Philadelphia, Pennsylvania: Scenic River Publishing, 2003, page 25.

In 1820, Little Rock became capital of the Arkansas Territory.

RESEARCH HANDBOOK

RESEARCH HANDBOOK

Write a First Draft

- Use your notes and your outline to write a draft of your report. Keep in mind that your purpose is to share information.
- Write in paragraph form. Develop your topic with facts, details, and explanations. Each paragraph should focus on one idea.
- Get all your ideas down on paper.

Proofreading Marks and Their Meanings	
Word	Meaning
^	Insert word.
^,	Insert comma.
¶	Start a new paragraph.
≡ cap	Use a capital letter.
ℓ	Delete.
lc	Use a lowercase letter.

Revise

- Read over your draft. Does it have a beginning, a middle, and an end?
- Rewrite sentences that are unclear or poorly worded. Move sentences that seem out of place.
- Add details to support your ideas.
- If too many sentences are alike, make some sentences shorter or longer.
- Check any quotations to be sure you have shown someone's exact words and that you have noted the source correctly.

Marta Berzina
Social Studies

A History of Little Rock, Arkansas

Little Rock is the capital of the state of Arkansas. the city has a rich history. In 1722, the site where Little Rock is located was explored by a French trapper. He named the area Little Rock after a rock formation that he saw there. About 100 years later, in 1820, Little Rock became the capital of the Arkansas Territory.

During the Civil War, Arkansas was one of the states in the Confederacy. In 1881, Confederate troops took over a Union arsenal in Little Rock. the Union captured Little Rock in 1883.

After the Civil War, Little Rock's economy grew. In the 1880s railroads began to connect the industries in Little Rock with the natural resources around Arkansas. Timber and coal, especially, were important natural resources for Little Rock. Also, farmers from around the state of Arkansas sold their produce in markets in Little Rock. In 1969 a network of canals and dams linked Little Rock to the Mississippi River, bringing more trade to the city.

Little Rock is also famous for what happened there during the Civil Rights movement. After the Civil War, Arkansas, like most other states in the South, became segregated. Segregation meant that African Americans and whites were separated. They ate in different restaurants, used different restrooms, and attended different schools. In 1954, the Supreme Court decided that segregation was unconstitutional. The Little Rock Nine were nine African American students from Little Rock who, in 1957, were the first to be sent to a school that before had only allowed white students to attend. Central High School, the school where this took place, is now a national historic site.

Proofread and Edit

- Proofread your report, checking for errors.
- Correct any errors in spelling, capitalization, or punctuation.

Publish

- Make a neat, clean copy of your report.
- Include pictographs, bar graphs, maps, or other illustrations to help explain your topic.

Oral Presentations

Sometimes you may be asked to give an oral presentation. The purpose of an oral presentation is to share information. These tips will help you prepare an oral presentation.

- Follow the steps described in Before Writing to gather and organize information.
- Use your notes to plan and organize your presentation. Include an introduction and a conclusion in your report.
- Prepare note cards that you can refer to as you speak.
- Prepare visuals such as illustrations, diagrams, graphs, or maps to help listeners understand your topic.
- Give your audience the main idea about your topic. Support your main idea with details.
- Practice your presentation.
- Be sure to speak clearly and loudly enough. Keep your listeners interested in your report by using facial expressions and hand movements.

Biographical Dictionary

The Biographical Dictionary provides information about many of the people introduced in this book. Names are listed alphabetically by last name. Pronunciation guides are provided for hard-to-pronounce names. After each name are the birth and death dates of that person. If the person is still alive, only the year of birth appears. A brief description of the person's main achievement is then given. The page number that follows tells where the main discussion of that person appears in this book. (You can check the Index for other page references.) Guide names at the top of the pages help you quickly locate the name you need to find.

A

Adams, John *(1735–1826)* The second President of the United States (1797–1801) and a signer of the Declaration of Independence. p. 206

Aesop (EE•sahp) *(620 B.C.?–560 B.C.?)* A Greek storyteller who was famous for telling fables. p. 348

Aldrin, Edwin "Buzz" *(1930–)* An American astronaut who was the second human to walk on the moon. p. 219

Alito, Samuel Anthony, Jr. *(1950–)* An American appointed as a justice of the United States Supreme Court. p. 284

Angelou, Maya (AN•juh•loo) *(1928–)* An African American poet and author. p. 60

Anthony, Susan B. *(1820–1906)* A leader in the women's rights movement who worked alongside Elizabeth Cady Stanton to earn women the right to vote. p. 165

Armstrong, Neil *(1930–)* An American astronaut who was the first human to walk on the moon. p. 219

B

Bell, Alexander Graham *(1847–1922)* An American, born in Scotland, who built a telephone in 1876. The next year he started the first telephone company. p. 171

Breyer, Stephen Gerald *(1938–)* An American appointed as a justice of the United States Supreme Court. p. 284

Buffalo Tiger *(1920–)* A leader of the Miccosukee tribe. p. 195

Burnham, Daniel *(1846–1912)* An American architect and urban planner who helped plan the city of Chicago. p. 50

Burr, Richard *(1955–)* A United States senator from North Carolina. p. 283

Bush, George W. *(1947–)* The forty-third President of the United States (2001–). p. 282

C

Camarena, Guillermo González *(1917–1965)* A Latin American scientist who invented color television and the remote control. p. 175

Carnegie, Andrew *(1835–1919)* A wealthy businessman who was known for his generous gifts to make the world a better place. p. 435

Carson, Benjamin S. *(1951–)* A leading brain doctor in the United States who grew up very poor. p. 435

Carter, James "Jimmy" *(1924–)* The thirty-ninth President of the United States (1977–1981). p. 254

Carter, Rosalynn *(1927–)* The wife of former President Jimmy Carter. p. 254

Cerf, Vinton *(1943–)* A scientist who helped create the Internet. p. 407

Chapman, John *(1775?–1845)* An American pioneer nicknamed "Johnny Appleseed" because he planted apple trees in large parts of Ohio, Indiana, and Illinois. pp. 349, 355

Chavez, Cesar *(1927–1993)* A farmworker and American leader who worked for fair treatment of all farmworkers. p. 258

Clark, George Rogers *(1752–1818)* An American military leader during the Revolutionary War. p. 23

Clark, William *(1770–1838)* An explorer who, with the help of Meriwether Lewis, led the Corps of Discovery in the exploration of the Louisiana Purchase. p. 213

Clinton, William Jefferson "Bill" *(1946–)* The forty-second President of the United States (1993–2001). p. 404

Cochran, Josephine *(1839–1913)* An American who invented the first dishwasher. p. 175

Coleman, Michael B. *(1954–)* A mayor of Columbus, Ohio, elected in 1999. p. 273

Columbus, Christopher *(1451–1506)* An Italian explorer, working for Spain, who sailed to the Americas while trying to reach Asia from Europe. p. 196

Corsi, Edward *(1896–1965)* An Italian immigrant who came to the United States in 1907. p. 326

de Soto, Hernando *(1496?–1542)* A Spanish explorer who explored southwestern Tennessee. p. 149

Dole, Elizabeth A United States senator from North Carolina. p. 283

Douglass, Frederick *(1817–1895)* A leader and writer who was born enslaved in Maryland. He escaped in 1838 and helped in the fight against slavery. p. 216

E

Earle, Sylvia *(1935–)* An American oceanographer who has written many stories and books about the ocean. p. 119

Edison, Thomas *(1847–1931)* An inventor who, along with Lewis Latimer, created the electric lightbulb. He also invented the phonograph, the movie camera, and the microphone. p. 174

Emerson, Jo Ann *(1950–)* A United States representative from Missouri. p. 63

Ford, Henry *(1863–1947)* The founder of the Ford Motor Company. He produced the Model T, the first affordable and widely available automobile. p. 172

Franklin, Benjamin *(1706–1790)* An American leader, writer, and scientist. He helped work on the Declaration of Independence. p. 210

Gandhi, Mohandas (moh•HAHN•dahs GAHN•dee) *(1869–1948)* An Indian leader who used peaceful tactics to change India into a free country. p. 166

Ginsburg, Ruth Bader *(1933–)* An American appointed as a justice of the United States Supreme Court in 1993. p. 284

Gomez, Joel *(1981–)* A United States soldier from Wheaton, Illinois, who was injured in the war in Iraq. p. 250

Granholm, Jennifer *(1959–)* The first female governor of Michigan, elected in 2003. p. 280

Grant, Ulysses S. *(1822–1885)* The eighteenth President of the United States. He was the leader of the Union army during the Civil War. p. 100

Hancock, John *(1737–1793)* The first signer of the Declaration of Independence. p. 206

Hatshepsut (hat•SHEP•soot) *(1503 B.C.–1482 B.C.)* A female Egyption pharaoh. p. 180

Herrera, Leticia An entrepreneur who runs a cleaning service company in Chicago. p. 392

Hreljac, Ryan *(1992–)* At the age of six, he started the Ryan's Well Foundation to help people gain access to clean water. p. 257

Huerta, Dolores *(1930–)* A teacher who worked alongside Cesar Chavez to help farmworkers become citizens, vote, and earn more money. p. 256

James I of England *(1560–1625)* King of England (1603–1625). Jamestown, the first lasting English settlement in North America, was named after him. p. 200

Jefferson, Thomas *(1743–1826)* The third President of the United States (1801–1809). He wrote the first draft of the Declaration of Independence. p. 210

Jenney, William *(1832–1907)* An American architect and engineer who designed the first steel-frame skyscraper. p. 164

Joseph *(1840–1904)* Known as Chief Joseph, a leader of the Nez Perce tribe. p. 194

Kennedy, Anthony M. *(1936–)* An American appointed as a justice of the United States Supreme Court in 1988. p. 284

Kennedy, John F. *(1917–1963)* The thirty-fifth President of the United States (1961–1963). p. 291

Key, Francis Scott *(1779–1843)* A lawyer and poet who wrote the words of "The Star-Spangled Banner." Congress adopted the song as the national anthem in 1931. p. 294

Khalfani, Lynnette *(1967–)* An African American author who has written several books about budgeting and saving money. p. 434

Khufu *(2500s B.C.)* A pharaoh in ancient Egypt. p. 180

Kid Blink A newsboy who led a strike against New York City newspapers in 1899. p. 423

King, B. B. *(1925–)* An African American guitarist and blues musician. p. 149

King, Dr. Martin Luther, Jr. *(1929–1968)* An American minister and civil rights leader who worked to change unfair laws. He received the Nobel Peace Prize in 1964. p. 167

Laclède, Pierre (lah•KLED) *(1729–1778)* A French explorer who founded St. Louis, Missouri. p. 198

Langdon, Phillip An American author who writes about communities and design. p. 63

Latimer, Lewis *(1848–1928)* An African American inventor who, along with Thomas Edison, created the electric lightbulb. p. 174

Lawrence, Jacob *(1917–2000)* An American artist who was famous for his paintings of historic events. p. 328

Lazarus, Emma *(1849–1887)* An American writer who wrote the poem printed at the base of the Statue of Liberty. p. 339

Leigh, Louise *(1914–)* A senior citizen from California who invented the idea for Constitution Day. p. 270

Lewis, Meriwether *(1774–1809)* An explorer who, along with William Clark, led the Corps of Discovery in the exploration of the Louisiana Purchase. p. 213

Lin, Maya *(1959–)* A Chinese American artist and architect who designed the Vietnam War Memorial in Washington, D.C. p. 342

Lincoln, Abraham *(1809–1865)* The sixteenth President of the United States (1861–1865). He was President during the Civil War. p. 217

Louis XV of France *(1710–1774)* King of France (1715–1774). St. Louis, Missouri, was named after him. p. 198

M

Maathai, Wangari *(1940–)* The first African woman to win the Nobel Peace Prize and the first woman in eastern or central Africa to earn a doctoral degree. She founded the Green Belt Movement in Kenya. p. 135

Madison, James *(1751–1836)* The fourth President of the United States (1809–1817) and a writer of the Bill of Rights, the first ten amendments to the Constitution. p. 270

Mansa Musa *(?–1332)* A ruler of ancient Mali. p. 184

Mead, Margaret *(1901–1978)* An American scientist who studied people and places. p. 62

Menéndez de Avilés, Pedro (may•NAYN•days day ah•vee•LAYS) *(1519–1574)* A Spanish explorer who founded St. Augustine, the oldest European settlement in the United States. p. 197

Moore, Richard H. The state treasurer of North Carolina. p. 434

Morganfield, McKinley. *(1915–1983)* An African American blues musician known as Muddy Waters. p. 149

Morse, Samuel *(1791–1872)* An American artist and inventor known for his work on the telegraph and Morse code. p. 171

Muir, John *(1838–1914)* An American naturalist, born in Scotland, who was largely responsible for the creation of many of the conservation programs in the United States. p. 106

N

Nelson, Gaylord *(1916–2005)* A Wisconsin senator who founded Earth Day in 1970. p. 134

Olmsted, Frederick Law *(1822–1903)* An American landscaper who designed many important parks. p. 50

Ortega, Katherine *(1934–)* The thirty-eighth treasurer of the United States (1983–1989). p. 421

Otis, Elisha *(1811–1861)* An engineer who designed the first elevator that could safely carry people. p. 164

Parks, Rosa *(1913–2005)* An African American civil rights leader. She refused to give up her seat on a bus to a white man. p. 255

Pocahontas (poh•kuh•HAHN•tuhs) *(1595–1617)* Indian chief Powhatan's daughter. p. 201

Ponce de Leon, Juan *(1460?–1521)* A Spanish explorer who claimed the land that is now Florida for Spain. p. 197

Powhatan (pow•uh•TAN) *(1550?–1618)* The chief of the Indian tribes who lived in the area where English settlers started Jamestown. p. 201

R

Ralston, Alexander *(1771–1827)* A city planner who planned Indianapolis. p. 237

Reinders, Jim *(1927–)* An American artist who created Carhenge in Nebraska. p. 381

Rivera, Diego *(1886–1957)* A Mexican painter known for his colorful murals. p. 350

Roberts, John *(1955–)* Chief Justice of the United States. He was appointed in 2005. p. 284

Rolfe, John *(1585?–1622?)* A citizen of Jamestown who began growing the first tobacco in North America. p. 201

Sacagawea (sa•kuh•juh•WEE•uh) *(1787?–1812)* A young Shoshone woman who helped the Corps of Discovery talk to Native Americans and led the explorers through paths in the Rocky Mountains. p. 213

Saicheua, Songsak (SAWNG•sag SY•choo•ah) The minister-counselor of Thailand. p. 405

Satanta *(1820–1878)* A Kiowa chief. p. 194

Scalia, Antonin *(1936–)* An American appointed as a justice of the United States Supreme Court. p. 284

Silko, Leslie Marmon *(1948–)* An author from the Laguna Pueblo tribe. p. 195

Smith, Jimmy Neil *(1947–)* An American who created the National Storytelling Festival. p. 356

Smith, John *(1579?–1631)* An early leader of Jamestown who helped maintain peace by trading for food with early Native Americans. p. 200

Souter, David Hackett *(1939–)* An American appointed as a justice of the United States Supreme Court in 1990. p. 284

Stanton, Elizabeth Cady *(1815–1902)* A leader in the women's rights movement who worked alongside Susan B. Anthony to earn women the right to vote. p. 165

Stephens, John Paul *(1920–)* An American appointed as a justice of the United States Supreme Court in 1975. p. 284

Stephenson, George *(1781–1848)* A British engineer and inventor who made the first modern locomotive. p. 163

Thomas, Clarence *(1948–)* An American appointed as a justice of the United States Supreme Court in 1991. p. 284

Tomlinson, Ray *(1886–1957)* An engineer who invented e-mail. p. 407

Tubman, Harriet *(1820–1913)* A person who escaped slavery and who used the Underground Railroad to lead more than 300 slaves to freedom. p. 216

Walker, Madame C. J. *(1867–1919)* An African American businesswoman who became the first female in the United States to make millions of dollars on her own. p. 393

Wangchuck, King Jigme Singye (JEE•mee SING•ee WANG•choo) *(1955–)* The King of Bhutan (1973–). p. 302

Washington, George *(1732–1799)* The first President of the United States (1789–1797). He is known as "the father of our country." p. 207

Weissenborn, Oscar An American entrepreneur who sold many pencils in the United States. p. 389

Wright, Orville *(1871–1948)* An American who, with his brother, Wilbur, built the first working airplane. p. 173

Wright, Wilbur *(1867–1912)* An American who, with his brother, Orville, built the first working airplane. p. 173

York *(1770?–1831?)* Enslaved African American who was a part of the Corps of Discovery. p. 213

Gazetteer

The Gazetteer is a geographical dictionary that can help you locate places discussed in this book. Place-names are listed alphabetically. Hard-to-pronounce names are followed by pronunciation guides. A description of the place is then given. The page number that follows tells where each place is shown on a map. Guide words at the top of the pages help you locate the place-name you need to find.

Afghanistan A country in south central Asia. p. 365

Africa The second-largest continent. p. 85

Akron A city in northeastern Ohio. p. 89

Alabama A state in the Southeast region of the United States. p. 103

Alaska A state of the United States, in the northwestern corner of North America. p. 103

Albany The capital of New York. p. 281

Ancient China An ancient civilization in Asia that developed into present-day China. p. 181

Ancient Egypt An ancient civilization in Africa. p. 180

Ancient Greece An ancient civilization where the world's first democracy was developed. p. 182

Ancient Mali An ancient civilization in Africa. p. 184

Ancient Mesopotamia An ancient civilization in southwestern Asia. p. 179

Ancient Rome An ancient civilization that ruled most of what is now Europe. p. 183

Annapolis The capital of Maryland. p. 266

Antarctica Continent located at the South Pole, covered by an ice cap. p. 85

Appalachian Mountains A low and rounded mountain range in the eastern United States. p. 99

Arctic Ocean The body of water surrounding the North Pole. p. 85

Arizona A state in the Southwest region of the United States. p. 103

Arkansas A state in the Southeast region of the United States. p. 103

Arkansas River A river that runs through Colorado, Kansas, Oklahoma, and Arkansas. p. 59

Asia The largest continent. p. 85

Atlanta The capital of Georgia. p. 281

Atlantic Ocean The body of water that separates North and South America from Europe and Africa. p. 85

Augusta The capital of Maine. p. 281

Austin The capital of Texas. p. 281

Australia The smallest continent. p. 85

Baltimore A city in Maryland. p. 49

Baton Rouge The capital of Louisiana. p. 281

Bhutan (boo•TAHN) A kingdom in Asia, located between India and China. p. 302

Bismarck The capital of North Dakota. p. 281

Bogor (BOH•gawr) A city in Indonesia. p. 28

Boise The capital of Idaho. p. 281

Boston The capital of Massachusetts. p. 281

Brazil A country in South America. p. 402

Buffalo National River A river in northern Arkansas. p. 59

California A state in the West region of the United States. p. 103
Canada A country in North America. p. 86
Carson City The capital of Nevada. p. 281
Chamblee A city in northern Georgia. p. 336
Charleston The capital of West Virginia. p. 281
Cheyenne The capital of Wyoming. p. 281
Chicago The third-largest city in the United States, located in northeastern Illinois. p. 331
Cincinnati A city in southwestern Ohio. p. 89
Cleveland A city in northeastern Ohio. p. 334
Coastal Plain A large area of plains in the United States that stretches along the Atlantic Ocean and the Gulf of Mexico. p. 99
Colorado A state in the West region of the United States. p. 103
Columbia The capital of South Carolina. p. 281
Columbus The capital of Ohio. p. 89
Concord The capital of New Hampshire. p. 281
Connecticut A state in the Northeast region of the United States. p. 103
Crater of Diamonds State Park A state park in southwest Arkansas. p. 59
Cuba A country in the Caribbean, south of Florida. p. 103

Delaware A state in the Northeast region of the United States. p. 103
Denver The capital of Colorado. p. 281
Des Moines The capital of Iowa. p. 281
Dover The capital of Delaware. p. 281

Eastern Hemisphere The eastern half of Earth. p. 83
Europe The second-smallest continent. p. 85

Fayetteville A town in northwest Arkansas, home to the University of Arkansas. p. 279
Florida A state in the Southeast region of the United States. p. 103
Frankfort The capital of Kentucky. p. 281

Georgia A state in the Southeast region of the United States. p. 103
Germany A country in Europe. p. 402
Great Lakes Large lakes located along the border of the United States and Canada; the largest body of freshwater lakes in the world. p. 99
Great Plains A large area of plains that stretches across the middle of the United States. p. 99
Greenland An island north of Canada, ruled by Denmark, part of North America. p. 86
Gulf of Mexico A body of water on the southeastern coast of North America. p. 103

GAZETTEER

Harrisburg The capital of Pennsylvania. p. 281
Hartford The capital of Connecticut. p. 281
Hawaii A state of the United States, made up of a string of volcanic islands in the north-central Pacific Ocean. p. 103
Helena The capital of Montana. p. 281
Helena Bridge A bridge in Helena, Arkansas. p. 59
Holla Bend National Wildlife Refuge A wildlife refuge in north central Arkansas. p. 59
Honolulu The capital of Hawaii. p. 281
Hot Springs National Park A national park in south Arkansas. p. 59
Hudson A county in New Jersey. p. 274

Idaho A state in the West region of the United States. p. 103
Illinois A state in the Midwest region of the United States. p. 103
Indian Ocean The smallest of the world's three major oceans, stretching between the southern tips of Africa and Australia. p. 85
Indiana A state in the Midwest region of the United States. p. 103
Indianapolis The capital of Indiana. p. 281
Iowa A state in the Midwest region of the United States. p. 103
Italy A country in Europe. p. 183

Jackson The capital of Mississippi. p. 281
Jamaica A country in the Caribbean, south of Florida. p. 364
Japan A country in northeast Asia. p. 365
Jefferson City The capital of Missouri. p. 281
Jersey City A city in New Jersey. p. 274
Jonesborough A city in eastern Tennessee. p. 356
Juneau The capital of Alaska. p. 281

Kansas A state in the Midwest region of the United States. p. 103
Kansas City The largest city in Missouri. p. 31
Kentucky A state in the Southeast region of the United States. p. 104
Knoxville A city in eastern Tennessee. p. 99

Lake Erie One of the Great Lakes. p. 89
Lake Huron One of the Great Lakes. p. 99
Lake Michigan One of the Great Lakes. p. 99
Lake Ontario One of the Great Lakes. p. 99
Lake Superior One of the Great Lakes. p. 99
Lansing The capital of Michigan. p. 281
Lexington A city in central Kentucky. p. 104
Lima (LY•muh) A city in northwest Ohio. p. 89
Lincoln The capital of Nebraska. p. 281
Little Rock The capital of Arkansas. p. 59
Los Angeles The second-largest city in the United States, located in southern California. p. 98
Louisiana A state in the Southeast region of the United States. p. 103

M

Madison The capital of Wisconsin. p. 281
Maine A state in the Northeast region of the United States. p. 103
Mali A country in western Africa. p. 365
Manica (mah•NEE•kah) A small farming region in Mozambique. p. 438
Maryland A state in the Southeast region of the United States. p. 103
Massachusetts A state in the Northeast region of the United States. p. 103
Mercer A county in New Jersey. p. 274
Mexico A country in southern North America that borders on the Pacific Ocean and the Gulf of Mexico. Mexico is on the United States' southern border. p. 85
Michigan A state in the Midwest region of the United States. p. 103
Millwood Lake A lake in southwest Arkansas. p. 59
Minnesota A state in the Midwest region of the United States. p. 103
Mississippi A state in the Southeast region of the United States. p. 103
Mississippi River The second-longest river in the United States. It runs from Minnesota to the Gulf of Mexico. p. 99
Missouri A state in the Midwest region of the United States. p. 31
Montana A state in the West region of the United States. p. 103
Montgomery The capital of Alabama. p. 281
Montpelier The capital of Vermont. p. 281
Mount Vernon A neighborhood in Baltimore, Maryland. p. 49
Mozambique (moh•zahm•BEEK) A country in southeastern Africa. p. 438

N

Nashville The capital of Tennessee. p. 281
Nebraska A state in the Midwest region of the United States. p. 103
Nevada A state in the West region of the United States. p. 103
New Hampshire A state in the Northeast region of the United States. p. 103
New Jersey A state in the Northeast region of the United States. p. 274
New Mexico A state in the Southwest region of the United States. p. 103
New York A state in the Northeast region of the United States. p. 103
Newark A city in New Jersey. p. 274
North America The continent that includes the United States, Canada, Mexico, and Central America. p. 86
North Carolina A state in the Southeast region of the United States. p. 103
North Dakota A state in the Midwest region of the United States. p. 103
North Pole The northernmost tip of Earth. p. 83
Northern Hemisphere The northern half of Earth. p. 83

O

Ohio A state in the Midwest region of the United States. p. 89
Ohio River A branch of the Mississippi River; runs from Pennsylvania to Illinois. p. 99
Oklahoma A state in the Southwest region of the United States. p. 103
Oklahoma City The capital of Oklahoma. p. 281
Olympia The capital of Washington. p. 281
Oregon A state in the West region of the United States. p. 103
Ouachita Mountains (WAHSH•uh•tah) A mountain range in Arkansas and Oklahoma. p. 59

GAZETTEER

P

Pacific Ocean The body of water that separates North America and South America from Australia and Asia. p. 85
Pennsylvania A state in the Northeast region of the United States. p. 103
Phoenix The capital of Arizona. p. 281
Pierre (PIR) The capital of South Dakota. p. 281
Poison Spring State Park A state park in south Arkansas. p. 59
Providence The capital of Rhode Island. p. 281

R

Raleigh The capital of North Carolina. p. 281
Rhode Island A state in the Northeast region of the United States. p. 103
Richmond The capital of Virginia. p. 281
Rocky Mountains A tall and sharply pointed mountain range in the western United States. p. 99
Russia A country in northern Europe and Asia. p. 365

S

Sacramento The capital of California. p. 281
Salem The capital of Oregon. p. 281
Salt Lake City The capital of Utah. p. 84
Santa Fe The capital of New Mexico. p. 281
Searcy (SER•see) A rural community in central Arkansas. p. 59
Sherwood A suburb of Little Rock, Arkansas. p. 59
South Africa A country in southern Africa. p. 365
South America The fourth-largest continent. p. 85
South Carolina A state in the Southeast region of the United States. p. 103
South Dakota A state in the Midwest region of the United States. p. 103
South Pole The southernmost tip of Earth. p. 83
Southern Hemisphere The southern half of Earth. p. 83
Springfield The capital of Illinois. p. 281
St. Louis A city in western Missouri. p. 28
St. Paul The capital of Minnesota. p. 281
Stillwater A town in north central Oklahoma. p. 71

T

Tallahassee The capital of Florida. p. 281
Tennessee A state in the Southeast region of the United States. p. 103
Texas A state in the Southwest region of the United States. p. 103
Tokyo A city in Japan that is also Japan's main business center. p. 437
Toledo A city in northwestern Ohio. p. 89
Topeka The capital of Kansas. p. 281
Trenton The capital of New Jersey. p. 274

U

United Kingdom A country in western Europe that includes England, Wales, Scotland, and Northern Ireland. p. 365
United States A country on the continent of North America. p. 86
Utah A state in the West region of the United States. p. 103

Venezuela A country in South America. p. 364

Vermont A state in the Northeast region of the United States. p. 103

Virginia A state in the Southeast region of the United States. p. 103

Washington A state in the West region of the United States. p. 103

Washington, D.C. The capital of the United States. p. 281

West Virginia A state in the Southeast region of the United States. p. 103

Western Hemisphere The western half of Earth. p. 83

Wisconsin A state in the Midwest region of the United States. p. 103

Wyoming A state in the West region of the United States. p. 103

Yellowstone National Park The world's first national park, located in the northwestern United States. It covers parts of Idaho, Montana, and Wyoming. p. 100

GAZETTEER

Glossary

The Glossary contains important history and social science words and their definitions, listed in alphabetical order. Each word is respelled as it would be in a dictionary. When you see this mark ´ after a syllable, pronounce that syllable with more force. The page number at the end of the definition tells where the word is first used in this book. Guide words at the top of the pages help you quickly locate the word you need to find.

add, **ā**ce, **câ**re, **pä**lm; **e**nd, **ē**qual; **i**t, **ī**ce; **o**dd, **ō**pen, **ô**rder; t**o͝o**k, p**o͞o**l; **u**p, b**û**rn; **y͞oo** as *u* in *fuse*; **oi**l; **pou**t; **ə** as *a* in *above*, *e* in *sicken*, *i* in *possible*, *o* in *melon*, *u* in *circus*; **ch**eck; ri**ng**; **th**in; **th**is; **zh** as in *vision*

absolute location (ab´sə•lo͞ot lō•kā´shən) The exact location of a place. p. 88

adapt (ə•dapt´) To change. p. 116

advertisement (ad´ver•tīz•mənt) A notice made to get people to buy something. p. 409

agriculture (a´gri•kul•chər) The growing of crops and the raising of farm animals for sale. p. 60

amendment (ə•mend´mənt) A change to something that is already written. p. 217

ancestor (an´ses•tər) Someone in a person's family who lived long ago. p. 34

ancient (ān´shənt) Happening or existing very long ago. p. 178

anthem (an´thəm) A patriotic song. p. 294

appointed (ə•point´əd) Chosen. p. 284

artifact (är´tə•fakt) An object that was used by people in the past. p. I2

assembly line (ə•sem´blē līn) A process to make a product in which each person adds one part as the product passes on a moving belt. p. 176

authority (ə•thôr´i•tē) The right given to leaders to give orders, make decisions, and take action for a community. p. 266

ballot (ba´lət) A list of the choices in an election. p. 246

bank (bangk) A business that keeps money safe. p. 25

bar graph (bär graf) A graph that uses bars to show amounts. p. 120

barter (bär´tər) To trade without using money. p. 418

biography (bī•ä´grə•fē) The story of a person's life. p. I2

border (bôr´dər) On a map, a line that shows where a state or a nation ends. p. 86

boycott (boi´kät) A decision by a group of people not to buy or use something. p. 255

budget (bu´jət) A plan for spending and saving money. p. 430

business (biz´nəs) An activity in which workers make or sell goods or do work for others. p. 16

canal (kə•nal´) A human-made waterway dug across land. p. 123

capital (kap´ə•təl) Money to start a new business. p. 394

capital resource (kap´ə•təl rē´sôrs) A tool or building that a business needs to make and deliver a product. p. 395

capitol (ka´pə•təl) The government building in a capital city where lawmakers meet. p. 281

cardinal directions (kär´də•nəl di•rek´shənz) The main directions *north*, *south*, *east*, and *west*. p. I13

century (sen´shə•rē) 100 years. p. 156

character trait (kar´ik•tər trāt) A quality that a person has. p. 253

citizen (sit´ə•zən) A person who lives in and belongs to a community. p. 14

civil rights (si´vəl rīts) Rights that give everyone equal treatment under the law. p. 167

civil war (si´vəl wôr) A war in which the citizens of a country fight each other. p. 216

civilization (si•və•lə•zā´shən) A large group of people living in a very organized way. p. 178

claim (klām) To say that something belongs to you. p. 197

climate (klī´mət) Weather that a place has over a long period of time. p. 20

GLOSSARY

colony (käl´ə•nē) A place that is ruled by another country. p. 204

common good (kä´mən go͝od) The good of everyone in a community. p. 250

communication (kə•myo͞o´nə•kāshən) The sharing of information. p. 27

communication link (kə•myo͞o•nə•kā•shən lingk) A kind of technology that lets people who are far apart share information instantly. p. 408

community (kə•myo͞o´nə•tē) A group of people who live and work in the same place. p. 14

compass rose (kum´pəs rōz) A drawing on a map that shows directions to help people use the map. p. I13

competition (käm•pə•ti´shən) The contest among businesses to sell the most goods or services. p. 423

compromise (käm´prə•mīz) When each person gives up some of what he or she wants in order to agree. p. 288

conflict (kän´flikt) A disagreement. p. 200

Congress (kän´grəs) The legislative branch of the national government. p. 283

consequence (kän´sə•kwens) Something that happens because of what a person does. p. 249

conservation (kon•sər•vā´shən) Working to save resources to make them last longer. p. 130

constitution (kän•stə•to͞o´shən) A written set of laws that describe how a government will work. p. 208

constitutional monarchy (kän•stə•to͞o´shən•əl män´är•kē) A kind of government that has both a monarch and a government elected by the people. p. 302

consumer (kən•so͞o´mər) Someone who buys a product or service. p. 390

continent (kon´tən•ənt) One of the seven large land areas on Earth. pp. I10, 82

continuity (kon•tə•no͞o´i•tē) Continuing without changing. p. 157

cooperate (kō•ä´pə•rāt) To work together. p. 252

cooperative (kō•ä´pə•rə•tiv) A group of workers who own a business together. p. 438

council (koun´səl) A group of people chosen to make laws. p. 273

county (koun´tē) A section of a state, including cities and towns in an area. p. 272

county seat (koun´tē sēt) The city or town in which the main government offices of the county are located. p. 274

court (kôrt) A place where a judge or a jury decides if someone has broken the law. p. 275

cultural identity (kul´chər•əl ī•den´ti•tē) A collection of traits that are seen in the members of a group. p. 364

culture (kul´chər) A way of life shared by members of a group. p. 15

custom (kus´təm) A way of doing something. p. 332

D

dam (dam) An earthen or concrete structure that holds back water. p. 126

decade (de´kād) Ten years. p. 156

decision (di•si´zhən) A choice. p. 260

demand (di•mand´) A willingness of consumers to buy goods and services. p. 424

democracy (di•mä´krə•sē) The form of government in which citizens have the right to vote. p. 182

deposit (di•pä´zət) To put money into a bank account. p. 429

desert (de´zərt) An area with a hot, dry climate. p. 21

diverse (dī•vûrs´) Different. p. 332

E

e-commerce (ē•kä´mərs) Buying and selling goods and services on the Internet. p. 408

economy (i•kä´nə•mē) The ways a country or community makes and uses goods and services. p. 60

ecosystem (ē´kō•sis•təm) The plants, animals, land, water, and climate that make up an area. p. 97

elect (i•lekt´) To choose by voting. p. 246

election (i•lek´shən) A time set aside for voting. p. 246

empire (em´pīr) All of the land and people under the control of a powerful nation. p. 184

engineer (en•jə•nir´) A person who designs ways to build and make things. p. 164

entrepreneur (än•trə•prə•nûr´) Someone who starts and runs a business. p. 389

environment (in•vī´rən•mənt) The physical and human features that make up a place. p. 114

equality (i•kwä´lə•tē) Equal treatment. p. 166

equator (i•kwā´tər) On a map or globe, a line that appears halfway between the North Pole and the South Pole. pp. I11, 83

erosion (i•rō´zhən) The wearing away of Earth's surface over a period of time. p. 96

ethnic group (eth´nik gro͞op) A group of people who share the same language, culture, and way of life. p. 333

executive (ig•ze´kyə•tiv) Having to do with the branch of government that sees that laws are obeyed. p. 268

explorer (ik•splōr´ər) A person who goes to find out about a place. p. 196

export (eks´pôrt) To send products and resources to other countries to sell. p. 402

F

fable (fā´bəl) A story in which animals speak and act like humans. p. 348

fact (fakt) A statement that can be proved. p. 354

factory (fak´tə•rē) A building where products are prepared and packaged. p. 396

festival (fes´tə•vəl) A joyful gathering for celebration. p. 359

fiction (fik´shən) A story that is made up. p. 354

flowchart (flō´chärt) A drawing that shows how to do something or how something works. p. 176

folk song (fōk sông) A song that expresses the culture of a group of people. p. 350

folktale (fōk´tāl) A story passed from one generation to the next. p. 349

free market (frē mär´kət) The freedom to make and sell any product or service that is allowed by law. p. 422

freedom (frē´dəm) The right to make your own choices. p. 204

fuel (fyo͞ol) A natural resource that is burned to make heat or energy. p. 108

G

geographic tool (jē•ə•graf´ik to͞ol) A tool that tells where a place is and what it looks like. p. 82

geography (jē•ä´grə•fē) The study of Earth's surface and the ways people use it. p. I8

globe (glōb) A model of Earth. p. I10

good (go͝od) Something that can be bought or sold. p. 24

government (guv´ərn•mənt) A group of people who make laws for a community. p. 19

government service (guv´ərn•mənt sûr´vəs) The work that the government does for everyone in its area. p. 267

governor (guv´ər•nər) The elected leader of a state's government. p. 280

grid system (grid sis´təm) A set of lines the same distance apart that cross each other to form boxes. p. 48

growing season (grō´ing sē´zən) The time in which plants can grow. p. 94

H

harbor (här´bər) A protected place with deep water that allows ships to come close to the shore. p. 45

hemisphere (hem´ə•sfir) Half of the globe when it is divided into either northern and southern halves or eastern and western halves. pp. I11, 83

heritage (her´ə•tij) A set of values and traditions handed down from those who lived earlier. p. 34

hero (hir´ō) A person who does something important and sets an example for others. p. 257

historic site (hi•stôr´ik sīt) A place that is important in history. p. 36

historical society (hi•stôr´i•kəl sə•sī´ə•tē) An organization of people who are interested in the history of their community. p. 36

history (his´tə•rē) The story of what has happened in the past. p. I2

history map (his´tə•rē map) A map that shows what a place looked like at an earlier time. p. 220

holiday (hä´lə•dā) A day set aside for remembering a person, an idea, or an event. p. 340

human feature (hyo͞o´mən fē´chər) Something that people add to a landscape. p. 114

human resource (hyo͞o´mən rē´sôrs) The workers who produce goods and services. p. 395

immigrant (im´ə•grənt) A person who comes to live in a country from somewhere else in the world. p. 218

import (im´pōrt) To bring in products and resources from other countries to sell them. p. 402

income (in´kəm) Money paid to a worker for the work he or she does. p. 392

independence (in•də•pen´dəns) Freedom from another country's control. p. 206

inset map (in´set map) A small map within a larger map. p. I12

interdependence (in•tər•də•pen´dəns) The reliance of producers and consumers on each other for products and resources they need. p. 391

interest (in´trist) The money a bank pays people for keeping their money there. p. 429

intermediate directions (in•tər•mē´dē•ət də•rek´shənz) The in-between directions that give more exact information about location, such as northeast, southeast, northwest, and southwest. pp. I13, 30

international trade (in•tər•nash´ə•nəl trād) The buying and selling between countries. p. 401

Internet (in´tər•net) A system that links computers around the world. p. 27

invention (in•ven´shən) Something that is made for the first time. p. 162

invest (in•vest´) To buy something that will grow in value. p. 429

irrigation (ir•ə•gā´shən) The moving of water to dry areas. p. 124

judicial (jo͞o•di'shəl) Having to do with the branch of government that decides whether laws are fair or are based on the Constitution. p. 268

jury (jo͞or´ē) A group of citizens that meets to decide whether a person has broken the law. p. 248

justice (jus´təs) Fairness. p. 253

land use (land yo͞os) The way most land in a place is used. p. 398

landform (land´fôrm) A physical feature, such as a mountain, valley, plain, or hill. p. 21

landform map (land´fôrm map) A map that shows a place's physical features. p. 98

landmark (land´märk) An important natural or human feature that marks a location. p. 338

language (lang´gwij) A set of words a group of people use to communicate. p. 190

latitude (la´tə•to͞od) Lines that run east and west around a globe. p. 88

law (lô) A rule that a community makes. p. 18

legend (le´jənd) A made-up story about a real person or event. p. 349

legislative (le´jəs•lā•tiv) Having to do with the branch of government that makes laws. p. 268

line graph (līn graf) A graph that uses a line to show patterns in information formed over time. p. 296

literature (li´tə•rə•chər) Stories and poems that people use to share their ideas. p. 348

locator (lō´kā•tər) A small map or picture of a globe that shows where an area on the main map is found in a state, on a continent, or in the world. p. I12

longitude (län´jə•to͞od) Lines that run north to south on a globe, from pole to pole. p. 88

majority rule (mə•jôr´ə•tē ro͞ol) Accepting the choice that more than half the people vote for. p. 247

GLOSSARY

manufacture (man•yə•fak´chər) To make something with machines. p. 397

map (map) A picture that shows the location of things. p. I3

map key (map kē) A box on a map in which map symbols are explained; also called a map legend. p. I12

map scale (map skāl) A part of a map that compares a distance on the map to a distance in the real world. p. I12

map title (map tī´təl) A title that tells what a map is about. p. I12

mayor (mā´ər) A leader of a community government. p. 273

mediator (mē´dē•ā•tər) A person who helps other people settle a conflict. p. 288

memorial (mə•môr´ē•əl) Something that helps keep a memory of a person or event alive. p. 292

migrate (mī´grāt) To move within one's country. p. 328

millennium (mə•len´ē•əm) 1,000 years. p. 160

mineral (min´ər•əl) A kind of natural resource found in the ground, such as iron or gold. p. 107

minority rights (mə•nôr´ə•tē rīts) The rights kept by a smaller group that did not vote for the same thing or person most people voted for. p. 247

mint (mint) A place where coins are made. p. 421

modern (mäd´ərn) Having to do with the time we live in today. p. 178

modify (möd´ə•fī) To change. p. 122

monument (män´yə•mənt) Something that is built to honor or remember a person or an event in history. p. 292

mountain range (moun´tən rānj) A large chain of mountains. p. 91

multicultural (mul•tē•kul´chər•əl) Having to do with many different cultures. p. 333

museum (myōō•zē´əm) A place that keeps and displays objects from other places and times. p. 17

myth (mith) A story made up to explain the world around us. p. 348

N

nation (nā´shən) An area of land with its own people and laws. Another name for a country. p. 26

natural disaster (nach´ər•əl di•zas´tər) An event in nature that causes great harm or damage to people and their property. p. 117

natural resource (na´chə•rəl rē´sôrs) Something from nature that people can use, such as trees, water, or soil. p. 106

nonrenewable (nän•ri•nōō´ə•bəl) Not able to be made again quickly by nature or people. p. 108

O

opinion (ə•pin´yən) A person's belief that can be supported by facts but cannot be proved. p. 410

opportunity (ä•pər•tōō´nə•tē) A chance to have a better way of life. p. 324

opportunity cost (ä•pər•tōō´nə•tē kôst) What someone gives up to get what he or she wants. p. 432

oral history (ôr´əl his´tə•rē) Spoken history. p. 190

P

Parliament (pär´lə•mənt) The legislative branch of Canada's government. p. 301

patriotic symbol (pā•trē•ä´tik sim´bəl) A symbol, such as a flag, that stands for the ideas in which people believe. p. 290

patriotism (pā´trē•ə•ti•zəm) A feeling of pride in one's country. p. 208

physical feature (fi´zi•kəl fē´chər) A feature of a place's land, water, climate, or plant life. p. 90

pictograph (pik´tə•graf) A graph that uses pictures or symbols to show the numbers of things. p. 120

pioneer (pī•ə•nir´) A person who settles a new land. p. 214

plateau (pla•tō´) A landform with steep sides and a flat top. p. 91

pollution (pə•lo͞o´shən) Anything that makes a natural resource dirty or unsafe to use. p. 128

population (pä•pyə•lā´shən) The total number of people in a place. p. 42

population density (pop•yə•lā´shən den´sə•tē) The number of people living in an area of a certain size. p. 330

port (pōrt) A place where ships dock to pick up goods or passengers. p. 185

prejudice (prej´ə•dis) The unfair treatment of a person because of his or her background, race, or religion. p. 325

preserve (pri•zərv´) To save. p. 104

President (pre´zə•dənt) The title given to the leader of the United States of America. p. 209

primary source (prī´mer•ē sôrs) A record of an event made by someone who saw or took part in the event. p. 168

prime meridian (prīm mə•rid´ē•ən) The meridian of 0 degrees longitude. p. 88

prime minister (prīm min´i•stər) The head of an executive branch of some countries' governments, such as Canada's. p. 301

problem (prob´ləm) Something that is difficult or hard to understand. p. 132

producer (prə•do͞o´sər) Someone who makes and sells a product or service. p. 389

product (prod´əkt) A good. p. 388

profit (prä´fət) The amount of money that is left over after all the costs of running a business have been paid. p. 422

public works (pu´blik wərks) A department of a community government that provides services to meet the daily needs of citizens, such as repairing streets, collecting trash, or making sure that there is clean water. p. 277

R

raw material (rô mə•tir´ē•əl) A natural resource that can be used to make a product. p. 394

recreation (re•krē•ā´shən) Any activity done just for enjoyment. p. 276

recycle (rē•sī´kəl) To reuse resources. p. 130

reference work (re´frəns wûrk) A source of facts. p. 33

region (rē´jən) A large area with at least one feature that makes it different from other areas. p. 42

relative location (re´lə•tiv lō•kā´shən) The location of a place in relation to another place. p. 86

religion (ri•li´jən) A person's belief system. p. 197

renewable (ri•no͞o´ə•bəl) Able to be made or grown again by nature or people. p. 108

representative (re•pri•zen´tə•tiv) A person chosen by a group of people to act or speak for them. p. 283

republic (ri•pub´lik) A type of government where citizens vote for leaders to make decisions for them. p. 183

reservoir (re´zə•vwär) A human-made lake used for collecting and storing water. p. 126

responsibility (ri•spon•sə•bil´ə•tē) Something a person should do because it is necessary and important. p. 248

revolution (re•və•lo͞o´shən) A fight for a change in government. p. 205

right (rīt) A freedom. p. 165

road map (rōd map) A map that shows the roads and other local features of a community. p. 278

rural (ro͝or´əl) Having to do with the countryside, farms, and small towns. p. 56

savings (sā´vingz) The money that people save. p. 429

scarcity (skâr´sə•tē) What happens when the supply of a product is not enough to meet the demand for it. p. 425

secondary source (se´kən•der•ē sôrs) A record of an event made by a person who was not present at the event. p. 168

service (sûr´vəs) Work that someone does for someone else. p. 24

settlement (se´təl•mənt) A new community. p. 197

settler (set´lər) One of the first people to live in a new community. p. 199

shelter (shel´tər) A home or building that protects people from the weather. p. 191

slavery (slā´və•rē) A system under which people have no choices. p. 201

slogan (slō´gən) A short phrase used to deliver a message. p. 165

solution (sə•lo͞o´shən) An answer to a problem. p. 132

statue (stach´o͞o) A monument built to honor or remember a person, an idea, or an event in history. p. 338

suburb (sub´ûrb) A smaller community built near a larger city. p. 52

suburban (sə•bûr´bən) Having to do with smaller communities around cities. p. 52

suffrage (suf´rij) The right to vote. p. 165

supply (sə•plī´) The products and services that businesses provide consumers. p. 424

supreme court (sə•prēm´ kôrt) The highest court in any state. The United States Supreme Court is the most important court in the nation. p. 281

tax (taks) The money that citizens pay to the government for goods and services. p. 205

technology (tek•nä´lə•jē) All of the tools people can use every day. p. 170

terrace (ter´əs) Giant steps cut into hillsides for farming. p. 124

territory (ter´ə•tôr•ē) Land that belongs to a government but is not a state or a colony. p. 217

time line (tīm līn) A drawing that shows when and in what order events took place. p. 160

trade (trād) To exchange one good or service for another. p. 184

trade-off (trād´ôf) The giving up of one thing in return for something else. p. 432

tradition (trə•di´shən) A custom that is passed on to others. p. 335

transportation (trans•pər•tā´shən) The movement of people, goods, and ideas. p. 46

tunnel (tun´əl) A path that runs through or under something. p. 123

urban (ûr´bən) Having to do with a city. p. 43

valley (va´lē) A lowland that lies between hills or mountains. p. 91

vegetation (ve•jə•tā´shən) The plants that grow in a place. p. 94

volunteer (vä•lən•tir´) A person who chooses to work without getting paid. p. 251

vote (vōt) A choice that gets counted. p. 165

wage (wāj) Money paid to a worker for the work he or she does. p. 392

worship (wûr´shəp) To pray together. p. 352

Index

The Index lets you know where information about important people, places, and events appear in the book. All key words, or entries, are listed in alphabetical order. For each entry, the page reference indicates where information about that entry can be found in the text. Page references for illustrations are set in italic type. An italic *m* indicates a map. Page references set in boldface type indicate the pages on which vocabulary terms are defined. Related entries are cross-referenced with *See* or *See also*. Guide words at the top of the pages help you identify which words appear on which page.

C

H

I

J

INDEX

R

INDEX

S

For permission to reprint copyrighted material, grateful acknowledgment is made to the following sources:

Atheneum Books for Young Readers, Simon & Schuster Children's Publishing Division: From *A Place Called Freedom* by Scott Russell Sanders, illustrated by Thomas B. Allen. Text copyright © 1997 by Scott Russell Sanders; illustrations copyright © 1997 by Thomas B. Allen.

Bloomsbury Children's Books, a division of Walker and Company: Cover illustration from *Hard Hat Area* by Susan L. Roth. Copyright © 2004 by Susan L. Roth.

Charlesbridge Publishing, Inc.: From *Be My Neighbor* by Maya Ajmera and John D. Ivanko. Text copyright © 2004 by SHAKTI for Children.

Children's Press, a Scholastic Library Publishing Company, Inc., a division of Scholastic Incorporated: Cover illustration from *mi barrio/my neighborhood* by George Ancona. Children's drawings © 2004 by Marc Anthony and Christina Ortiz; photograph © 2004 by George Ancona.

Dial Books for Young Readers, a Division of Penguin Young Readers Group, a Member of Penguin Group (USA) Inc., 345 Hudson Street, New York, NY 10014: "Walk Lightly" from *A World of Wonders: Geographic Travels in Verse and Rhyme* by J. Patrick Lewis, illustrated by Alison Jay. Text copyright © 2002 by J. Patrick Lewis; illustrations copyright © 2002 by Alison Jay.

Farrar, Straus and Giroux, LLC: Cover illustration by Jerome Lagarrigue from *Going North* by Janice N. Harrington. Illustration copyright © 2004 by Jerome Lagarrigue.

Grosset & Dunlap, a Division of Penguin Young Readers Group, a Member of Penguin Group (USA) Inc., 345 Hudson St., New York, NY 10014: Cover illustration by Thor Wickstrom from *Money: A Rich History* by Jon Anderson. Illustration copyright © 2003 by Thor Wickstrom.

Harcourt, Inc.: Cover illustration by Wendell Minor from *Rachel: The Story of Rachel Carson* by Amy Ehrlich. Illustration copyright © 2003 by Wendell Minor. Cover illustration by Emily Arnold McCully from *Old Home Day* by Donald Hall. Illustration copyright © 1996 by Emily Arnold McCully.

HarperCollins Publishers: Cover illustration from *Market!* by Ted Lewin. Copyright © 1996 by Ted Lewin. Cover illustration by Frané Lessac from *Capital! Washington D. C. from A to Z* by Laura Krauss Melmed. Illustration copyright © 2003 by Frané Lessac. Cover illustration from *The Train of States* by Peter Sís. Copyright © 2004 by Peter Sís.

Henry Holt and Company, LLC: Cover illustration from *Mapping Penny's World* by Loreen Leedy. Copyright © 2000 by Loreen Leedy.

Houghton Mifflin Company: Cover illustration by Claire A. Nivola from *The Flag Maker* by Susan Campbell Bartoletti. Illustration copyright © 2004 by Claire A. Nivola.

Kids Can Press Ltd., Toronto: Cover illustration by Shelagh Armstrong from *If the World Were a Village: A Book about the World's People* by David J. Smith. Illustration © 2002 by Shelagh Armstrong.

Philomel Books, a Division of Penguin Young Readers Group, a Member of Penguin Group (USA) Inc., 345 Hudson St., New York, NY 10014: Cover illustration by Ted Lewin from *High as a Hawk* by T. A. Barron. Illustration copyright © 2004 by Ted Lewin. Cover illustration by William Low from *Henry and the Kite Dragon* by Bruce Edward Hall. Illustration copyright © 2004 by William Low.

Scholastic Inc.: From *Dreaming of America: An Ellis Island Story* by Eve Bunting, illustrated by Ben F. Stahl. Text copyright © 2000 by Edward D. Bunting and Anne E. Bunting, Trustees of the Edward D. Bunting and Anne E. Bunting Family Trust; illustrations copyright © 2000 by Ben F. Stahl. Cover photograph by Russ Kendall from *Sarah Morton's Day: A Day in the Life of a Pilgrim Girl* by Kate Waters. Photograph copyright © 1989 by Russell Kendall.

Jay Scott: From *Alex and the Amazing Lemonade Stand* by Liz and Jay Scott with help from Alex Scott, illustrated by Pam Howard. Text copyright © 2004 by Liz and Jay Scott; illustrations copyright © 2004 by Pam Howard.

Tilbury House, Publishers: Cover illustration by Lea Lyon from *Say Something* by Peggy Moss. Illustration copyright © 2004 by Lea Lyon.

PHOTO CREDITS FOR GRADE 3 SOCIAL STUDIES

Placement Key: (t) top; (b) bottom; (l) left; (r) right; (c) center; (tl) top left; (tc) top center; (tr) top right; (cl) center left; (cr) center right; (bl) bottom left; (bc) bottom center; (br) bottom right; (bg) background; (fg) foreground; (i) inset

COVER

ENDSHEET

FRONTMATTER

Blind (b) David Lawrence/Panoramic Images; iv (bg) Joe Sohm/PictureQuest; vi (bg) Photodisc Red/Getty Images; (b) Kwame Zikomo/SuperStock; vii (t) Royalty-Free/Corbis; (fg) David Young-Wolff/PhotoEdit; viii (fg) David W Hamilton/Getty Images; (bg) Steve Vidler/SuperStock; (b) Richard T. Nowitz/Corbis; xii (bg) Index Stock Imagery; (fg) John Wang/Getty Images; xiii (fg) Kevork Djansezian/AP Images; x (b) PhotoDisc/Media Bakery; (bg) Maryland Historical Society; (fg) Michael Ventura/PhotoEdit; xi (fg) Comstock/PictureQuest; xiv (bg) Minnesota Historical Society/Corbis; (b) Jamie & Judy Wild/Danita Delimont Stock Photography; (t) Joe Tree/Alamy; I2 (bc) Brand X/SuperStock; (bl) Corbis; (br) Library of Congress; I3 (bl) Alan King/Alamy; (br) Jeremy Woodhouse/Getty Images; I8 (c) Danny Lehman/Corbis; (b) Age fotostock/SuperStock; I9 (t) Gail Mooney/Masterfile; (c) Peter Christopher/Masterfile; (b) age fotostock/SuperStock.

UNIT 1

1 (bl) Used with permission from The Biltmore Company, Asheville, North Carolina (t), (b) Panoramic Images; 2 (t) Robert Harding World Imagery/Getty Images; 3 (tl) Gary Conner/PhotoEdit; (c) Lenny Ignelzi/AP Images; (tr) Masterfile Royalty-Free; (b) Artiga Photo/Corbis; 5 (t) Greg Pease/Photographer'sChoice/Getty Images; (b) Bruno Barbey/Magnum Photos; 6 (c) Josef Polleross/The Image Works; (b) Ken Cavanagh/Photo Researchers, Inc.; 7 (b) Nik Wheeler Photography; (t) Momatiuk-Eastcott/Woodfin Camp; 8 (t) Robert Frerck/Woodfin Camp; (b) Adam Tanner/The Image Works; 9 (t) Ray Roberts/Topham/The Image Works; (b) Robert Fried/Alamy; 10 (b) Richard Hutchings/Photo Researchers, Inc.; (t) Sean Sprague/Sprague Photo Stock; 11 (b) Jim Mahoney/The Image Works; (t) David Austin/Woodfin Camp; 12 (b) James Lemass/Index Stock Imagery; (br) HIRB/Index Stock Imagery; (bl) Diaphor Agency/Index Stock Imagery; (bg) J Sohm/Voa LLC/Panoramic Images; 14 (b) Jon Arnold/Danita Delimont; 15 (t) Rudi Von Briel/PhotoEdit; 16 (b) Jacqueline Larma/AP Images; (c) Terry Gilliam/AP Images; 17 (b) Scott Barrow,Inc./SuperStock; (t) Monika Graff/The Image Works; 19 (t) Toby Talbot/AP Images; 20 (bl) Charles Crust Photographer; (br) Claver Carroll/Panoramic Images; 21 (bc) age fotostock/SuperStock; (bl) Jim Wark/AirPhoto; (br) Rafael Macia/Photo Researchers, Inc.; 22 (t) Beverly Palau/City of Greenbelt; (b) Tom Carter/PhotoEdit; 23 (b) Clarksville Historical Society; (t) Indiana Historical Society; 24 (bl) Jack Kurtz/The Image Works; (br) Masterfile Royalty-Free; 25 (t) Pickerell/Folio; 26 (b) Peter Adams/Panoramic Images; 27 (t) Evan Collis/Australian Picture Library; 28 (tr) Medio Images/Getty Images; (tl) Bjorn Grotting/Indonesia Photo; (b) St.Louis Center for International Relations; 29 (t) Jordan R. Beesley/US Navy/NewsCom 33 (t) Mark Richards/PhotoEdit; 34 (bg) Gerald L. French/Panoramic Images;36 (bg), (inset) North Carolina ECHO; 37 (t) Michael Jaenicke/The Robesonian/AP Images; 38 (t) Jacqueline Larma/AP Images; 39 (tl) age fotostock/SuperStock; 40 (bg) SpotWorks, Inc.; (bl) Henry T. Kaiser/Stock Connection/Workbook; (bc) Michael Melford/Getty Images; (br) Grandmaison Photography; 42 (b) SpotWorks, Inc.; 43 (c) Joe Sohm/PictureQuest; 44 (bg) age fotostock/SuperStock; 45 (t) Photodisc Green/Getty Images; (c) Gail Mooney/Masterfile; 46 (b) Julie Jacobson/AP Images; (c) SpotWorks, Inc.; 47 (t) Michael Newman/PhotoEdit; 50 (b) AP Images; 51 (t) Walter Bibikow/Getty Images; (c) U.S. Postal Service/AP Images; 52 (b) BerylGoldberg; 53 (t) Emily Shur/Getty Images; 54 (b) Peter Byron/PhotoEdit; 56 (bg) Gary McMichael/Grant Heilman Photography; 57 (t) Philip Holsinger/The Daily Citizen; 58 (b) Randall Hyman/AGPix; 59 (br) R. Kaubner/Robertstock.com; (t) Paul Rezendes Photography; 60 (t) John Elk III; 61 (t) Steve Warble/Mountain Magic Photography; 62 (c) Bettmann/Corbis; 63 (tl) Knight Programing Community Building/University of Miami School of Architecture; (tr) U.S. Representative JoAnn Emerson; 64 (cl) Paul Barton/Corbis; (cr) Susan Van Etten/PhotoEdit; 66 (t) Joe Sohm/PictureQuest; 67 (tl) Beryl Goldberg; (tr) Gary McMichael/Grant Heilman Photography; 70 (t) age fotostock/SuperStock; (b) Tom Carter/PhotoEdit.

UNIT 2

73 (b) The Granger Collection, New York; (bg), (t) Chad Ehlers/Stock Connection/ Workbook; 74 (t) Royalty-Free/Corbis; (br) Ariel Skelley/Masterfile; 75 (tl) Jupiter Images/PictureQuest (tr) Stockbyte/Media Bakery RF; (c) Sal Maimone/SuperStock; (b) Douglas Peebles/Corbis; 77 (b) Jeremy Frechette/The Image Bank/Getty Images; 80 (bg) Adam Jones/Danita Delimont Stock Photography; (bc) Paul Rezendes; (br) Macduff Everton/Iconica/Getty Images; 84 (t) Tim Thompson/Corbis; 90 (b) Photodisc Red/Getty Images; 91 (t) Kwame Zikomo/ SuperStock; 92 (t) Darrell Gulin/Getty Images; 93 (t) Tom Bean/Corbis; 94 (c) Art Wolfe/Getty Images; (bl) Gary Conner/Index Stock Imagery; (br) Frank Krahmer/zefa/ Corbis; 95 (bl), (br), (tr), (tl)Todd Pearson/ Getty Images; 96 (t) David Muench/Getty Images; 97 (t) Norbert Wu/Minden Pictures; 100 (bg) Willard Clay/Getty Images; (b) Bob and Suzanne Clemenz/AGPix; 101 (tr) Gunter Marx/Corbis; (cr) Byron Jorjorian/Alamy; (tl), (c) Paul Uhl; (cl) Dewitt Jones/Corbis; 102 (bl) Tim Fitzharris/Minden Pictures; (br) Yva Momatiuk/John Eastcott/Minden Pictures; 103 (bl) Glen Allison/Getty Images; (b) Masterfile Royalty-Free; (br) Digital Vision/Getty Images; 104 (t) Jeff Rogers Photography; 105 (c) Kevin R. Morris/Corbis; (t) Jeff Spradling/University of Kentucky Appalachian Center; 106 (bg) Ike Geib/Grant Heilman Photography; (c) Denny Eilers/ Grant Heilman Photography; 107 (fg) Peter Dean/Grant Heilman Photography; 108 (t) Jason Turner/The Journal/AP Images; (b) Grant Heilman/Grant Heilman Photography; 109 (t) Photodisc Collection/Getty Images; 110 (t) Photodisc Red/Getty Images; 111 (tl) Digital Vision/Getty Images; (tr) Jason Turner/The Journal/AP Images; 112 (bg) James M Phelps, Jr/ShutterStock; (bc) Denny Eilers/Grant Heilman Photography; (bl) Yann Arthus-Bertrand/Corbis; (br) Karl Weatherly/Corbis; 114 (b) James Schwabel/ Panoramic Images; 116 (t) W. Robert Moore/ Getty Images; (c) Bryan & Cherry Alexander Photography; 117 (b) Mario Tama/Getty Images; 119 (b) Macduff Everton/Corbis; 120 (t) Weatherstock/Peter Arnold, Inc.; (b) Stephen Holman/Stillwater News Press/AP Images; 122 (b) Sergio Pitamitz/Getty Images; 123 (b) Hulton Archive/Getty Images; 124 (t) Tom Brownold/AGPix; (b) Johan Elzenga/Foto Natura/Minden Pictures; 125 (t) Kevin R. Morris/Corbis; (b) Bernhard Lang/The Image Bank/Getty Images; 126 (b) Photos courtesy of Lake of the Ozarks CVB/800-FUNLAKE/ funlake.com; (t) Royalty-Free/Corbis; 127 (t) Glen Allison/Getty Images; 128 (b) Photodisc Collection/Getty Images; 129 (c) Hand Out/ AP Images; 130 (b) JP Laffont/Sygma/Corbis; (t) David Young-Wolff/PhotoEdit; 131 (t) Shipley's Choice Elementary/Maryland Department of the Environment; 134 (b) Tom Lynn/Journal Sentinel Inc.; (c) Gregory Berger/Pomegranate Design/Sacramento Area Earth Day Network; 135 (b) Ron Wurzer/Nature Consortium/AP Images; (t) Karen Prinsloo/AP Images; 138 (t) Mario Tama/Getty Images; 139 (tl) Photos courtesy of Lake of the Ozarks CVB/800-FUNLAKE/ funlake.com; (tr) David Young-Wolff/ PhotoEdit; 142 (b) Hand Out/AP Images.

UNIT 3

145 (bl) Jean Leon Jerome Ferris/Private Collection/Bridgeman Art Library; (bg) Prisma/SuperStock; 146 (t) Bettmann/Corbis; (br) Mark Richards/PhotoEdit; 147 (tl) Masterfile Royalty-Free; (c) Larry Ulrich; (tr) Art Resource, NY; (b) Paul Johnson/ Index Stock Imagery; 149 (b) Sylvia Pitcher Photolibrary/Alamy; 154 (bg) K. Yamashita/ PanStock/Panoramic Images/Workbook; (bc) Brad Wrobleski/Masterfile; (bl) Noel Hendrickson/MasteFile; (br) Scala/Art Resource, NY; 156 (b) Adam Jones/Getty Images; 157 (cl) New York Public Library Picture Collection; (cr) Hisham F Ibrahim/ Photodisc Green/Getty Images; 158 (tl) Corbis; (tr) Scala/Art Resource; 159 (t) Bob Landry/Time Life Pictures/Getty Images; (c) Herb Levart/SuperStock; 160 (bl) Lawrence Carmichael Earle/Chicago Historical Society/Bridgeman Art Library; (br) Chicago Historical Society; 161 (bl) Library of Congress; (b) Bettmann/Corbis; (br) Images. com/Corbis; 163 (t) John Seymour Lucas/ Institute of Mechanical Engineers/Bridgeman Art Library; 164 (b) Raymond Patrick/Getty Images; 165 (br) California Historical Society; (b), (bl) National Museum of Women's History; 166 (c) Robin Nelson/PhotoEdit; (t) Douglas Miller/Getty Images; 167 (t) Bob Fitch/Stock Photo; 168 (br) Stephen Chernin/ Getty Images; (bl) Flip Schulke/Corbis; (c) Ted Spiegel/Corbis; 169 (inset) Getty Images; 170 (b) Gilcrease Museum; 171 (tl) Corbis; (tr) Bettmann/Corbis; (bl) Ryan McVay/Getty Images; (c) Scott Milless/ShutterStock; (br) Getty Images; (b) The Granger Collection, New York 172 (t) Bettmann/Corbis; 173 (t) Underwood & Underwood/Corbis; 174 (c) J. Walter Thompson/AP Images; (b) Queens Borough Public Library; (tl), (tr) The Granger Collection, NY; 175 (t) Judy Rosella Edwards/Ecolitgy Communications; 178 (b) Nik Wheeler Photography; 179 (tr) Réunion des Musées Nationaux/Art Resource; (tl) Werner Forman/TopFoto/The Image Works; 180 (b) Travel Ink Photo Library/Index Stock Imagery; (t) Deir el-Bahri, Temple of Hatshepsut/Metropolitan Museum of Art Excavations; 182 (b) Johnny Stockshooter/Robertstock.com; 184 (b) Ali Murat Atay/Coral Planet/AGPix; (t) Bibliotheque Nationale de France, Paris; 185 (t) Bruno Morandi/Getty Images; 186 (t) Bob Fitch/Stock Photo; 187 (tl) Bettmann/Corbis; (tr) Réunion des Musées Nationaux/Art Resource; 188 (bg) John Neubauer/PhotoEdit; (bl) Scott Olson/Getty Images; (bc) Michael Pasdzior/The Image Bank/Getty Images; (br) John Elk III/Lonely Planet Images/Getty Images; 190 (b) David W Hamilton/Getty Images; 191 (b) Private Collection/Peter Newark Western Americana/Bridgeman Art Library; 193 (t) Nathan Benn/Corbis; 194 (cl) Picture History, LLC; (cr) W.S. Soule/Picture History, LLC; 195 (tl) http://www.mrp.txstate.edu/mrp/publications/hillviews/2001/ winter/page4.html; (tr) Marilyn "Angel " Wynn/nativestock.com; 196 (br) Private Collection, Index/Bridgeman Art Library; (bl) Sebastiano del Piombo/Metropolitan Museum of Art/Bridgeman Art Library; 197 (c) Bettmann/Corbis; (t) Steve Vidler/ SuperStock; 198 (t) MPI/Getty Images; (b) David Schultz/Missouri Historical Society; 199 (b) The Granger Collection; (t) Airphoto; 200 (b) Richard T. Nowitz/Corbis; 201 (t) David Muench/Corbis; 202 (bl) Snark/Art Resource, NY; (cl) Jeff Greenberg/PhotoEdit; (cr) Bettmann/Corbis; (br) Tom Horlacher; (t) Brand X/SuperStock; 203 (t) Burstein Collection/Corbis; 204 (b) Bettmann/ Corbis; 206 (t) Bettmann/Corbis; 207 (t) Morristown National Historic Park/National Park Service Museum Collection; (b), (c) Military and Historical Image Bank; 208 (b) The Granger Collection, New York; 209 (t) Arsene Hippolyte Rivey/New-York Historical Society/Bridgeman Art Library; 210 (bl), (br) The Granger Collection, New York; 211 (t) Courtesy of the Historical Society of Pennsylvania; (c) The Granger Collection, New York; 212 (b) "Lewis and Clark at Three Forks" by E.S. Paxson, Oil on Canvas 1912, Courtesy of the Montana Historical Society, Don Beatty photographer; 213 (b) National Museum of American History, Smithsonian Institution; 214 (b) Comstock Images/Alamy; 215 (b) Montana Historical Society, Helena.; 216 (c) National Archives; (t) Library of Congress; 217 (t) National Portrait Gallery, Smithsonian Institution/Art Resource, NY; (b) Library of Congress; 218 (b) Royalty-Free/Corbis; 219 (fg) NASA Kennedy Space Center; (bg) Worldspec/NASA/Alamy; 220 (c) David Schultz/Missouri Historical Society Collections; 222 (bl) Geography and Map Division/The Library of Congress; (br) Oregon Historical Society; 223 (bl), (br) Oregon Historical Society; (t) Erich Lessing/ Art Resource, NY; (c) The Granger Collection, New York; 226 (t) Bettmann/Corbis; 227 (tr) National Portrait Gallery, Smithsonian Institution/Art Resource, NY; 229 (tc) U.S. Postal Service, HO/AP Images; (c) NASA Kennedy Space Center; (cl) Picture History LLC; (cr) Kean Collection/Getty Images; (bl) AP Images; (bc) Bettmann/Corbis; 230 (t) Scott Milless/ShutterStock; (b) National Museum of Women's History.

UNIT 4

233 (bg), (t) San Rostro/AGE Fotostock; 234 (t) David Butow/Corbis Saba; (br) Getty Images;

235 (tl) Jeffrey Greenberg/Photo Researchers, Inc.; (c) Gary Conner/PhotoEdit; (tr) C Squared Studios/Getty Images; (b) Park Street/PhotoEdit; 237 (b) George & Monserrate Schwartz/Alamy; 238 (b) Lawrence Migdale; 239 (tl), (tr) Lawrence Migdale; 240 (bl), (br) Lawrence Migdale; 241 (t) Lawrence Migdale; 242 (bg) Nanine Hartzenbusch/Getty Images; (bl) St. Cloud Times, Kimm Anderson/AP Images; (bc) John Neubauer/PhotoEdit; (br) Paul Conklin/ PhotoEdit; 244 (b) Alex Wong/Getty Images; 245 (t) The Granger Collection, New York; (br), (cl) David Young-Wolff/PhotoEdit; (cr) Richard Hutchings/PhotoEdit; (bl) Lisa Law/The Image Works; 246 (t) Spencer Platt/Getty Images; (b) Jeff Greenberg/The Image Works; 247 (t) Jonathan Nourok/ PhotoEdit; 249 (t) John Neubauer/PhotoEdit; (b) Bob Stern/The Image Works; 250 (b) Jesse Chehak; (t) Tanit Jarusan/The Daily Herald Photo Archives; 251 (t) Jesse Chehak; 252 (b) David Schmidt/Masterfile; 253 (t) Beach/Kentucky Transportation Cabinet; (c) Vincent/Kentucky Transportation Cabinet; 254 (t) Pat Roque/AP Images; (b) Bjoern

Sigurdsoen/Pool/AP Images; 255 (t) Take Stock; (b) Paul Warner/AP Images; 256 (t) Bob Fitch/Take Stock; (c) Library of Congress; 257 (t) Ryan's Well Foundation; 258 (b) Najlah Feanny/Corbis; 259 (t) Sakuma/AP Images; (c), (b) Spotworks; 263 (tl) John Neubauer/PhotoEdit; (tr) Pat Roque/AP Images 264 (bg) Mark Gibson Photography; (bc) Ted Soqui/Corbis; (bl) Rebecca Cook/ Reuters/Corbis; (br) Ron Chapple/Taxi/ Getty Images; 266 (b) Office of the City Clerk/Annapolis, Maryland; 267 (c) Douglas Kirkland/Corbis; (b) Marland State Archives; 268 (tl) PhotoDisc/Media Bakery; (tr) Larry Fisher/Masterfile; (b) Ron Edmonds/AP Images; 269 (t) Ed Reinke/AP Images; 270 (br) Jim Rider/South Bend Tribune/AP Images; (bl) Musee Franco-Americaine, Blerancourt, Chauny, France, Giraudon/Bridgeman Art Library; 271 (b) Bob Child/AP Images; (t) National Archives; 272 (b) Lee Snider/Photo Images/Corbis; 273 (t) Columbus City Council; (b) Terry Gilliam/AP Images; 274 (b) Warren County Public Information & Tourism Department; 275 (b) Brian Rose; 276 (t) Kayte M. Deioma/PhotoEdit; (b) Comstock Images/PictureQuest RF; 277 (t), (c) Stephen Wirt; 280 (b) Jim LeMays/Michigan Department of Transportation/Gov. Jennifer M. Granholm; 281 (b) SuperStock; 282 (b) Getty Images; 283 (b) 2005 Getty Images; (t) U.S. Senator Richard Burr; 284 (t) Jason Reed/Reuters/Corbis; (c) Bettmann/Corbis; 285 (t) Jeffrey Greenberg/Photo Researchers, Inc.; (c) Byron Jorjorian Photography; 286 (bg) Lester Lefkowitz; (b) Royalty-Free/Corbis; 287 (c) Peter Gridley/Getty Images; (br) Mark Wilson/Getty Images; (tl) Brand X Pictures/ Alamy; (tr) Kelly-Mooney Photography/ Corbis; (bl) Craig Aurness/Corbis; 288 (inset) Catherine Karnow/Folio, Inc.; 290 (b) PhotoEdit; 291 (c) Bob Daemmrich/The Image Works; (b) Comstock/PictureQuest; 292 (t) National Geographic/Getty Images; 293 (c) Pablo Martinez Monsivais/AP Images; (t) Photo Disc/Media Bakery; (c) Richard T. Nowitz/Corbis; 294 (t) Library of Congress Prints and Photographs Division Washington, D.C. 20540 USA; 295 (b) Maryland Historical Society; (t) Michael Ventura/PhotoEdit; 296 (b) age fotostock/SuperStock; 298 (c), (b) Flags: The Americas/PictureQuest; 299 (tl), (b) Vector-Images.com; (tr) Stockbyte/ PictureQuest; 300 (b) J. Scott Applewhite/ AP Images; 301 (t) Business Wire/Getty Images; 302 (t) Robert Nickelsberg/Time Life Pictures/Getty Images; (b) National Geographic/Getty Images; 303 (t) Anupam Nath/AP Images; 304 (cl) Peter Arnold, Inc./ Alamy; (b) Robert Harding Picture Library Ltd/Alamy; (cr) Colin Young-Wolff/PhotoEdit; 306 (t) Lee Snider/Photo Images/Corbis; 307 (tl) 2005 Getty Images; (tr) Comstock/ PictureQuest; 309 (l) Library of Congress Prints & Photographs Division; 310 (t) The Granger Collection, New York; (b) Douglas Kirkland/Corbis.

UNIT 5

313 (t) Panoramic Images/Getty Images; 314 (t) James J. Bissell/SuperStock; (br) Bill Aron/PhotoEdit; 315 (tr) Creatas/SuperStock; (c) North Wind Picture Archives/Alamy; (b) Jack Kurtz/The Image Works; (tl) Ryan McVay/Getty Images; 317 (b) Tom Stewart/ Corbis; 318 (b) The Mariners' Museum; 319 (c) AP Images; 321 (c) Ellis Island Immigration Museum; 322 (bg) Gary Conner/PhotoEdit; (bl) Photodisc Red/Getty Images; (br) Howie McCormick/AP Images; (bc) Michael Goldman/The Image Bank/Getty Images; 324 (b) Bettmann/Corbis; 325 (b) Royalty-Free/ Corbis; 326 (t) National Archives Washington DC/The Art Archive; (b) Underwood & Underwood/Corbis; 327 (b) Kathy Willens/AP Images; 328 (b) Digital Image © The Museum of Modern Art/Licensed by Scala/Art Resource, NY; 329 (t) Pluriel Phototheque/ SuperStock; 330 (c) Jim Hartman/ Division of Streets/ Department of Public Properties/City of Aurora; 332 (b) Elliot Teel Photography; 333 (t) Index Stock Imagery; 334 (tl), (tr) Cleveland Public Library Photograph Collection; 335 (b) John Kuntz/The Plain Dealer; (t) Jeff Greenberg/Courtesy of Convention & Visitors Bureau of Greater Cleveland; 336 (b) SpotWorks, Inc.; 337 (t) SpotWorks, Inc.; 338 (bl), (br) Corbis; 339 (br) John Wang/Getty Images; (t) age fotos-tock/SuperStock; (bl) Bettmann/Corbis; 340 (b) Janet Hostetter/AP Images; (t) Spencer Platt/Getty Images; 341 (c) Comstock/Media Bakery RF; (t) Ariel Skelley/Corbis; 342 (b) Ohio University; 343 (t) Dennis Brack Photography; (c) Andre Jenny/Alamy; 344 (t) Bettmann/Corbis; 345 (tl) Index Stock Imagery; (tr) Ariel Skelley/Corbis; 346 (bg) Russell Gordon/Danita Delimont Stock Photography; (br) Catherine Karnow/Corbis; (bc) Pat & Chuck Blackley; (br) Myrleen Ferguson Cate/PhotoEdit; 348 (b) Syracuse Newspapers/John Berry/The Image Works; 349 (t) Bonnie Kamin/PhotoEdit; (c) Carol Cunningham/AP Images; 350 (b) Erin Patrice O'Brien/Getty Images; (t) Gift of Edsel B. Ford(33.10.N)/Detroit Institute of Arts; 351 (t) Gibson Stock Photography; (b) Robert Frerck and Odyssey Productions, Inc; 352 (cr) age fotostock/SuperStock; (cl) John Elk III; (tr) Martin Puddy/Getty Images; (tl) Spotworks, Inc; 356 (bg) Fresh Air Photo; 357 (tl) Hillhouse Graphic Design; (cl), (tr), (cr) Fresh Air Photo; 358 (b) Thomas Cain/Getty Images; 359 (b) Dave Scherbenco/Citizens Voice/AP Images; (t) Kevork Djansezian/AP Images; 360 (t) Julie Jacobson/AP Images; (b) Liu Liqun/Corbis; 361 (t) AFP Photo/ Pornchai Kittiwongsakul/Getty Images; 362 (b) Dave Bartruff/Corbis; 363 (b) Brian Seed/Alamy; (t) Jon Hicks/Corbis; 364 (t) Galen Rowell/Corbis; (cl) Ned Frisk Photography/Brand X Pictures/Adobe Stock Photos; (b) Mark Eveleigh/Alamy; (cr) Gen Nishino/Taxi/Getty Images; 365 (t) Richard Kolker/Getty Images; (c) Adam Buchanan/ Danita Delimont Stock Photography; (br) Darroch Donald/Alamy; (cl) Ariadne Van Zandbergen/Lonely Planet Images/Getty Images; (tr) Oleg Nikishin/Getty Images; (cr) J Kim/Stone/Getty Images; (bl) Peter Turnley/Corbis; (tl) Tony Latham/Getty Images; 366 (t) Akira Kaede/Getty Images; (b) Sylvain Grandadam/Stone/Getty Images; 367 (t) travelstock44/Alamy; 370 (t) Erin Patrice O'Brien/Getty Images; 371 (tl) Thomas Cain/Getty Images; (tr) Adam Buchanan/Danita Delimont Stock Photography; 374 (t) Comstock/Media Bakery RF; (b) Royalty-Free/Corbis.

UNIT 6

377 (t) David R. Frazier/PhotoLibrary Inc/ Alamy Images; 378 (t) Getty Images; (br) Laura Rauch/AP Images; 379 (tl) Gift; State Historical Society of Colorado, 1949/Library of Congress; (br) Royalty-Free/Corbis; (bl) Francisco Cruz/SuperStock; 381 (b) Glen Allison/Stone/Getty Images; 385 (t) Alex's Lemonade Stand; 386 (bg) Jeff Greenberg/ Courtesy of Convention & Visitors Bureau of Greater Cleveland; (br) J. Silver/SuperStock; (b) Richard Shock/Stone/Getty Images; (bl) Michael Newman/PhotoEdit; 388 (b) Minnesota Historical Society/Corbis; 389 (tl), (tr) The General Pencil Co.; 391 (t) Barbara Stitzer/PhotoEdit; (b) Lawrence Migdale; 392 (t) ECI; 393 (b) A'Lelia Bundles/Walker Family Collection/Wash, DC; 394 (b) Andre Jenny/The Image Works; 395 (t) Hans Strand/ Corbis; (c) Mark E. Gibson/Corbis; (b) Roy Ooms/Masterfile; 397 (t) Bob Krist/Corbis; 398 (b) Christine Osborne/Worldwide Picture Library/Alamy; 400 (b) Jamie & Judy Wild/ Danita Delimont Stock Photography; 401 (t) Bob Krist/Corbis; 402 (b) Joe Tree/Alamy; 403 (t) SpotWorks, Inc.; 404 (b) Ethan Miller/ Getty Images; 405 (t) Gautam Singh/AP Images; (b) Rogelio Solis/AP Images; 406 (fg) Royalty-Free/Corbis; (bg) Franz Marc Frei/Corbis; 407 (t) Photodisc Blue/Getty Images; (b) Index Stock/Alamy; 408 (cr) Ed Wheeler/Corbis; (br) Scott Sady/AP Images; (bl) Chuck Savage/Corbis; 409 (t) Gary Conner/Index Stock Imagery; 412 (bl) National Museum of American History, Smithsonian; (br) Index Stock RF; 413 (c) Smithsonian Institute, Computers and Communications; (t) Wikimedia Foundation Inc.; 414 (t) Lawrence Migdale; 415 (tl) Bob Krist/Corbis; (tr) Gary Conner/Index Stock Imagery; 416 (bg) Doug Mills/AP Images; (bc) Ariel Skelley/Corbis; (bl) Royalty-Free/ Corbis; 419 (t), (inset) Royalty-Free/Corbis; (b) Bill Bachmann/Index Stock Imagery; 420 (tl) Helene Rogers/Alamy; (bl) The British Museum; (tr) Werner Forman/Art Resource, NY; (cr) Gary Conner/PhotoEdit; (b) The British Museum; 421 (t) Scott Stewart/AP Images; (bg) SpotWorks, Inc.; 422 (b) Owaki - Kulla/Corbis; 423 (b) Frances Roberts/Alamy; 424 (b) John Dominis/Index Stock Imagery; (t) Hulton Archive/Getty Images; 425 (t) Don Smetzer/PhotoEdit; 429 (t) Royalty-Free/ Corbis; 434 (cl) The Money Coach; (cr) North Carolina Department of State Treasurer; 435 (tr) Bettmann/Corbis; (tl) Carson Scholars Fund; 436 (b) José Fuste Raga/zefa/Corbis; 437 (t) David Guttenfelder/AP Images; 438 (b), (c) John Robinson; 439 (t) John Robinson; 442 (t) Royalty-Free/Corbis; 443 (tl) Hulton Archive/Getty Images.

All other photos from Harcourt School Photo Library and Photographers: Ken Kinzie, Weronica Anakaron, Eric Camden, Doug Dukane.

All Maps created by MAPQUEST.COM.